Same-Sex Marriages

Same-Sex Marriages

New Generations, New Relationships

Brian Heaphy, Carol Smart and Anna Einarsdottir
University of Manchester, UK

palgrave
macmillan

First published 2013 by
PALGRAVE MACMILLAN

Palgrave Macmillan in the UK is an imprint of Macmillan Publishers Limited, registered in England, company number 785998, of Houndmills, Basingstoke, Hampshire RG21 6XS.

Palgrave Macmillan in the US is a division of St Martin's Press LLC, 175 Fifth Avenue, New York, NY 10010.

Palgrave Macmillan is the global academic imprint of the above companies and has companies and representatives throughout the world.

Palgrave® and Macmillan® are registered trademarks in the United States, the United Kingdom, Europe and other countries.

ISBN 978–0–230–30023–1

This book is printed on paper suitable for recycling and made from fully managed and sustained forest sources. Logging, pulping and manufacturing processes are expected to conform to the environmental regulations of the country of origin.

A catalogue record for this book is available from the British Library.

A catalog record for this book is available from the Library of Congress.

10 9 8 7 6 5 4 3 2 1
22 21 20 19 18 17 16 15 14 13

Printed and bound in Great Britain by
CPI Antony Rowe, Chippenham and Eastbourne

Contents

List of Tables

Preface

This book is about formalised same-sex relationships – what in the UK are legally termed 'civil partnerships' and what in the media and everyday life are termed 'gay marriages'. Our aim is to show how younger generations of same-sex couples, who see their lives and relationships as relatively ordinary, have responded to new opportunities for legally recognising their relationships by creating meaningful 'marriages'. We also aim to shed light on the social and biographical factors that influence these relationships, and the significance of their formalisation for partners themselves, their families and personal communities. The book documents couples' and individuals' accounts of their relating ideals, imaginaries and practices, and in analysing them makes links between partners' relational biographies and broader developments in personal life.

The book is based on joint and individual interviews with partners in same-sex couples who were aged up to 35 when they entered into civil partnership. The interviews were carried out as part of a research project titled 'Just like Marriage? Young Couples' Civil Partnerships' that was undertaken in 2009 and 2010 and was funded by the British Economic and Social Research Council (ESRC reference: RES-062-23-1308). In discussing the couples' formalised relationships we often use the terms 'civil partnerships' and 'marriages' interchangeably. We do this not to deny the important legal differences between these, but to reflect the ways in which our participants used the terms and conceived their relationships. As is discussed in the book, most partners saw and described themselves as married on the basis of their entry into civil partnership, and the overwhelming tendency was to use the terms interchangeably. As is also discussed in the book, there is a case to be made for seeing civil partnerships as a form of marriage. However, where participants, or we as sociologists, determined the distinctions between civil partnerships and marriages to be significant, we have explicitly flagged this up. In discussing the couples we studied, we also regularly use the term 'young' to describe them, which may sound as if we are stretching the term beyond its reasonable limits. It is not entirely satisfactory to us as authors, but it is difficult to find a better overarching term to indicate how the couples were generationally located. Similarly, we sometimes use the term 'sexual minorities' in a descriptive way to include a range of (non-hetero) sexualities organised around different identities and practices where appropriate. While it is commonplace to use LGBTI (lesbian, gay, bisexual, transgender, intersex) to describe a range of sexual identities, our study took *relationships* as the primary unit of analysis and not identity. In narrating their relationships, participants often made reference to their sexual identities (and in some cases individuals referred to several identities) but it was sometimes the case that a specific sexual identity was not explicitly articulated as such. The study did not seek to impose or fix sexual identities, and where 'gay', 'lesbian' and 'bisexual' identities are attributed to partners this reflects how they defined themselves (see Appendix 2).

In the study we sought to do two things. First, we wanted to explore the meanings and practices associated with younger cohorts' formalised same-sex relationships. The everyday possibilities for doing same-sex relationships have altered radically in recent decades, and we sought to explore how these were engaged with by 'new' generations: generations that included people who had grown up with the relative visibility and ordinariness of same-sex relationships from an early age, and who could claim relational citizenship via civil partnership or 'marriage' for most of their adult lives. Second, we sought to explore these relationships and marriages in their own right, and not as either 'mimicking' or 'queering' heterosexual ones. We aimed to situate them in terms of changing meanings and practices associated with same-sex *and* heterosexual relationships. This raised the issues of gender and power.

The tendency in existing analyses of relationships has been to view heterosexual marriage through the lens of gender difference, power imbalances and inequality and to view same-sex relationships through the lens of gender sameness, mutual negotiation and equality. While the norms, values and practices of heterosexual marriages are often assumed to be socially 'given' along gendered lines, those linked to same-sex relationships are often assumed to be creatively 'made' in the absence of clear-cut gender differences. This is a crude take on relational agency and power that undermines developments in heterosexual and same-sex relationships which are intrinsically interlinked. The fact is that social changes are reconfiguring marriage, heterosexuality, homosexuality and gender in situated ways on the ground, and legal developments in same-sex marriage are linked to these. Younger cohorts of same-sex married partners highlight how in practice marriages involve the interplay between 'the given' *and* 'the made'. It would be mistaken to see marriage as a static and omnipotent institution *or* to ignore that marriage continues to speak to relational ideals, imaginaries and practices in powerful ways. The 'ordinary' same-sex marriages that are considered in this book emerge from conversations between the given and the made in situated contexts. In this respect they are not so different from heterosexual marriages. However, they bring into sharp focus how in some circumstances ordinariness can be a political act. In the chapters of this book we seek to develop this argument and draw out its implications for understanding the flow of power with respect to relationships, gender and sexuality today.

Acknowledgements

We would like to thank the Economic and Social Research Council for generously funding the research on which this book is based. The project was based at the Morgan Centre for the Study of Relationships and Personal Life, in Sociology at the University of Manchester, and we thank our colleagues for their support. Lisa Jenkins administered the project, and we are especially grateful to her and to Hazel Burke and Victoria Higham. We are also grateful to the members of our research-user and advisory group including Meg Barker, Susan Botcherby, Scott Cuthbertson, Samantha Days, Petra Nordqvist, Martin Mitchell and Paul Simpson. We would like to thank Jeffrey Weeks for his interest in the project, and are grateful to Wendy Bottero for her comments on an early draft of the book. We would also like to thank the many academics and research users who listened to our presentations and helped us think through our findings, and the young LGBTI support groups and other organisations that talked to us about the research. We are indebted to the registrars across Britain, who generously helped us to recruit our interviewees, and we are especially grateful to Paul Parr, Deputy Registrar General, GROS, whose advice and help in recruiting was invaluable. Most importantly, we want to thank the partners who took part in the research and who generously gave their time to the study. We dedicate the book to them.

Introduction

Changing Contexts

A couple decide to holiday in a popular tourist district. Having tried to book into a hotel they end up fighting a discrimination case for two-and-a-half years. They are refused a double bedroom on the grounds that they are unmarried. The devoutly Christian owners of the hotel are opposed to sex before marriage and therefore deny unmarried couples rooms with double beds. The couple are shocked, and after a court rules that they had been discriminated against, one partner recounts: 'we have stayed in places that you might think would be far more traditional and religious [...] and had double beds with no worries at all' (*The Guardian*, 19 January 2011: 1).

A surprising tale? In this day and age few couples would expect to be denied their preferred sleeping arrangements on the basis of their marital status. However, there are complicating dimensions to this couple's story: they are a same-sex couple in a legally recognised civil partnership. Thus what began as an ordinary holiday turned out to be what the media represented as a battle between those at the vanguard of post-traditional secular lifestyles and the defenders of 'traditional' religious mores. The outcome of the case is noteworthy for a number of reasons. First, while hotels in the jurisdiction can legally refuse double beds to unmarried couples, they cannot do so on the basis of a distinction between marriage and civil partnership. Second, in his ruling the judge recounted that until recently the beliefs of the defendants would have been those 'accepted as normal' by society at large, but now 'it is the other way around'. Third, while the defendants, predictable organisations and elements of the media decried the marginalisation of Christian 'rights', even tabloid journalists (historically the most vitriolic opponents of political correctness) were keen to inform their readers that 'there is no difference between a civil partnership and marriage'

1

and that in this case it was the hoteliers who were 'loonies' (Parsons, 2011). Overall, the case illuminates how, in the interpretation of law and in public discourse, marriage and civil partnership are for many intents and purposes one and the same thing. It also touches on the power of marriage-like legal arrangements as a strategy for claiming same-sex relational 'rights' on a par with those afforded heterosexuals. Further, it points to changing conceptions of who belongs to the mainstream: in this case, 'married' same-sex couples do while traditionalist and religious 'loonies' do not. Historically, the mainstreaming of same-sex relationships via marriage-like arrangements is a surprising development. As Weeks recounts:

> In the 1970s, with the rise of gay liberation ideas across most Western countries, but especially in the United States, no-one, whether inside or outside the movement mentioned the possibility of same sex marriage. It seemed beyond the horizon of possibility and even of desirability in the context of fierce lesbian and gay critiques of the family and heterosexual marriage.
>
> Weeks (2010: 129)

Marriage, a core institution through which the norms and privileged status of heterosexuality were enshrined, has become more open. Same-sex marriage is one expression of this as it signals a detachment from the requirements of sexual and gender difference. While some commentators celebrate this development as indicative of the moment of sexual (or lesbian and gay) citizenship and equality, others have linked it to the broader modernising, renewal and reinvigoration of marriage along more democratic and egalitarian gendered lines. The development has not, or course, escaped criticism or resistance. For some, it illustrates how the 'natural' order of things, based on clearly defined gendered differences and values, is being undermined. For others, it is indicative of something altogether different: the triumph of hetero-patriarchy where rights and respectability are bestowed on same-sex couples on the basis of adopting heterosexual conventions. For others still, it represents the redrawing of relational citizenship in line with market-driven neo-liberal values. In the latter respect, through marriage, same-sex couples take on the financial and caring responsibilities that the neo-liberal state seeks to shed.

However one views it, there is no doubt that same-sex marriage is a life-political story of our time. By this we mean that it has become an important focus of debates about how the diverse ways in which people 'do' their relationships, and the meanings and values they attach to them, can or should be recognised in law, policy and in day-to-day life. It would be mistaken to see this as concerning solely, or even primarily, the politics of same-sex relationships. At the heart of debates about same-sex marriage is a broader scoping of the meaning and significance of formalised relationships that cuts across homosexual–heterosexual difference. Sociologically, there are a number of questions that lie at the centre of debates about same-sex marriage that are as pertinent to heterosexual life as they are to same-sex relationships. First, what difference does legal recognition make to relationships on the ground nowadays? Second, how are contemporary orientations to marriage, and the relating practices they involve, socially shaped and/or linked to personal agency? Third, in what ways are contemporary marriages indicative of new constraints and/or freedoms with respect to gender, sexuality and relating?

In this book, we attempt to address these questions from the hitherto unexplored perspective of the new experiences of younger generations of people who have entered into civil partnership, and who mostly see themselves as married. Younger same-sex couples' accounts of their relationships tend to highlight the value of the couple above other adult relationships. They emphasise the personal importance of maintaining connections with families of origin, of couple-focused personal lives and of 'ordinary' practices of commitment. They are narratives of 'ordinary' relationships that are linked to, but that are not wholly determined by, generationally located personal histories. They are stories of relationships that are vital to a sense of self-security and of interpersonal connectedness, and of marriage as route to affirming and recognising the personal significance of these relationships. Sociologically, these accounts and stories point to how couple relationships and marriages are vital in another sense: they are dynamic and emergent, and do not simply follow a script. Rather, young same-sex partners actively structure and 'do' their relationships and marriages in a diverse range of ways, as is likely to be the case for heterosexual relationships and marriages today. This is linked to how different 'relating selves' interact, and how relational conventions, constraints and choices are negotiated in situated circumstances.

Despite this diversity, in actively modelling their relationships on the ordinary, the couples whose relationships are analysed in this book often adopted 'conventional' standards. As we shall see, this was evident where partners' tended to invest in the couple as the ideal relational form, linked monogamous couple relationships to maturity, drew on their parents' and others' 'ordinary' relationships to articulate their relational imaginaries, and ceremonialised their 'marriages' in mainstream and sometimes self-consciously conservative ways. It was also evident in how the couple as the focus of relational life tended to trump all other relationships, including friendships. Compared to previous generations of same-sex relationships as reported by a number of studies, the younger couples we studied appeared to be more actively invested in convention than in radical relational experimentation. In this book we suggest that there are contradictions and convergences between convention and experimentation, and between diversity and commonality, that are linked to broader developments (variously termed 'postmodernisation', 'individualisation' or 'neo-liberalisation') that are reconfiguring relational life today and that give rise to new experiences.

New experiences

This book analyses younger same-sex partners' accounts of their formalised relationships. It considers couple and individual narratives of being formally partnered or 'married', and situates these with respect to partners' relational biographies, the meaning and practices they attach to money and finances, sexual and intimate commitments and to being coupled. These are important new stories because they were told by people who in many cases have grown up with the relative visibility of diverse sexual identities, who will have more or less full access to the kind of sexual and relational citizenship that marriage affords for most of their adult lives, and who have a strong sense of the ordinariness of same-sex relationships. In this sense, they indicate *some* of the possibilities for same-sex relationships after sexual and relational citizenship has been recognised through marriage or marriage-like arrangements. But they also provide insights into the broader question about what contemporary relationships, and marriage in its increasingly more open form, mean today.

On the one hand, these stories suggest that same-sex marriage potentially troubles the assumptions about natural gender differences that underpinned the modern institution of marriage. Historically, such assumptions have been central to shaping gender practices and inequalities. On the other hand, the stories suggest that same-sex marriage potentially reinforces assumptions about the naturalness of couple-centred relationships, families and kinship. Such assumptions shore up a couple-centred relational panorama whereby more radical relational experiments are potentially made invisible. On the surface, the mainstreaming of same-sex couples through marriage-like arrangements seems to signal that marriage as an institution has become more democratic, and this fits well with popular assumptions about the inherently progressive nature of social developments with respect to gender and sexuality.

Indeed, notable findings from our research include the common belief among younger same-sex partners that gender and sexual inequalities in relationships have largely been overcome, and that *couple-centred* life remains the obvious and natural answer to life-political questions about how to live and relate. These beliefs partly influenced many partners' claims to have 'ordinary' marriages, which in turn were grounded in a conviction that contemporary heterosexual and same-sex relationships were much the same. This is linked to a conviction that heterosexual and same-sex relationships are now equal in the eyes of the law, and are generally accepted as on a par with each other in day-to-day life. It is also linked to the strong sense that active commitments are more important than gender and sexuality in the making of 'good' relationships and marriages. Such beliefs and claims were thought to be evidenced by real changes that had taken place with respect to sexuality in law and in everyday life, which enabled younger same-sex couples to live their lives relatively free from the constraints encountered by previous generations. While previous generations of feminist and lesbian and gay liberationists linked the cultural privileging of the couple and marriage to constraining power, the tendency among our younger same-sex partners was to link their personal privileging of the couple and marriage to the historically increased quanta of power that sexual minorities have over their ordinary lives. At the same time, their beliefs that their relationships were more similar to, rather than different from, their heterosexual generational peers were grounded in a conviction that the latter tended to be less 'traditional' and more equal relationships than was the case for their parents' generation. This implied that gender was nowadays relatively insignificant in shaping heterosexual relationships and marriages. This is the imagined social world that many younger same-sex partners invoke in telling their stories of their 'ordinary' relationships.

New narratives of ordinary lives

Despite the ways in which the media represented the couple discussed at the beginning of this chapter, as being at the vanguard of post-traditional secular lifestyles, the publicising of their personal story about being in a marriage-like relationship had its beginnings in an commonplace experience that would raise few eyebrows: going on holiday. Reflecting on the court ruling in their favour, one partner recounted: 'Had we not been in a civil partnership it would have been a different decision'. Their holiday would have been marred by their experience, but they would have had no legal recourse. Legal recognition can enable the living of ordinary lives and this, some argue, has been at the heart of claims to same-sex relational rights. For some, such rights are at the heart of lesbian and gay equality, and recent legal developments are said to signal the achievement of (non-hetero) sexual citizenship. The speed with which such developments have taken place in some contexts is notable, even if, overall, they are uneven.

'Gay Rights. Job Done?' was the question asked by the headline of an article reporting of the raft of legislation on same-sex relationships and sexual orientation in Britain in recent years (BBC News Magazine, 30 April 2007). As well as the Civil Partnership Act (2004), the lowering of the age of consent (2000), and the repeal of 'Section 28' that prevented local schools and councils from promoting homosexuality as 'pretended family relationships' (2000 in Scotland, 2003 in the remainder of the UK), there was the Equality Act (2007) that protected against discrimination on the basis of sexual orientation. The Civil Partnership Act and the Human Fertilisation and Embryology Act 2008 also recognised same-sex parents (see Harding, 2011). While there have been similar developments in some parts of the United States, the overall situation is more varied. Following the US Supreme Court ruling in *Lawrence v. Texas* (2003), same-sex sexual acts became legal nationwide. More recently, the passing of the Don't Ask, Don't Tell Repeal Act permitted openly homosexual men and women to serve in the US military.Many states have outlawed discrimination on the grounds of sexual orientation, and hate crimes based on sexual orientation are punishable by federal law. Policies on same-sex parenting are very varied. As of early 2012, six states perform same-sex marriages (Massachusetts, Connecticut, Iowa, Vermont, New Hampshire, New York, as well as the District of Columbia) and four states (Illinois, New Jersey, Rhode Island and Delaware) recognise civil unions. At the same time, other states have enacted constitutional amendments that explicitly forbid same-sex marriage, or have passed legislation that bars civil-union-type arrangements. In the United States, President Obama has recently supported same-sex marriage, as has Britain's Prime Minister, David Cameron. Their stance has divided their political allies and enemies alike. In light of these uneven transatlantic developments, it is clear the gay rights job is not wholly done and dusted in legislative and policy terms (Harding, 2011), and globally the job may just be beginning (see Chapter 1). This is especially the case in terms of embedding rights on the ground, where same-sex relationships and minority sexualities continue to be subject to marginalisation, harassment, denigration and the like.

Despite this, in Western democracies, many sexual minorities are now living more 'ordinary' lives than were imagined possible 20 years ago. While they may still encounter prejudice, heterosexism or homophobia, this is not the *defining* story that many tell about their lives. Rather, it is one story among others of the challenges encountered in living their everyday lives. Such challenges often concern relationships with family, partners and friends; emotional, home and work lives; money, resources and lifestyle aspirations; and the balancing of various demands to do with parenting, health and care. Previously sexual minority life stories tended to emphasise marginalisation, exclusion and prejudice. Nowadays we are hearing fuller stories of multi-dimensional lives. Among these are diverse and multi-faceted stories of same-sex relationships, and accounts of 'ordinary' same-sex marriages are a part of these where the opportunity for legal recognition is available. These accounts are not so dissimilar from stories told about heterosexual relationships and marriage: of romance, love and relational aspirations; of trials and tribulations, successes and failures; of plans, contingencies and surprises; of grappling with the challenges and rewards that couple and married relationships involve. Such accounts highlight how in same-sex relationships, like heterosexual ones, women and men must actively grapple with conflicting demands, pressures and ideals, and juggle the expectations, tensions, contradictions, emotions, joys, disappointments, constraints *and* possibilities associated with partnerships. In these respects, all adult partnerships nowadays – same-sex and heterosexual, married and otherwise – share a degree of sameness.

While it might be tempting to think that same-sex couples' claims and practices of ordinariness are indicative of how homosexual relationships have become more like heterosexual ones, the issue could be viewed the other way around. Indeed, some theorists have argued that heterosexual relationships have become more like same-sex ones in that they no longer follow given formulae or have conventional supports. Put another way, heterosexual marriages in practice have become more like same-sex relationships in that they do not simply follow a set of given rules. Rephrased again, nowadays heterosexual relationships and marriages have become more intensely vitalised: like same-sex partners, heterosexual partners must actively and intensively participate in *creating* their relationships and marriages. At the heart of this are the ways in which marriage is no longer always a necessity for reproduction or economic and social status. Also, marriage does not necessarily presume a lifelong commitment, and people nowadays enter into marriages with previous experiences of sexual and intimate relationships. Thus, they are likely to be familiar with the doubts, cynicism and the bad press that marriage receives in the media and day-to-day life. In these respects, marriage is not a given script that people simply follow. In principle, for heterosexual and same-sex partners alike, 'ordinary' marriages are vital projects that necessarily involve heightened degrees of agency. Agency in this respect refers to the requirement to be an active participant in the structuring of one's relationship and personal life, but agency does not imply freedom *from* power. Rather, one of the implications of the findings outlined in this book is that accounting for the agency people have with respect to their relationships necessitates a more vital conception of power than the gender reductive one that has often underpinned studies of heterosexual *and* same-sex relationships.

While the 'new' similarities between heterosexual and same-sex relationships are noteworthy, it is also important to remain attuned to the differences between relationships. In general terms, heterosexual relationships are still privileged over same sex ones in most contexts. But there are also differences *between* same-sex relationships that are linked to how they are socio-culturally located. As well as the historical, cross-national, state and district differences that influence variations in legislation and the knock-on effects they have for experiences on the ground, same-sex relationships are also shaped by differences to do with gender and sexual identity (LGBTQI), class, ethnicity, geography, age and the like. We consider these differences as they emerge as significant in our analysis, but by focusing specifically on younger generations' same-sex marriages our aim is to bring *generationally* inflected differences in experience to the fore. Thus, prior to discussing the new experiences that are the main focus of this book, it is important to situate them generationally, and we do this in Chapter 1. Before this, we briefly situate these new experiences with respect to the study that we undertook to explore them.

Situating young same-sex marriages

Despite international interest, and the wealth of literature debating formalised same-sex relationships, relatively few detailed empirical studies of the actual experience of these relationships have been published (but see Badgett, 2009; Bates Deakin, 2006). This book is based on a qualitative study that sought to explore formalised same-sex relationships from the perspective of life on the ground. The study involved joint and individual interviews with 50 same-sex couples (in total 50 men and 50 women) who were aged up to 35 when they entered into civil partnership. It also involved group discussions with members of a LGBTI youth group, representatives of agencies involved in LGBTI lives and international academics who study minority sexualities and same-sex relationships. By focusing on the experiences of younger cohorts, we aimed to adopt a generationally situated view of formalised same-sex relationships, based on the belief that the historical period when one recognises one's same-sex desires and becomes involved in same-sex relationships is likely to be a major influence on how one views and experiences them.

Within the age range, we sought to make our study as inclusive as possible of a diversity of experiences, contexts and backgrounds (see Appendices 1 and 2). With the help of registrars, we contacted couples across mainland UK in urban and rural areas. Our interviewees were drawn from diverse family, class, ethnic and cultural backgrounds, from different economic and occupational groups, and represented a diversity of age ranges between the early 20s and late 30s. Of our interviewees, 16 were parents and had come to parenthood in a range of ways. Some partners had had no or limited experience of previous relationships, while others had had experience of long, short, serial and/or multiple relationships. Many partners had only same-sex desires and relationships, while others had previously been in heterosexual relationships and some had had relationships with both women and men. The study therefore reflected a wide range of situated experiences. However, it is not a statistically representative study that makes claims about *all* younger civil partnerships, not least because it was not possible to access the contact details of all of those aged up to 35 who had entered into civil partnership for the purposes of sampling. Instead, we relied on the willingness of registrars to forward information about the study to couples on our behalf, and where we were given the details of couples the stringent nature of the ethical guidelines that we followed meant that only certain couples could be contacted. At this point, the couples could choose to ignore the information or signal that they were interested in taking part in the study. Even if a statistically representative sample were possible, we aimed for something else: an in-depth qualitative exploration that would generate personal narratives of formalised same-sex relationships to illuminate their influences and operation and the insights they generate for the links between gender, sexuality and marriage more generally.

The motivation for our qualitative study came from our sense that it was necessary and timely to explore the multi-dimensionality of formalised same-sex relationships in a situated way: to study meanings as well as everyday practices in a way that included the socio-culturally-shaped biographical contexts that influenced them. To do this, we developed an approach that was very loosely based on one of the few existing studies that grappled fully with the ordinariness, complexity and power of heterosexual marriage: Mansfield and Collard's research on young married couples published in *The Beginning of the Rest of Your Life* (1988). Taking Mansfield and Collard's ground-breaking research as our inspiration enabled us to make some direct comparisons between the meanings and practices of previous generations of young heterosexual marriages and contemporary young civil partnerships, but it also allowed us to make comparisons with research findings about previous cohorts of same-sex couples that had explicitly engaged with Mansfield and Collard's work (Dunne, 1997; Weeks et al., 2001). We were especially convinced by Mansfield and Collard's argument that strong efforts should be made to view marriage as anthropologically strange, and to eschew already established commonsense and sociological 'givens' about its significance.

Following Mansfield and Collard, we sought to understand what the experience of being formally partnered or 'married' was for the individual and the couple, but 'without underestimating the influence of the public context of marriage' (1988: 4). There were a number of specific questions that Mansfield and Collard (1988: 6) sought to explore that were central to our own concern to situate formalised same-sex relationships: What ideas about marriage and formalised relationships are absorbed from outside, in addition to personal and familial experience of marriage? How do young partners compare their partnerships and marriages to other marriages – favourably or problematically? How do young partners assert and practice difference and sameness, and to what other imagined partnerships and marriages? What external standards of marriage are evoked by young partners and what variety of images of formal partnerships are amalgamated? Preempting later theoretical debates, Mansfield and Collard noted that the moral pressure to conform with respect to marriage has weakened. However, instead of proposing the normative ideal of the pure or reflexive relationship (as Giddens, 1992, has done), they sought, as we did, to explore which is most frequently preferred in practice.

The young married people in Mansfield and Collard's study showed a wide range of influences which had contributed to their image of marriage in general and their own marriage in particular. These included explicit and implicit definitions in law; general knowledge of other people's marriages generated via gossip or media; views of marriage by experts; and the impression of marriages to which they were closest, which was usually their own parents'. The incorporation of these insights into our own study alerted us to the range of possible influences on younger couples' civil partnerships. Thus, we were able to investigate the assumption that same-sex relationships are relatively uninfluenced by such sources, or *primarily* by counter-discourses generated by lesbian and gay communities (Blasius, 1994; Heaphy, 2008; Weeks, 1995; 2007).

A key finding of Mansfield and Collard's study was that when an analytical shift is made from meanings to practices (e.g. with respect to finances, expressions of commitment and family-making), despite newly married couples' ideals about equal marriage, their accounts of their day-to-day lives and plans for the future showed 'clearly that social and economic structures are still highly influential in shaping the worlds of women and men and therefore in shaping the private relationships between husbands and wives' (1988: 16). Marriages, they noted, were *created* by the individuals involved in the relationship, but married lives were worked out within the context of the wider society and there was continual interaction between their participants' images of what marriage should be like, could be like and would probably be like. In portraying their marriages, their interviewees played with different images and interwove morality, idealism and reality (1988: 19). By keeping in mind these insights, our study aimed to move beyond the concern with 'egalitarian ideals' that are often of primary interest in studies of same-sex relating, and to explore more thoroughly how such ideals interweave with and/or contradict everyday realities, especially with reference to finances, sexuality, couple and broader commitments.

While Mansfield and Collard argued that the very ordinariness of married life could become a pitfall for those who wish to explore it (1988: 36), we thought that, in contrast, the often assumed 'exceptionality' of same-sex relationships could be a similar pitfall. Thus, we attempted to put some critical distance between our own approach to analysis and existing ones (see Chapter 1). By this we mean that we were careful not to simply follow any particular sociological script about same-sex relationships or marriage. Rather, following Plummer (1995), we treated the interview accounts in a pragmatic way as 'narrative' truth, asking what work these accounts did in terms of relational selves, relationships themselves and the broader social order. By bringing our findings and analysis into conversation with the findings of previous research, we were then able to identify continuities and differences between contemporary young same-sex 'married' couples, previous heterosexual married and non-formalised same-sex relationships. In doing this, we were able to address issues to do with socio-cultural change, but also to identify aspects and areas where existing frames for comprehending same-sex and heterosexual relationships (and the links between them) were less than insightful.

The book

This book is concerned above all with how new generations of same-sex couples have responded to the opportunity to have their relationships legally recognised by creating meaningful 'marriages'. Each chapter situates and explores different dimensions of the process of interweaving the 'given' and the 'made' that is the heart of creating same-sex marriages. Throughout, we draw parallels between our own findings and those from previous cohorts of heterosexual married couples and same-sex relationships, highlighting what is distinctive about younger cohorts' 'married' same-sex relationships and what is not.

Chapter 1, 'Ordinary lives, vital relationships', analyses some of the international, socio-historical and political contexts that are the backdrop to young same-sex couples' claims and practices of ordinary marriages. It situates these claims and practices in terms of developments in heterosexual and non-heterosexual cultures; political and academic debates about the significance of marriage; and the methodological approach we adopted to the study. Key to the latter was an interactionist focus on the work the personal stories do. From this perspective, personal accounts of ordinary and vital relationships can be explored for the work they do in people's lives, relationships and social ordering.

Chapter 2, 'Relationships, partnerships and marriages', outlines the diverse ways in which partners narrated their formalised relationships as 'marriage', as akin to marriage or – more rarely – as different to marriage. It situates marriage within the broader context of couples' relationships on the ground, and considers how same-sex marriages are linked to an enhanced sense of acceptance by personal communities. Socio-cultural positioning could influence the degree to which relationships were deemed to be accepted as ordinary, but the overall meanings and practices associated with marriage were not reducible to gender, class and the like in any straightforward way. The chapter illuminates how static institutional and structural frames cannot account for the diverse, situated and dynamic nature of marriages in practice.

Chapter 3, 'Relational biographies', considers the ways in which relational ideals and practices are embedded in, but are not wholly determined by, socio-culturally shaped personal histories, and the ways in which partners articulated their relating ideals and practices with reference to their parents' relationships. This highlights continuities in assumptions about 'good' relationships. Partners shared their parents' commitments to the couple as the focus of family life, although many conceived their own relationships to be more freely chosen than their parents' relationships. However, there was only limited evidence of the kind of chosen or friendship families that have been documented among previous cohorts of lesbians and gay men. This is partly linked to the ways coming out tended not to fundamentally disrupt 'given' relationships with kin, and the ways in which same-sex relational ideals and practices were embedded in and supported by personal communities rather than critical sexual communities.

Chapter 4, 'Forming and formalising relationships', focuses on the formation and development of commitments that lead to 'marriage', and on the ceremonialism that surrounds the formalisation of relationships. In line with romantic notions of love, many couples linked the formation of their relationships to chance and fate, while others emphasised reason and choice. For the majority, partnership choices were linked to romance *and* reason. Nevertheless, decisions to marry were most often cast in the language of love and confirming commitment, with legal rights often a secondary – or in some cases a relatively insignificant – consideration. While most couples emphasised that they married to confirm their mature commitments to each other, ceremonies themselves often represented a critical moment where familial and personal community inclusion and the reality of the marriage could be affirmed or negated.

Chapter 5, 'Relationships, money and the self', considers the relational significance of money. It situates young married couples in terms of their incomes, and suggests that money can be an important part of the story of becoming a couple and of the bonding process. It is also a significant aspect of relational biographies and linked to a mature sense of self. Money management is commonly linked to independence in the literature on same-sex relationships, where it has been argued that non-heterosexuals seem to be able to 'write and enact their own financial "scripts"'. It is also an important element in theories about the egalitarian nature of same-sex relationships. However, among young same-sex couples, equal earnings were not linked to power-free relationships. Money, and especially debt, illustrate how same-sex couples, like all couples, are not free from cultural, social or biographical constraints.

Chapter 6, 'Sex and security', situates young couples' sexual commitments with respect to partners' previous sexual relationships and the meanings they attach to sex in their current relationships. Couples' sexual commitments were often narrated with reference to partners' previously immature 'promiscuity' or to serial monogamy. In modelling their relationships on the ordinary, most young couples assumed that their relationships would be monogamous from the outset. The chapter explores couples' narratives of (non-)monogamy in some detail as well as changing meanings that partners give to sex over time. It considers the ways in which sexual practices and their meanings are linked to the temporal rhythms of couples' day-to-day lives. Sex could also be experienced as a problematic issue for some partners, and the ways in which this undermined a sense of relational security goes some way to explaining why couples were so invested in sexual monogamy.

Chapter 7, 'Couple worlds', focuses on young civil partners' day-to-day practices of love and commitment, and considers couple life as it involves children and plans for the future. It explicitly explores the difference that civil partnership and marriage makes to being a couple, and considers the extent to which 'married' same-sex couples might be viewed as being engaged in radical life experiments or not. While couples display a relatively heightened degree of reflexivity and agency compared to previous cohorts of heterosexual marriages, this seems to be focused on producing 'convention' as opposed to undermining it. In most cases, couples actively modelled their relationships on a concept of the ordinary rather than the radically different. In this respect, they refused the burden of being at the vanguard of radical innovation with respect to relationships. At the same time, by doing marriage in very ordinary ways, they trouble core tenets of an institution that has historically been intrinsic to modern gender, sexual and relational inequalities.

Finally, in the concluding chapter, 'New experiences of ordinariness', we revisit some of the core issues discussed in the book to draw out the themes of ordinariness and difference and their relational, political and sociological implications. In doing so, we highlight the implications of our analysis for thinking about same-sex *and* heterosexual relationships in the context of contemporary social change. By bringing the themes of ordinariness and difference into conversation, we suggest that ordinariness is a privilege that is not automatically given by virtue of the legal recognition of relationships. We also suggest that ordinariness is a political claim about difference and commonality that is about much more than assimilation. Rather, ordinariness concerns the ways in which relational experiences – same-sex and heterosexual – emerge through the interplay of embeddedness *and* agency.

1

Ordinary Lives, Vital Relationships: Same-Sex Marriage in Context

In this chapter we consider some of the international, socio-historical and political contexts that are the backdrop to new generational claims about the ordinariness of same-sex relationships and marriages. Our aim is to situate these claims, and the relating practices they involve, in terms of developments in heterosexual and non-heterosexual cultures, in terms of political and academic debates about the significance of marriage, and in terms of the methodological approach of the study that generated these claims and accounts of practice. The chapter begins by situating same-sex marriages with respect to the diverse meanings and practices associated with relationships and marriages more generally today. It then considers developments in same-sex relational worlds that have facilitated a shift from being 'other' to 'ordinary' in some contexts, and links this to developments in heterosexual relationships and marriage. Both sets of developments can be linked to processes of social change that have been variously conceptualised as postmodernisation, individualisation or neo-liberalisation. However, rather than following the sociological scripts suggested by any of these frames, we highlight the important point that stems from these as far as our analysis is concerned: that relationships and marriages, both same-sex and heterosexual, have become intensely vitalised. This links to our approach to analysing the experiences discussed in the book, which is loosely based on interactionist ideas about how ways of doing – or scripting – relationships *emerge* through interaction.

Meanings of marriage

In October 2010, under the headline 'Couples bid to overturn gay marriage law' (24/10/2010: 25), *The Observer* newspaper reported on a campaign in Britain to overturn the restrictions that prevent same-sex couples from being formally married and heterosexual couples from entering into civil partnerships. The report quoted the campaign's coordinator, the Outrage! activist Peter Thatchell, as saying that civil partnerships and civil marriage bans violated the Human Rights Act. As part of the campaign, eight couples filed applications at register offices for ceremonies that were forbidden. One applicant, who was in a same-sex relationship, was reported as saying 'We want marriage – that is an institution we believe was divined by God and for me that's important, and I don't see why we should be denied it because of our gender [...] Love is love at the end of the day and that should be honoured'. This is just one of the many media reports about couples seeking legal equality that have appeared for well over a decade in Western democratic countries. On the surface, it is just one more story about campaigns for same-sex marriage, but it touches on broader developments.

While the reported campaign advocates same-sex couples' rights to marriage, it also supports heterosexual couples' rights to civil partnership: to have their relationships legally sanctioned without marriage. Thus, the campaign points to how for both heterosexuals and sexual minorities alike relationship recognition can be a matter of life-politics: where people seek recognition for their relationships on the basis of the meanings *they* attach to them and not on the basis of definitions 'imposed' by the state and/or religious authorities. The meanings given to relationships are diverse, as is evident in how claims to recognition are currently framed. In this short article alone they include human rights, Divine rights, gender equality, the 'chosen' or 'imposed' nature of marriage, and the naturalness and universality of love. These claims point to how in contemporary contexts established frames for understanding couple commitments and their legitimacy intermingle and jostle with new ones. Diverse meanings are in turn linked to the range of opportunities that now exist for living and 'doing' relationships in practice.

However, amidst these developments, marriage continues to be central to cultural and political discourse about socially valued relationships. Whether people are in favour of it, opposed to it, or are ambivalent about it, marriage remains an ideological reference point in debates about how intimate and family relationships could and should be lived; how some relationships are or should be privileged over others; and how relationship commitments could or should be recognised at legislative and personal levels. These debates signal that marriage is no longer (if it ever were) a straightforward matter. They illustrate that marriage as a legal and social institution is radically contested, and that public discourse about marriage is, above all, contested discourse. However, the centrality of marriage to public debates about couple and family relationships points to its continuing salience as a touchstone for cultural imaginings of the relational order. This partly explains why same-sex civil unions, which are technically not marriage, are often represented in the media and public discourse *as* 'gay marriage'. This is certainly the case in Britain since the Civil Partnership Act was introduced in 2005. The language of marriage has also been speedily absorbed into everyday life, not least by many of those who have entered civil partnership:

> Robert got down on one knee and said, okay, I know we've sort of said this before but went down on one knee, 'will you marry me?' It was like 'Absolutely. But I don't want to wait a long time. Let's do it now, let's do it within six months'.
>
> Daniel (202a)

Kamilia (103b):	Started to live together and the relationship just got better and better.
Radinka (103a):	Yeah.
Kamilia:	And then we decided to get married [...] I think that's about it, isn't it? And now we are together, happy. I think, I hope.
Radinka:	Yes, definitely [...] it feels different [...] I'm not saying about security, because basically that's what we shared before but the actual fact that we are committed to each other.

Stories like these, from people who were aged up to 35 when they entered civil partnership, point to a relative unselfconsciousness about the use of the term 'marriage' in same-sex relationships. They deploy the language of marriage with ease when describing their decision to formalise their relationships, the nature of their commitment and the everyday practices through which their relationships are embedded. They also tell culturally familiar stories of marriage as a key life event and as bolstering couple commitments. Many young couples in civil partnerships tell 'ordinary' marriage stories like these.

It would be surprising if some same-sex couples did not view marriage as an extraordinary way to discuss same-sex relationships, and studies have documented some same-sex couples' opposition to and ambivalence about the notion of marriage (Hull, 2006, Mitchell et al., 2009). Prior to the availability of civil partnership, research by Weeks et al.

(2001) on non-heterosexual relationships in the UK, undertaken in the mid-1990s, found high levels of personal discomfort with the notion of same-sex marriage. While those studied supported the availability of same-sex marriage, the majority recounted that they would not chose it themselves because they saw it as a heterosexual institution. Later, in the mid-2000s, a UK study of pre-civil partnership recognition arrangements found greater ease among same-sex couples with the notion and terminology of same-sex marriage (Shipman and Smart, 2007). A similar ease among same-sex couples undertaking do-it-yourself recognition ceremonies has been documented in US studies (Hull, 2006, Lewin, 1998), but also ambivalence and opposition among others (Hull, 2006). A more recent cross-national study (where LGB respondents were mostly from Australia, Canada, the UK and the USA) also found a range of views, but with significant support for the idea of gay marriage (Harding, 2011; see also Clarke et al., 2006). As marriage-like arrangements become a real possibility, it seems that people are more likely to support them and that couples more seriously entertain the idea of entering into them.

However, different attitudes remain that are partly rooted in different political and cultural traditions. These are partly reflected in different national responses to claims for same-sex relationship recognition. Discussing the latter, Weeks (2010: 130) argues that while the French PACS legislation follows 'classic republican traditions' by refusing to recognise the separate cultural identities of lesbians and gay men, the Dutch recognition of same-sex civil partnerships and after that marriage is a logical move in The Netherlands' 'institutionalised liberalism'. In the UK, he suggests, the Civil Partnership Act in 2004 continued a tradition of 'liberalisation by stealth' by reproducing marriage law but naming it something else, thus 'avoiding much religious opposition [...] a classic case of, and a very British compromise' (2010: 130). In the USA, which Weeks sees as the most neo-liberal of cultures, with the most affirmative LGBT identities and communities, the intensity of debate about same-sex marriage is linked to its being 'the most religious of Western societies'. This, he argues, can partly explain the degree of opposition from conservative Christians and why advocates for same-sex relationship recognition in the USA often hold out for full recognition of marriage 'compared to the more secular British or Scandinavians' (2010: 131). Where marriage is in decline, he suggests:

> [T]he LGBT population seems more likely to be satisfied with less than marriage, because marriage itself is less sanctified. Where religious

traditions remain strong, as in Spain and the USA, so it is likely to go for full marriage rights when same-sex unions are recognised.

Weeks (2010: 131)

Other differences in attitudes to same-sex marriage intermingle with and cut across national, cultural and religious ones. Chief among these are generational ones related to cohort differences and the historically situated nature of sexual identities and cultures (cf. Edmunds and Turner, 2002: 6). In this respect, different attitudes to same-sex marriage are likely to be related to when and how people formed their minority sexual identities.

Generationally situated meanings

Among many of those whose sexual identities were formed through an active engagement with lesbian, feminist, gay, bisexual and queer critical communities and cultures, there is likely to be an enduring reluctance to embrace marriage as a way of understanding or recognising their relationships (cf. Adam, 2004). This is linked to how such communities and cultures were often critical of marriage as the lynchpin of heteronormativity and of 'homosexual' oppression. Of course, it is also the case that people can review their opposition in light of changing legal, social, political and personal developments (see Kitzinger and Wilkinson, 2004).

Among younger cohorts, and especially those whose sexual identities were not formed through active engagement with critical cultures and communities, there can be more general comfort with the idea of same-sex marriage. This was evident in how the same-sex partners we spoke to view the marriage/civil partnership distinction (for socio-legal analyses see Barker, 2006; Harding, 2011; Stychin, 2006). The majority were untroubled with the legal distinction between marriage and civil partnership. They viewed themselves as married, and saw the distinction as a relatively insignificant technical one, even if some would prefer it to be dissolved. A small number who viewed themselves as married were more outraged by the distinction, as they saw it as an affront to their ordinariness. Others still were ambivalent about the issue. A small minority were keen to keep the distinction on the basis that they did not want to be married. Most of the couples we spoke to would have agreed with Doris (104a), who said: 'it [is] a civil partnership and we feel it's a marriage'. Even those who were wary of marriage as a heterosexual institution could describe themselves as married. This was the case for a couple we spoke as part of our pilot study (where one partner was aged over 35 when they entered into civil partnership) who were at the cusp of different generational experiences of same-sex relationships:

Sue (102b): when we got married I was [...] still not sure about using the terminology of marriage [...] I did have quite big problems with the notion of [...] marriage as an institution.

Beverley (102b): Yeah, I'm not a big fan of marriage as an institution and I'd always sworn that I was never ever getting married. Of course, what I meant was to a man [...] I'm not particularly keen on the implications. But we are just like a married couple really, aren't we?

Sue: [...] even though legally [marriage and civil partnership are] pretty much the same, it is the same, there wasn't that baggage of what marriage should mean that you get with a heterosexual marriage.

While these partners are not technically married, they describe themselves thus and see marriage and civil partnership as 'the same'. While they are familiar with, and espouse, political criticism of marriage as 'an institution', on the basis of the gender differences it has 'traditionally' assumed and the gender inequalities it promoted, they describe themselves as 'just like a married couple' in practice (Harding, 2011, also found a 'major attachment' to arguments about same-sex and heterosexual relational sameness among lesbians and gay men). Confused thinking? Perhaps. A more likely explanation is that this couple, like many others, are grappling with complex realities that stem from the changing possibilities that have opened up for some same-sex *and* heterosexual relationships. By formalising their relationships, couples like Beverley and Sue are engaged in new ways of conceiving and doing same-sex relationships, and are differently positioned in relation to marriage than they were previously (but see Adam, 2004, 2006). As opposed to viewing marriage in mostly institutional terms, as they imply they once did, Beverley and Sue also now see it from another perspective: from the perspective of life on the ground. This more multi-dimensional perspective is signalled by the complexity of their exchange. One the one hand they are keen to critically distance themselves from marriage as a heterosexual institution because of its baggage of gender and sexual differences and inequalities (its 'shoulds'). On the other hand, they are keen to embrace the similarities between their own and others' marriages on the basis that they are not *necessarily* subject to its institutional baggage in practice.

Another couple, Kevin (205a) and Jorge (205b), also touched upon the ordinariness of same-sex relationships and partnerships when discussing the similarities and differences between their partnership and their parents' marriages. As opposed to identifying these as being intrinsically different on the basis of their gendered make-up, as older cohorts have done in previous studies (see Dunne, 1997; Sullivan, M. 2004; Weeks et al., 2001), they emphasised the commonalities. They saw them as rooted in the interpersonal challenges that all partnerships – whether married or not – involved:

Jorge: I suppose because they've been together many years. They've had their up and downs but they always manage to pull through [...]

Kevin: I mean I think the key thing, I mean my mum and dad [...] had difficulties throughout their marriage but I think the key thing is that [...] being in a partnership is you're a team and you kind of, deal with the good and bad stuff as a team and it's kind of what it's about really. And generally there's more, you know you hope for more good than bad, but you know life's a bit full of surprises, so [...] the partnership thing is about working through stuff together and being a team really.

Some will be cheered, and others depressed, by same-sex couples' stories of being 'married', of being like other married couples, and of the continuities between heterosexual marriages and their own. In sociological terms, these stories can be difficult to hear in their own right, without slotting them into existing frames that see marriage through the lens of gendered and (hetero)sexual domination and inequalities, and that see same-sex relationships in terms of gender equality and (non-hetero)sexual agency (see below). Thus, it may be tempting to see such stories as evidence of the undermining *or* the triumph of heterosexual norms, and to interpret stories of ordinariness as evidence for either side of the debates about the value or dangers of claims to normality and assimilation (Adam, 2004; Rauch, 2004; Sullivan, A. 1996, 2004; Warner, 2000). We will discuss the frames and debates in more depth in due course. For the moment, however, we argue that understanding these stories requires situating them generationally.

Unlike previous generations of lesbians and gay men who, because of the lack of cultural guidelines and social supports for their identities and relationships, had little choice but to engage in life experiments, the partners in our study neither claimed nor wanted to be at the vanguard of radical relational life. This does not mean that their relationships were not radical in practice. In some situations they clearly were, especially where their visibility as a 'married' couple disrupted the heterosexual assumption and where their very ordinariness troubled constructions of homosexual pathology and depravity. Nevertheless, the ways in which most modelled their relationships on the ordinary was linked to the broader ways in which they saw their lives as ordinary. This is not because they are the unthinking victims of heterosexual ideologies (cf. Warner, 2000), but because their generational circumstances made it possible to *feel* relatively ordinary compared to previous generations of lesbians and gay men. Young same-sex couples' claims to be ordinary may well feed 'the fears of queer critics that what same-sex unions are all about is assimilation into the status quo' (Weeks, 2008: 792). However, Weeks argues that 'we should never underestimate the importance of being ordinary. It has helped to transform the LGBT and broader worlds' (2008: 792). A more important point, we suggest, is that there is the need to interrogate the 'status quo' as it is imagined and deployed by queer and other critics.

We aim to do this by putting personal stories of ordinary same-sex 'marriages' at the centre of the frame for comprehending developments that *cut across* the homosexual–heterosexual dichotomy. These developments are linked to the diversity and vitality of ordinary relationships, and trouble the notions of a simply given or universal status quo or set of relational values. To explain this, in the following sections we consider the historical, legislative and broader socio-cultural developments with respect to same-sex relating and marriage that are the backdrop to contemporary young same-sex couples' experiences. We also outline the analytical strategy we deployed to explore these experiences.

From 'other' to 'ordinary'

Modern histories of same-sex relationships and heterosexual marriage are deeply intertwined. Historically, same-sex relationships have been construed as the 'other' of heterosexual ones, and since the nineteenth century homosexual relationships have been intensively defined, outlawed and pathologised as unnatural, unhealthy and abnormal. As Foucault (1979) observed, the discursive invention of homosexuality as socially and personally threatening went hand-in-hand with the codification of normal (re)productive sexualities as a property of the heterosexual married couple. The modern sexual hierarchy (Rubin, 1992), with heterosexual married couples at the top and same-sex relationships near the bottom, was never wholly unchallenged (Adam, 2004). However, current possibilities for minority sexualities and same-sex relationships are most directly rooted in the feminist, lesbian and gay and sexual-liberation movements of the late 1960s and 1970s, and in the historical, socio-cultural and economic developments that gave rise to them (Adam, 1987; 2004; Altman, 1971; D'Emilio, 1983; Weeks, 1977). These movements gave rise to sexual communities and cultures that were critical in a number of senses. First, they challenged the heterosexual assumption (or compulsory heterosexuality, Rich, 1983) and the sexual and gender ideologies that underpinned it (Blasius, 1994; Connell, 1987). Second, they enabled the formation of strong, although still marginalised, minority sexual identities (Adam, 2004; Weeks, 1995). Third, they were the source of political claims for sexual-minority rights and the legitimacy of same-sex relationships (Adam, 2004; Cruickshank, 1992). While they opened up new ways of identifying, it has also been argued that lesbian and gay critical communities provided the context for a distinctive ethos of relating.

It has been argued that coming out as lesbian or gay has entailed 'coming into' lesbian and gay culture and community (see Plummer, 1995). This, Blasius (1994: 219) argues, involves 'rejecting one's own subjection [...] that is the product of historical processes of domination by heterosexism' through the resources that critical lesbian and gay cultures and communities provide. For Blasius, coming out assumes a critical reorientation to dominant heterosexual practices of relating that are linked to ideologies of natural gender differences and interdependence and that support gender inequalities. Lesbian and gay approaches to intimate relating, he argues, are 'derived from an erotics that decentres genital sexuality and de-essentialises gender' and through this 'the possibility of a different relational ethic emerges: reciprocity' (ibid). Also, the absence of institutional supports and cultural guidelines for same-sex relating implies that lesbians and gay men are engaged in *creating* novel, vital and more egalitarian relationships (see also Dunne, 1997; Sullivan, M. 2004). Since these have 'no other support than the willingness of partners to enter into it [...] they are not in themselves power relationships' (Blasius, 1994: 219). At the heart of Blasius's analysis is an often repeated argument: that by virtue of gender sameness, lesbian and gay relationships are more creative than heterosexual ones, and are, in principle, reciprocal and equal (Dunne, 1997; Sullivan, M. 2004).

The themes of creativity, reciprocity and equality have also been a feature of discussions of developments in sexual-minority cultures that have most immediately and directly influenced current claims for the legal recognition of same-sex relationships and same-sex marriage. These include AIDS, same-sex parenting and the 'family turn' in non-heterosexual cultures. AIDS was a catalyst in mobilising a new lesbian and gay relational politics in the 1980s. These politics were initially focused on the recognition of same-sex partners' vital caring commitments, and protecting 'rights' in relation to property and next of kin. Community responses to AIDS facilitated the institution-building and political confidence that made same-sex relationship recognition seem like a realisable political objective. Combined with this, new possibilities opened up for lesbian and gay parenting from the 1980s (through self and assisted insemination, surrogacy, fostering, adoption, and so on) that led to a growing number of same-sex couples (mostly women) choosing to parent. Relationship recognition was seen as vital for recognising and protecting co-parenting commitments.

Initially, Moral Right responses to AIDS and same-sex parenting in the UK and the USA reinforced the historical construction of lesbians and gay men as a threat to the family. In the United Kingdom, for example, legislation was introduced in the late 1980s (commonly known as Section 28) that explicitly sought to ban the promotion by local authorities of homosexuality 'as a pretended family relationship'. Such interventions, however, had the reverse effect of mobilising a lesbian and gay relationship-oriented politics that was organised around family issues such as couple and family recognition, parenting, adoption and other rights. Weeks et al. (2001) conceptualised these developments in terms of the practices and politics of 'families of choice' (see also Weston, 1991). Whereas same-sex relationships were once seen as the antithesis of family, in the 1980s and 1990s sexual minorities began to reclaim the language of the family to refer to the relationships they chose, created and invented: relationships that were vital in giving meaning to their day-to-day lives. In doing so, they challenged the idea that family was defined by biologically or legally sanctioned relatedness, and instead suggested that what mattered most was who people 'do' family with (see Morgan, 2011).

Key to Blasius's (1994) analysis, and to Weeks's (Weeks, 1995; 2007) elsewhere, is the idea that by the end of the twentieth century lesbians and gay men had arrived at the cusp of 'equality'(Blasius) or the moment of 'citizenship' (Weeks, 1995). Both theorists argue that this was rooted in the personal politics of coming out and the strong lesbian and gay communities that facilitated and partly grew from this. This, in turn, led to a 'felt need for same-sex relationship rights [that] grew from the ground upwards' (Weeks, 2010: 129). While some observers link same-sex marriage campaigns to the activities of global elites, Weeks stresses that the latter are themselves 'a response to changing social realities, not an anticipation of them' (Weeks, 2010: 129). While Blasius's and Weeks's broad analyses are convincing to some extent, they gloss over the more messy complexities of the politics of coming out and of sexual communities that are central to understanding same-sex marriage as *one* (highly visible) direction that same-sex relational politics has taken (Adam, 2004). Most importantly, they overplay the coherence of imagined lesbian and gay communities, underplay the radical diversification of sexual identities and politics, and ignore generational developments with respect to sexual communities, identities and politics.

One of the key features of sexual-minority cultures in recent years has been their fragmentation by 'internal' claims for the recognition of diverse sexualities and relationships. Nowadays it is broadly accepted that there is no one lesbian and gay culture of the kind that Blasius seemed to assume, and even the plural notion of lesbian and gay 'cultures' has been troubled by the identities and experiences encompassed by the acronym LGBQTI. While there are dominant sexual stories (Plummer, 1995), in practice *a* lesbian and gay community and ethos was always unlikely – not least because of the significance of gender, class, 'race' and ethnicity and other differences in influencing diverse experiences (cf. Hennessy, 2000; Taylor, 2007). Nevertheless, the critical lesbian and gay communities that emerged in the 1970s were largely populated by those who were distinctively located in historical, cohort and generational terms (Rosenfeld, 2003). This was a founding generation of lesbians and gay men in the sense of 'a cohort that comes to social significance by virtue of constituting itself as cultural identity' (Edmunds and Turner, 2002: 7). This founding generation can be distinguished as a political generation 'in its rejection of the status quo and in its attempts to overturn current political values usually in response to historical circumstances' (ibid). Generations are linked to cohort experiences, and the constraints and opportunities that shape life chances and worldviews. They do not necessarily share one worldview (or ethos), as generations contain internally differentiated 'generation units' (Mannheim, quoted in Edmunds and Turner, 2002: 9). As far as sexualities and relationships are concerned, there is no 'one' generational experience, and within any generation there are diverse experiences. The experience that most successfully articulates itself as *the* generational one is the one that is best resourced to do so (cf. Edmunds and Turner, 2002). Sociologically speaking, the generations that have so far defined sexual-minority experience since the 1970s are the founding lesbian and gay generation and the queer generation that followed it (Warner, 2000). The raises an important question: Can the defining frames of interpretation generated by previous generations adequately explain the experiences of contemporary younger generations?

The cohorts that we are concerned with are those that were born between the mid-1970s and the late 1990s, who entered into their teens between the mid to late 1980s and the early 2000s, and who entered into their 20s between the mid-1990s and the late 2000s. If one of the defining experiences of earlier cohorts was that of a more-or-less absolute heterosexual landscape (where the public visibility of homosexuality was highly policed and enforced), one of the differentiating aspects of younger cohorts' experience is the increasing visibility of sexual minorities. By the mid-1980s, homosexuality had entered the public consciousness through AIDS, but also through lesbian and gay battles against negative representations of same-sex relationships. By the late 1980s, public debates about lesbian and gay families were in full swing, and Denmark had legalised same-sex unions. By the mid-1990s (when the oldest of the younger cohorts were aged in their mid-20s and the youngest were still young children), same-sex relationships were being represented in the media and television programmes like *Friends, Ellen, Brookside, Queer as Folk* and the like. By the mid-2000s, civil partnership was seen as akin to marriage in the UK. Thus, these cohorts have to a greater or lesser degree grown up with the cultural visibility of lesbian and gay identities and same-sex relationships, and will have legal recognition for their identities and relationships (in a variety of ways) for most of their adult lives. Many had grown up with a sense of the relative ordinariness of lesbian and gay identities and same-sex relationships, or developed this fairly early on in their lives.

These experiences can go hand-in-hand with the belief that heterosexualities and minority sexualities themselves are not so different. This appeared to us to be the underlying assumption where several of our interviewees spent hours discussing their relationships but made little or no mention of their sexual identities. It might also partly explain the *relatively* less significant ways (compared to previous studies) in which 'coming-out' out stories featured in interviewees' background narratives to their relational lives. As one woman put it 'I've never had this kind of big realisation that I'm gay' (Theresa, 110b), and as another woman recounted 'I just went with it, like with Stacey I just went with it [...]

it never really felt strange to me' (Angela, 106a). Further, it may partly explain why many people felt little need to socialise with others on the basis of a shared sexual identity. Many partners recounted having mostly heterosexual friends. Callum (203b), for example, preferred the company of his own and his partner's 'straight friends [who] see us as Mark and Callum, rather than [being gay]'. His partner, Mark (203a), commented that 'you would never know that we were any different to the straight friends that we've got'. On the one hand, some analysts could view this couple's comments as unwelcome evidence of normalisation or assimilation. On the other hand, the above quotations taken together could be viewed as evidence for something else: that minority sexual communities and identities are becoming less essential or vital in an era where the work for recognition has been done by previous generations. This may partly explain why some theorists are now discussing the decline of the modern regime of sexuality, and suggesting that the politics of sexual identity and sexual difference is being superseded by the politics of intimacy (Weeks, 2005) or becoming a spent force (Noys, 2008).

At the heart of Weeks et al.'s (2001) analysis of the family turn in non-heterosexual life, as discussed earlier, was another argument that loosely links to generational experience: that creative developments in families of choice and same-sex relationships, and the *ideals* of reciprocity and equality that they aspired to, should not be seen as isolated from developments that were reconfiguring relationships in the 'heterosexual world'. This points to a problematic assumption that underpins some arguments (like Blasius's) about a *distinctive* lesbian and gay ethos of – or approaches to – relating: that heterosexuality and marriage, and the links between them, have remained historically and generationally static. Thus, marriage and heterosexuality are primarily viewed in static institutional terms as 'givens', and not in terms of dynamic meanings and practices. Hence, while the creativity and vitality of lesbian and gay relationships are applauded, little credence is given to historical agency as far as heterosexuality is concerned. This undermines the ways in which definitions and practices of marriage have in some contexts become more flexible and open, which partly accounts for why same-sex relationships can be incorporated into marriage.

The politics of marriage

Same-sex marriage and the recent proliferation of marriage-like arrangements, along with continuing struggles for and against these, are often seen as representing a critical moment in the history of marriage as an institution (Oerton, 2008). While this can be viewed in negative, positive and ambivalent ways, it cannot be understood in isolation from longer-term and broader developments in the diversification and vitalisation of ordinary ways of relating on the ground. Before discussing this, let us briefly review the current state of affairs with respect to same-sex relationship recognition. Few countries currently afford same-sex couples the opportunity to fully participate in marriage. As of late 2011, those that do include Argentina, Belgium, Canada, Iceland, the Netherlands, Norway, Portugal, South Africa, Spain and Sweden. In addition, same-sex marriages are performed in Mexico City and in six states of the USA. Additionally, marriages are recognised but not performed in countries like Israel and France. As well as a growing number of European states, Australia, Brazil, Mexico, New Zealand and other countries have either nationwide or regional facilities for the recognition of same-sex or cohabiting relationships. Civil unions, civil partnerships and registered cohabitation, which often include exemptions from the automatic rights afforded heterosexual married couples, are the most common forms of legal recognition. To varying degrees they offer some of the legal, symbolic and material advantages associated with marriage, but often with more limited legal status. Same-sex marriage and civil unions are being debated, planned for *and* legislated against globally where most same-sex partners currently rely on 'do-it-yourself' affirmation and commitment ceremonies, or seek religious blessings where available. In short, the global picture is a patchy but dynamic one.

Where marriage now includes same-sex couples or sits alongside other ways of legally formalising adult couple and family relationships, heterosexual marriage's place at the top of the sexual hierarchy looks decidedly precarious. In these contexts, marriage is beginning to look like just one way among many of recognising and doing relationships. But this is not new. For many decades now, marriage has increasingly become the focus of contingent commitments, and sits alongside cohabitation, serial and more ad hoc partnering as one way of doing heterosexual relationships (Mansfield and Collard, 1988; McRae, 1999). While it is relatively usual for couples to live together before they are married, others don't marry because they are ambivalent about it, and others still choose not to marry because personal commitment is sufficient. Instead of seeing diverse ways of doing heterosexual relationships as alternatives *to* marriage, or indicative of its demise, some have argued they can be conceptualised as 'informal' marriages (Mansfield and Collard, 1988: 4). Thus, Mansfield and Collard argued in the late 1980s that the definition of marriage was changing, and being extended to encompass a broad range of relationships in practice (Mansfield and Collard, 1988: 4).

This notional extension of marriage to include all manner of relationships may be problematic, as it still privileges the normative frame and language of marriage to make sense of relationships. However, it does point to how the meanings of marriage are 'open', flexible and diverse. In the 1980s, Mansfield and Collard (ibid) argued that this was linked to changes in the public image of marriage, where there was a shift 'in emphasis from the external structure of married life to the private meaning of the marital relationships: the public institution of marriage is being privatised'. While the distinction between 'marriages' that are formalised or not is an important one, there are also radically diverse ways of conceiving and doing formalised marriage in practice. As well as those differences linked to class, ethnicity, religion, nationality and the like, there are other differences linked to family formation, the presence or absence of children, the demands of work and other commitments, personal preferences and interpersonal arrangements. It might be tempting to see the radical diversification, or privatisation, of meanings and practices of marriage as evidence of social instability and moral degeneration. However, as early as the 1960s, when discussing cohabitation, some argued that such diversification could be equally viewed as 'signs of moral regeneration' (Fletcher, cited in Mansfield and Collard, 1988: 5). Similarly, Giddens (1991) has seen such developments in terms of the life-politics of 'remoralising social life'. We prefer to see it as an aspect of the broader vitalisation of personal life, where models and meanings of relationships are not simply given but have to be actively grappled with. Indeed, frames for giving meaning to relationships are never straightforwardly imposed or taken up. Rather, they are vital in that they are emergent and have to be grappled with as such.

Once marriage has become so extended that it can, notionally at least, include radically diverse of ways of doing and giving meaning to heterosexual relationships, it is unsurprising that same-sex relationships should be included within it. If changes in marriage are indicative of the moral regeneration and vitalisation of personal life, then why not see same-sex marriage as an aspect of this? Viewed in this way, same-sex marriages can be seen as one aspect of what Stacey terms the postmodern family (Stacey, 1997; 2006), and as linked to the reconfiguration of gender, sexuality and personal relationships more broadly. Where modern frames and concepts are deployed to make sense of contemporary

marriages – same-sex or otherwise – this invariably entails overempha-
sising marriage as an ordering and homogenous institution, and impos-
ing a conceptual coherence on marriage that is deeply at odds with the
multiple, and often contradictory, meanings and practices associated
with ordinary marriages on the ground. This problem is inherent in
many of the existing debates about same-sex marriage, where modernist
frames continue to be deployed to understand the links between marriage and the politics of family, sexuality and gender. To emphasise this
point, it is worth briefly reviewing these debates.

While some constituencies see same-sex marriage and civil unions
as an ultimate marker of social and political tolerance, others see it as
indicative of the decline of religious and moral values in an increasingly secular world. Among conservative religious and social groups
especially, same-sex marriage is often interpreted as an attack on the
primacy and 'naturalness' of the heterosexual married bond that is
assumed to underpin a stable society. One dominating frame for academic debates about same-sex marriage is centred on the dichotomies
of accommodation and resistance. This concerns the extent to which
same-sex marriage represents a radical challenge to heteronormativity
or a triumph of heterosexual norms (see Harding, 2011: 41–3; Oerton,
2008). On the one hand, marriage is viewed as the legitimate aim of
lesbian and gay politics, and as the most appropriate strategy for non-
heterosexual citizenship (Calhoun, 2000; Eskridge, 2002; Sullivan, A.
1996). This position often understands the marriage contract as symbolising an emotional, financial, and psychological bond, highlights
the economic and social advantages of marriage, and the advantages
for the social inclusion of sexual minorities. Some analyses suggest that
legalising same-sex unions can reshape and modernise the institution
of marriage in keeping with gender and sexual equality (Kitzinger and
Wilkinson, 2004). On the other hand, some feminist, liberationist and
queer critics have argued that same-sex marriage represents the dominance of heterosexual values and undermines the distinctiveness of lesbian and gay cultures (Auchmuthy, 2004; Warner, 2000). They view the
extension of marriage to same-sex couples as a form of social regulation,
with profound normalising implications for same-sex relationships and
queer identities (Warner, 2000).

The political desire for marriage, some argue, is based on outmoded
notions of commitment. Ultimately, it may lead to normative constructions of socially responsible and irresponsible homosexuals, and
to the imposition of rules that may stifle the creativity of same-sex
partnerships (Donovan, 2004). Some feminist critics have further

argued that the valorisation of marriage as 'full citizenship' for lesbians and gay men is a naïve political strategy. They point to the historical role of the institution of marriage in the reproduction of patriarchal structures, and its grounding in gendered inequalities (Jackson, 1996; Jeffreys, 2004). Other feminists argue for 'full marriage' on the basis that civil unions and other forms of recognition reinscribe the superiority of heterosexual married relationships. In line with a progressive view of socio-legal developments, they see same-sex marriage as a global inevitability:

> The movement toward equality and justice for LGBT people has become a global one. It is no longer a question of 'whether' we will have the right of equal access to marriage worldwide; it has become a question of 'when'. For feminists, the question is now what will we do with this right once we have it – and what does it mean for our politics of sexuality, marriage and the family?
>
> Wilkinson (2004: 14)

These debates deploy many of the tropes of modernist thinking: progression/decline, structure/agency; regulation/resistance; dominance/submission. Diverse as they are, viewed together they express enduring themes and core tensions in modernist thinking about disintegration and order, emancipation and the impoverishment of personal culture (Heaphy, 2007). Overall, in line with conceptions of marriage as a lynchpin of modern (Foucault, 1979), patriarchal (Jackson, 1996) or capitalist projects, they view marriage as an *ordering project* that is linked in various ways to family, gender, sexual and broader social ordering. While continuity *and* discontinuity are two sides of the 'intricate relationship between the present social condition and the formation that preceded and gestated it' (Bauman, 1992: 187), each of these responses tends to overemphasise one side of the coin over the other. Taken together, they continue traditions of dichotomous framing of social issues to impose order on the meaning and implications of same-sex marriage. In addition, they imply that same-sex marriage is something that *demands* a position – *either* pro *or* con. In doing so, they tend to underemphasise radically diverse, uncertain and ambivalent meanings and attitudes associated with both heterosexual and same-sex marriage, and the radically diverse, uncertain and ambivalent directions that developments in marriage might take. A key challenge for understanding contemporary experiences involves a departure from inherited categories, conceptions and models of society and the social (Bauman,

1992). This involves developing new ways of conceiving the world and a new vocabulary for doing so. In important ways, the responses to same-sex marriage above fail to meet this challenge. What about other more nuanced responses?

Oerton (2008) suggests that since the 1990s there have been two waves of academic responses to same-sex marriage. The first, in evidence until the early to mid-2000s, was partly defined by debates of the kind we have considered here 'about the extent to which same-sex relationship recognition, in whatever guise it came, was radical, transgressive and destabilising of heteronormativity' (2008: 783). The second, in evidence from the mid-2000, 'is more open to constructive dialoguing across the political spectrum' (ibid: 784). In the later wave, Oerton includes 'analyses of the regulatory frameworks operating in and across different contexts, and the multiple drivers underpinning them' (ibid; see Harding, 2011; Hull, 2006; Stychin, 2003) and scholarship that comprises 'critical analyses [...] that contextualize the various meanings that recognition, commitment and ritual has for those whose lives are touched by existing and emergent laws' (ibid; see Lewin, 1998; 2008; Smart, 2008; Shipman and Smart, 2007; Weeks et al., 2001). She also notes how feminist academics have interwoven their lived experience with theoretical and political analyses (see the collection edited by Clarke and Finlay, 2004). Thus, she argues that recently there has been a shift towards the production of more highly nuanced academic scholarship on same-sex relationship recognition (see special issue of *Sexualities*, 2008). While there may be a shift occurring, it is fair to say that Oerton (2008) probably overstates the distinction between the first and second 'waves' she identifies. While there are some notable exceptions (including many of the works cited above), and while some recent responses may be more situated, complex and nuanced, the tendency is for academics to continue to deploy many of the tropes of modernist thinking, and especially the modernist regulation/resistance frame. For example, one of the most recent and nuanced contributions, entitled *Regulating Sexuality* (Harding, 2011), uses such a frame for comprehending legal consciousness with respect to same-sex relationship and parenting recognition.

Ordinariness and vitality

A core argument of this book is that understanding same-sex marriages and their social and political significance requires an understanding of the developments discussed so far in this chapter, combined with an exploration of the experiences of same-sex marriages on the ground. By taking these together we aim to generate insights into same-sex marriage as one expression of the new politics of ordinary and vital relationships. What do ordinariness and vitality mean in this context? As we have seen, in terms of contemporary sexual-minority and mainstream heterosexual cultures of relating, diversity is the order of the day. There is no homogenous lesbian and gay experience, or ethos of relating, that can be counterposed to any homogenous heterosexual one. Sexual-minority experience, like heterosexual experience, is radically diverse. Plummer (1995) acknowledges this in discussing late modern sexual stories, where 'different kinds of stories [are] emerging *alongside* the older ones' (1995: 131, his emphasis):

> In the late modern world, the very idea of 'being gay' may increasingly get transformed into the idea of a multiplicity of sexual/gendered/ relational/emotional, etc. beings in the world. Enter the time of post-gay and the post-lesbian? And, as importantly, the awareness of the dispersal of homosexualities must also mean the awareness of the dispersal of hetrosexualities. Indeed, late modernist stories dissolve such distinctions at base. The separate genders and their separate sexualities cannot so clearly be sustained.
>
> Plummer (1995: 142)

Continuity *and* change are important. While people continue to tell stories about being 'gay' or 'heterosexual', or being in a lesbian or heterosexual relationship, this cannot be taken as short-hand to describe any one way of living or relating. Similarly, stories about being partnered or married cannot be read as indicating any one way of organising or 'doing' a relationship. Claims to ordinariness can be read in multiple ways (Heaphy, 2011; Savage et al., 2000), and it would be mistaken to read young same-sex couples' claims to be 'like any other marriage' in any straightforward way as evidence of the normalising/regulating or queering/resisting potentials or effects of same-sex marriage. This would be a reductive view of these claims. In contrast, our argument is that claims to ordinariness are sometimes an explicit, and more often an implicit, recognition that 'all' marriages are the same *and* different to the extent that they are vital in terms of interpersonal affect, and the meanings and practices they involve.

Marriages nowadays – same-sex or otherwise – need to be understood in terms of the *vitality* of the relational landscape. Marriage as an institution no longer has the universal ordering and constraining power that is commonly associated with modern marriage. Elsewhere it has been argued that one of the defining features of late modernity is how gender and sexual identities, meanings and practices have become so open (or individualised) that heterosexualit*ies* have become radically diverse (cf. Giddens, 1991; 1992) and that marriage is a zombie institution (Beck, 2000). It has also been suggested that because of interlinked processes of detraditionalisation and individualisation, heterosexual married couples nowadays meet as equals (in principle at least) in negotiating relationships (Giddens, 1992). While the assumptions underpinning these arguments have been the subject of trenchant criticism (Adkins, 2002; Heaphy, 2007; Jamieson, 1998), the core arguments themselves point to how heterosexualit*ies* nowadays cannot be reduced to the omnipotent heterosexuality that is often imagined in critical socio-cultural analyses of modern marriage. In this respect, Henning Bech has argued that it is the changing nature of heterosexuality that needs to be placed at the heart of analyses about same-sex marriage. He argues that heterosexual experience is becoming more and more like modern homosexual experience:

> 'The heterosexuals' [...] know that that the family is not an eternal institution into which they have entered once and for all; they may divorce, establish another family, live outside the family, use the world of strangers as a resource, a place where one can go and find other people to build up new kinds of relationships. They, too, experience promiscuity, broken relationships and serial monogamy, and they have established networks of friends other than relatives.
>
> Bech (1997: 195–6)

Bech argues against the idea that same-sex marriage should be seen as 'normalisation', 'bourgeosification' or 'straightification'. On the contrary, he says, same-sex marriage has become possible because of decline of modern constructions of marriage and 'the family', which is influencing a 'basic *homo*-genisation of ways of life' (1997: 203). From Bech's perspective, new personal stories about the ordinariness of same-sex relationships reflect the ways in which heterosexual experiences have come into line with homosexual ones. Whether we accept or reject Beck's, Giddens's or Bech's approaches to explaining the issue, they are agreed that the differences and distinctions between heterosexual and homosexual relationships may be less important than the 'new' similarities. As we discussed in the previous section, this is a point that many younger same-sex couples who see themselves as married agree with.

Same-sex marriage is not the end of the creativity of same-sex relation-ships, but is linked to the intensive vitalisation of heterosexual ones. At the root of this is how marriages have become increasingly vitalised in practice – where people must grapple with conflicting demands, pres-sures and ideals, expectations, emotions, disappointments *and* possibili-ties associated with partnerships. Thus, the vitality of marriage is linked to the vitality of relational life and personal life more broadly – same-sex or otherwise – in advanced modernity. This is expressed in the broader culture where relationships and marriages are now regularly represented and storied in radically diverse ways. Media representations of relation-ships and marriage, for example, reflect the multiple meanings and prac-tices associated with them. While headlines may often link the current state of marriage to social progress or demise, the real stories beneath the headlines are the personal ones of relational vitality: of emotional commitments, struggles, changes and the like. Plummer has captured the dynamics at play through the metaphor of the personal story, none of which he argues 'are true for all time and space':

> We invent our stories with a passion, they are momentarily true, we may cling to them, they may become our lives and then we may move on. Clinging to the story, reworking it, denying it. But some-where behind all this story telling there are real, active, embodied, impassioned lives.
>
> Plummer (1995: 170)

This points to an important story about same-sex marriage that often gets lost in abstract debates about the issue and the reductive terms in which they are often framed: the *vital* relationships that people in same-sex marriages have, and how these are linked to real, active, embodied, impassioned lives. This is not to say that such lives and relationships are not socially shaped or patterned or are not linked to the workings of power. Indeed, vitalism as a philosophical tradition has been modi-fied and taken up in critical theoretical work to explore how lives are socially shaped relationally, where 'subjects, concepts are composed of nothing more-or-less than relations' (Fraser et al., 2005), and to under-stand power in the sense that Foucault understood it when he discussed the 'turn to life', bio-politics and bio-power (Olma and Koukouzelis, 2007). The point is that same-sex marriages as they are lived are more complexly shaped, patterned and *made* than many of those in favour of or against same-sex marriage suggest. By focusing on their vitality, we can explore the social influences and power that same-sex marriages involve in emergent and relational ways. The focus on relationality, in turn, implies that it would be mistaken to equate the vitality of relationships and personal life with the contemporary disembeddedness of personal life as some theorists do (Bauman, 2003; Beck and Beck-Gernsheim, 1995, 2002; Giddens, 1992). Rather, it can partly be viewed as an aspect of the interplay of embeddedness *and* openness, which was a core concern of the study which is at the heart of this book.

Conceptualising the vitality relationships

In line with modernist frames for understanding relationships, existing empirical studies of heterosexual married relationships suggest they are highly gendered and support unequal relations between men and women (Duncombe and Marsden, 1993; Duncombe et al., 2004; 1999; Mansfield and Collard, 1988). Despite changes in the ideologies of gendered work, intimacy and democratic personal relations, research suggests the continuation of distinctively gendered relational cultures, especially with respect to finances, monogamy and family-making (child care, domestic work, emotion work and the like). Such studies indicate women and men's continuing *struggles* for equal and mutually fulfilling personal relationships. In contrast, studies on same-sex relations generally suggest a smoother incorporation of egalitarian ideals into day-to-day relational practice. Research on same-sex couples has also explicitly focused on finances, monogamy and family-making, and suggests these are more-or-less 'freely' negotiated in accordance with egalitarian ideals, and that the struggles and disappointments documented in married heterosexual relationships are less prevalent in same-sex ones (Dunne, 1997; 1999; Heaphy et al., 1999; 2004; Sullivan, M. 2004). Gender sameness, as well as an egalitarian relational ethos (as discussed earlier), are often held to explain the more equal and mutually satisfying operation of same-sex relations.

Such interpretations of research data are relatively convincing when viewed through the lens of abstract theoretical debates about the resilience of gender structures, institutionalised heterosexuality and the possibilities that same-sex relations offer for reworking gender. They do not, however, account for or illuminate the vitality and complex workings of either contemporary heterosexual *or* same-sex relationships in sufficiently situated ways, and fail to fully illuminate the ordinary, but nevertheless complex, influences on expectations, meanings and practices at the level of day-to-day relating. This, we suggest, is partly because inherited (modernist) sociological models for understanding intimate relationships have tended to become congealed as fairly solidified normative frames that dominate research on personal life and interpretations of it (Heaphy, 2007; Smart, 2007). As a consequence of this, heterosexual married relationships tend to be interpreted through overarching structural (gender) frames that do not illuminate the *range* of influences on personal experiences, meanings, values and practices (such as those related to finances, monogamy and family-making), how these interact with and contradict each other, and how they become embedded and/or open to change. Same-sex relationships, in comparison, have tended to be interpreted through 'liberationist' (Blasius, 1994), 'post-emancipatory' (Giddens, 1991; 1992) or 'queer' (Roseneil, 2002) frames that often ignore the embeddedness of meanings, values and practices per se. This has resulted in an overemphasis on their creative and 'freely' agentic qualities that fails to fully account for the mundane influences and practices that constrain and shape such creativity and agency and enable it. It also fails to account fully for the multi-dimensionality of same-sex relationships (the expectations, tensions, contradictions, joys, disappointments and possibilities).

To capture a sense of this multi-dimensionality and develop a more situated understanding of the socio-cultural implications of civil partnership, the study discussed in this book set out to explore how civil partnerships are 'made' and experienced in practice; how 'partnered' or 'married' life is defined, constructed and linked to various areas of living (e.g. work, family, friendship, parenting, finances, sexuality, leisure and so on); and how personal and couple meanings and practices associated with civil partnership are influenced by biographical, social, cultural and temporal factors. This, we hoped, would generate insights into the meanings, experiences and practices associated with civil partnership in day-to-day life, and enable the exploration of the implications for change and continuity with respect to marriage.

As noted in the Preface and Introduction, we interviewed 50 same-sex couples where partners were aged up to 35 when they entered into civil partnership. We interviewed them together and apart to generate three relationship stories about each relationship: a couple one and two individual ones. It was not our primary intention to look for contradictions between the stories partners tell in different interview contexts, although they do exist and can be sociologically interesting. Rather, our aim was to explore the conarrated (and emergent) couple story of the relationship via the joint interview, and to link this to partners' socially shaped relational orientations and habituated practices that were explored via the personal narratives generated in individual interviews (see Appendix 1). Central to our approach to interviewing couples and to analysis was an interactionist understanding of scripting (see Atkinson and Housley, 2003; Kimmel, 2007; Plummer, 1983; Simon and Gagnon, 2004), and an exploration of its potential value in generating 'new' stories of couple relationships. This allowed us to conceptualise young couples' civil partnerships as vital relational projects that involve multi-dimensional dynamics of scripting and power. Scripting here refers to the stories that are told about relationships, but it is also a metaphor for how relationships are 'done' in practice. We adopted a pragmatic approach to conceptualising the link between the stories that our interviewees told and their actual lives. This was based on Plummer's (1995) argument that personal stories can be explored less for their literal truth or aesthetic qualities than for the part they play in the life of the person, social relationships and the social order. From this perspective, partners' narratives could be viewed as a 'cite' (Gubrium and Holstein, 2009) for exploring how relational practices are shaped by the culture (cultural scripts), how cultural scenarios are taken up, negotiated, reworked or contested between partners (interpersonal scripts) and how partners process interpersonal experience and cultural scenarios (intrapsychic scripts) (Jackson and Scott, 2010a, 2010b; Simon and Gagnon, 2004).

More specifically, we deployed scripting as an analytical tool for thinking about how young couples' civil partnerships are linked to mainstream and marginal, queer, personal community and other relational discourse at a cultural level (cultural scripts), involve the socially shaped relating orientations and practices that people bring to their relationships (personal scripts), and how through *interaction* in relationships couple stories and practices emerge (couple scripts). These discourses, orientations, stories and practices can be conceptualised as interlinked orders of relational scripting that are involved in young same-sex couples' marriages. Generating couple and individual interview stories enabled us to explore how personal and couple relating scripts are influenced by cultural scripts, but also how interlinked personal, couple and cultural scripts are reaffirmed, altered and generated *through* interactions. To explore young same-sex marriages as scripted is to acknowledge that they are neither wholly predictable nor wholly creative, but are vital in how they are socially shaped *and* dynamic. This vitality is partly linked to different partners' sense of how their relationships should, could and might be like; to the interplay of constraints and possibilities that partners encounter; and to the range of responses (cognitive and affective) that they (and others) have to such constraints and possibilities. In the past, scripting has been associated with a kind of symbolic interactionism that was concerned with how social actions and interaction follow scripts. This is an impoverished view of scripting theory, as Plummer argues about sexual scripting theory:

> In the hands of some researchers, it [scripting theory] has become a wooden mechanical tool for identifying uniformities in [...] conduct: the script determines activity, rather than emerging through activity. What is actually required is to show the nature of [...] scripts as they *emerge* in encounters.
>
> Plummer, quoted in Knapp et al. (2004: 132)

The interplay of embeddedness and openness is important in understanding same-sex partners' emergent stories and scripts. Personal stories of same-sex marriage are linked to family discourse at a sociocultural level, and this is itself composed of multiple and often contradictory discourses. Such discourses are historically embedded but also underscore the diverse possibilities for relating. In line with the notion of 'habitus' (Bourdieu, 1977), people bring their biographically rooted and socially shaped orientations – their embedded 'naturalised' meanings, values and practices – to their relationships. But also in line with the notion of habitus which, as Bourdieu acknowledges, is to some degree open, people's relating orientations are subject to modification over the lifecourse. While changing cultural norms and values influence relating orientations, personal relationships are likely to be a key site of interaction through which 'new' relationship scripts emerge and feed back into the culture. It would be naïve to ignore the significance and power of relational scripting at the levels of culture and habituated practice (Bourdieu, 1977). Personal stories always reference such scripting. However, it would be equally naïve to ignore how new relational scripts (at the level of culture, and social and personal practice) emerge through interpersonal interaction. Thus, it is crucial to acknowledge continuities *and* changes in how same-sex relationships *and* marriages are done, and that the flow of power with respect to marriage is not uni-directional: same-sex marriages are not simply conventional *or* creative, they are both. In the following chapters we explore how same-sex partners put convention and creativity to work in narrating and doing their relationships and marriages.

2
Relationships, Partnerships and Marriages

In our study of young same-sex partners in formalised relationships, we partly set out to explore the ways in which the partners conceived and practised their relationships as 'like' and/or 'unlike' marriage. In light of the findings of previous studies of same-sex relationships, and some of own research on previous generational experiences, we were taken aback by the extent to which our interviewees saw their relationships *as* marriage or as akin to it. By the same token we were also surprised by how so few interviewees were keen to emphasise the distinction between civil partnership and marriage. Our surprise was no doubt linked to our own 'older' generational experience and positioning. This chapter begins by providing an overview of the ways in which partners described their formalised relationships as marriage, as akin to it or as different to it. It then describes in depth three couples' relationships to illustrate how same-sex marriage stories emerge from embedded lives and relationships on the ground. Following this, we consider how claims and practices of ordinary relationships are linked to a sense of 'assumed acceptance' of same-sex relationships in the situated contexts in which people live, but also the ways in which socio-cultural positioning (in terms of ethnicity and race, economic resources and class, disability and religion) could constrain a sense of ordinariness, acceptance and new relational possibilities. Gender, in and of itself, did not structure a sense of ordinariness or acceptance in any straightforward way, and this points to how static institutional and structural frames cannot account for the diverse, situated and dynamic nature of marriages in practice.

Civil partnerships and marriages

Overall, the personal stories generated by our study highlight how, in practice, civil partnership can be understood as a form of marriage.

Despite the fact that civil partnership is technically distinct from marriage, the majority of partners viewed themselves as married and had taken to 'marriage' like ducks to water. Of the 100 partners, 74 saw and presented themselves as married. It is not that they were unaware of the legal distinction between civil partnership and marriage, but for the most part they deemed the distinction to be insignificant. The general tendency was to use the terms interchangeably, with the emphasis being on the fact that they saw themselves as married:

> Diego (208b):   actually I felt that being in a civil partnership, or being married – I don't necessarily distinguish between the two, I don't really see the point [...]
>
> Jan (208a):   we use them interchangeably.

> I do tend to use them interchangeably but I know that really, you know in the eyes of the state they're not necessarily the same thing but that's pretty much how we see it. So yeah, yeah so we use them interchangeably.
>
> Lucas (221a)

> I mean civil partnership it's a mouthful. Marriage comes right out. Rolls off the tongue.
>
> Sara (121b)

For some partners, like Sara, the language of civil partnership was cumbersome. It was easier to describe yourself as married rather than 'civilly partnered', and to refer to your husband, wife or spouse as opposed to 'civil partner' in everyday interactions. 'Partner' on its own was viewed as too vague. Even if people understood the term to refer to an intimate relationship, and not a business one, it did not signify the loving and committed nature of the relationship in the way marriage did. In everyday contexts, using 'civil partnership' to describe the relationship seemed too technical and obtuse, whereas marriage needed little explanation. More important, for many, was the fact that they did not see their civil partnership and relationship as marriage-like: as far as they were concerned they *were* married. Generally speaking, this was confirmed by the couples' close and broader circles:

> But the thing is I think in my experience of being a gay man entering into civil partnership, I think most of my friends, the people that I'd discussed it with, were also referring to it [...] as getting married.
>
> Otto (212a)

If you're already out to the person and you say you're getting married to your girlfriend, I think everybody knows what that means. Very few people I've met have a problem with [using the words] marriage or wedding about gay people.

Olga (126b)

What makes these stories historically distinctive is the extent to which young same-sex couples' narratives of being married are encouraged and supported by their personal and broader social networks. Also, unlike previous generations of non-heterosexuals, the young partners saw little or no differences between their relationships and formalised heterosexual marriages in terms of what they involved in day-to-day living. As Sara (121b), quoted earlier, remarked: 'I just think that we were both raised with parents who were married and we've been around people who are married and we consider we have a marriage'. Most partners believed that civil partnership gave them full recognition and protection in line with heterosexual married couples. In this respect, civil partnership and marriage were different 'only in name'. For most, the legal distinction was insignificant, as Jorge recounted:

some people ask me 'oh don't you, mind, that it's not called marriage' but we've never really felt it [...] maybe it's discriminatory but I've never felt it that way [...] we've never really ever felt discriminated against in that it [is] a civil partnership and not full marriage, the rights are the same, only the name.

Jorge (205b)

Only 15 out of 100 partners did not see themselves as married on the basis of the technical distinction between civil partnership and marriage. Of these, seven partners viewed the distinction as a good thing: they did not want marriage because they saw it as intrinsically linked to plans for having children or as rooted in religion. As Ben (210a) put it:

[I] don't have a problem with – in fact I positively think that civil partnership is a good thing [...] I see marriage as being one thing, I see civil partnership as being another thing – the important thing for me was they had the same legal status and they afford the same rights and the name actually is quite healthy, as a different name. I mean marriage carries with it a lot of connotations including a lot of religious connotations.

Ben's comments illustrate the striking way in which partners who supported the distinction between civil partnerships and marriage were *not* explicitly critical of marriage as a heterosexual institution. Eight of those who did not see themselves as fully married wanted formal marriage: two on religious grounds and the remaining six on the basis that the distinction did not reflect the realities that same-sex and heterosexual committed relationships were the same. In these senses, civil partnership was 'second class'. Doris (104a), who saw her 'real' marriage as dating from the religious commitment ceremony she and her co-parent (Maria, 104b) entered into before civil partnership was available, recounted:

> It's our relationship and they call it a civil partnership and we feel it's a marriage [...] that was why I was against civil partnerships in the first place 'cause it's not marriage, if it was marriage then just call it marriage but it's not, it's something else, it's less than that.

As well as the two partners who expressed discontent with the distinction between civil partnership and marriage on religious grounds, four people were unhappy with the fact that they could not hold their ceremonies in a church. However, this was not on the basis of strong religious belief as such but was linked to a sense of exclusion from the 'traditions' associated with marriage and because church weddings would have been easier and cheaper to organise. Mark (203a) and Callum (203b) were one such couple:

> Callum: I said I would never get married unless I got married in a church and when I realised that through research after research, eye wracking, eye hurting stuff, I realised that it would never change in a church 'cause I always want to be recognised, not as a gay man getting married but as another human being getting married, like a straight couple, like a man gets married to a woman and they can have this big church service and choir and everything and that's what I wanted, but we decided, yeah.
>
> Mark: To settle for the ship.

Ten people were highly ambivalent or unsure what they thought about the legal distinction between civil partnership and marriage. However, whether they viewed it as marriage or not, the majority (77) seemed more-or-less fully content with current arrangements for recognising same-sex relationships. Given that the majority viewed themselves as *already* married, it was unsurprising that only two brought up their intention to formally marry if the opportunity presented itself in the future. Others were unlikely to go through the 'whole thing' again:

Olga (126b):	The whole thing was a big job. We're not getting married again.
Mandy (126a):	No.
Olga:	Oh (laughs).
Mandy:	Oh, it's far too stressful.
Olga:	Yeah, it was just months and months of hyper-organisation.

In discussing same-sex marriage in the context of the contemporary politics of sexuality, kinship and family, Butler (2002) has argued that it is a topic that requires double thinking: it is both important and risky as a political strategy. It is a topic that requires even more multiple ways of thinking when same-sex marriage is viewed from the perspective of lives on the ground. This is especially the case when we consider that while civil partnership and marriage are not one and the same in law, civil partnerships and civil unions are often seen and lived as a form of marriage in everyday lives. Despite the historical links between the institution of marriage, institutionalised heterosexuality and marginalised homosexualities, many same-sex couples are now actively deploying the linguistic and social conventions associated with marriage in actively making the nature of their commitments intelligible to themselves and others, actively claiming their ordinariness and actively structuring their relationships in interaction with others. On the one hand, this deployment of convention has radical implications for disrupting the heterosexual panorama and destabilising ideologies of gender and sexual difference with respect to marriage. On the other hand, the risks of deploying convention in this way are that non-heterosexual commitments, claims to ordinariness and relational structuring are understood as an issue of parity with heterosexual marriage. This potentially shores up the idea of the couple as the natural focus of adult relational commitments and makes its personal, social and legal privileging seem inevitable. Also, while the effort and agency that same-sex couples put into claiming and creating ordinary marriages could be seen as a commitment to the life-politics of relational and sexual choice, they risk making invisible the social and cultural dynamics that make couple-centred lives seem like an 'obvious' and 'natural' choice. The challenge that personal stories of civil partnership and 'ordinary' marriages present for multiple ways of thinking stems partly from the ways in which they seem to emerge 'naturally' from embedded lives on the ground. In the following section we offer some examples of this.

Situating stories: marriages in lives

Hanna and Tammy (108a and 108b)

Hanna is a 26-year-old white woman who works in social care and has a low income. She is in a partnership with Tammy, aged 29, a white woman who also works in social care and earns an average income. They 'married' ten months before the interview. Neither use 'lesbian' to describe their identities, although they do talk about 'gay marriage'. They met when Hanna struck up a conversation with Tammy in a bar. The relationship developed from a first date where 'we were both chuffed with each other 'cause we didn't have a drink and we still kept a conversation going' (Hanna). Both were living with their parents when they met. Tammy recalls: 'about a fortnight or something [after our first date] I more-or-less moved into your Mam's'. The living conditions were cramped with no privacy. As Hanna puts it:

> I always thought I could never afford to live like on me own but then Tammy got herself a new job [...] so like we went to council and said that we was overcrowded, and it took like a year to get this place and then like we moved in here and it's been the best thing we've ever done hasn't it?

Three or four months after they met, Hanna recalls Tammy had 'asked us to marry you, hadn't you? [You] made this nice romantic meal for us and everything and went down on one knee'. But as Hanna puts it they did not 'set a date or anything 'cause again we always thought we never had enough money to do it 'cause we thought it would be too expensive'. However, Hanna's sister was diagnosed with a terminal illness and 'really wanted us to get married while she was still alive'. As Hanna recounts:

> It was me sister who give us all the ideas of how to do it, like cheaply and how to save money on things and, and like Tammy's Mam paid for the food, my Mam paid for like the hall and the disco and like [...] we'd asked for presents to help towards the wedding so then we could like save us money and we could afford it and that but we

managed [...] were getting married and me sister like died a week later but at least she knew we were getting married, and that's all that she was bothered about.

While these specific circumstances influenced them to marry when they did, they were 'always' keen to marry each other. For Tammy 'it was just the next step wasn't it? It was just "oh why can't we get married" [...] we loved each other so'. Hanna wanted to marry because:

this might sound corny and things like that, but like I felt like [...] I finally found me soul mate, that's how it feels like, we've got a really strong bond and I've never had that with anybody before and I just loved her so much and like Tammy says we just felt it was the next step to take [...] to sort of like sort of show each other how much we love each other.

Both partners feel that they have faced many challenges as a couple 'compared to like some other couples out there'. In the first two weeks Hanna 'got taken into hospital 'cause I wasn't very well and I was saying [...] she'll not want a girlfriend that's always sick [...] but she [...] was there every day that she could be there [...] all visiting hours she was there [...]. I'm thinking "What's going on here?", like I've never had someone like this before'. As well as Hanna's sister's death, they have had money worries to do with a family member's bankruptcy. Hanna believes 'it's just brought us together'. Both of their families have been supportive of them, but Tammy also recounted that 'all the sort of caring responsibilities always seem to end up on us'. They find themselves 'trying to do as much for everyone as we can' but that, together with work, means 'that sometimes it feels like we're spreading ourself too thinly and not having time with each other'. But being there for family is crucially important and family care underpins the values they share. As Hanna puts it:

I think I share the same values as me parents you know, try and work things out if we can, and kind of like in it for the long run [...] I'd like to think that if anything happened to Hanna if she had any kind of disability or anything that I'd like stand by her through thick and thin you know like me Dad stood by me Mam [...]. When [Mam's disability] started coming on [...] their friends all started to disappear [...] they've just got each other and obviously like me and me brother [...] they're quite happy and I think sometimes that's all you need if you've got like the love of your family

Kathryn and Louise (105a and 105b)

Kathryn is a white woman aged 37 who works as a service manager and earns an above average salary. Her partner of almost eight years is Louise, a white woman who is four years older and works part time as an administrator and earns a low salary. They were 'married' over five years ago. They have one child together and another on the way. They refer to themselves as 'gay'. They met through friends, and fairly immediately hit it off. They were struck by a number of coincidences in their tastes. Also, as Louise put it, they: 'just happened to be very similar, because of the similar type of [...] middle-class upbringing [...] very similar values'. Louise continues:

> And I think that linked, very much linked to [...] family life and whether we wanted children or not. I know that was a very early conversation we had, was about family and children and stuff, 'cause I knew, I certainly knew that I wanted children.

After a year they had a humanist commitment ceremony, as civil partnership was not yet available. The commitment ceremony was their 'real' wedding. Their families attended and were pleased for them, 'but probably a little bit apprehensive and didn't know quite what to expect'. Most of their friends are heterosexual, and even their few gay friends hadn't been to a commitment ceremony before. There were about 120 people there, and Kathryn and Louise were especially pleased because the woman presiding over the ceremony was 'brilliant':

> she actually said, "you know, at the end of the day, we're here because two people love each other and [...] they want to show, in front of all of you, that they're very serious about their relationship, they want to be together forever, they want you [...] to share in that and be part of it and will you support them" [...] I think it really got people thinking, quite a few people came up to us, on the day and since and said, "oh it really got me thinking, of course your relationship is as important as anybody else's".

A couple of months after the ceremony they 'went to the doctors and said, we're gay [...] where do we need to go and how do we go about having a baby?' As Kathryn recounts: 'I'm four years older than Louise, so we thought "Oh, I'll go first and see what can happen"'. They went 'complete NHS just the same as anyone else having treatment' and had very positive experiences. After some disappointments about not conceiving through the first donor, they were offered another and 'got pregnant on the second attempt with that donor [...] And we just moved into this house, I must have been pregnant but we didn't know'. Louise is now pregnant. As Kathryn puts it:

> now it's not just about our relationship, it's about our family's, so the shift has very much gone from our relationship to our family and [their daughter] notices differences and all her little friends notice a difference, but not in a negative way it's just factual for them [...] "We're just a different type of family" [...] tends to be the stock phrase isn't it, that we're just a different type of family?

Civil partnership itself did not figure highly in Kathryn and Louise's story. In some ways they see it as a marriage and in some ways they don't. On the one hand, in terms of everyday practices they recount:

Kathryn: I probably view it in exactly the same way as a marriage.
Louise: Yep, don't see it any differently [...] you get on my nerves sometimes, I get on yours, other times we don't.
Kathryn: You've got decisions to make about your family
Louise: Decisions to make, yeah, you're knackered at the end of a day, [...] running around doing a hundred and one things
Kathryn: Yeah, and, and as we've said before, the majority of our friends are married and heterosexual and we just
Louise: Don't see any difference.

Elsewhere, however, Kathryn recounted: 'when we use the terms 'marriage' or 'wife' it's more about conforming to make it easier for other people I guess to understand, but for me, we're not married, we've got a Civil Partnership and you're my life partner'. They are agreed that it's the legal side of things 'that is most important': As Kathryn puts it:

> if we were in that situation with a hospital, the police, whatever it is, applying for mortgages or whatever it is, I don't have to say 'Yes, she's my partner, we've been together seven years' [...] by saying Civil Partner people know what that means and I think they know that it's, that there's the same [...] level of importance as a marriage.

While Kathryn and Louise were drawn together by similar family experiences and shared values, their own relational values are distinct from those they grew up with. As Kathryn puts it: 'even before I'd even considered a relationship with a woman, I [...] remember [...] thinking I'm not gonna be the sort of woman that will be at home and doing the cooking, cleaning and everything while the husband comes home and sits down in front of the telly [...] I wanted very much a relationship that was a partnership, not two different roles'. Similarly, Louise recounts:

> we're Jewish and there was quite a pressure in those days to marry somebody else that was Jewish, [my dad] was a little bit older, time was running out sort of thing and he wasn't married yet, [my mum] was still living at home, and was looking for a bit of an escape [...]. They married for the wrong reasons [...] they're both incapable of communicating really [...] I want to share my life with somebody [...] share everything, that's thoughts, feelings, emotions, money, experiences, all of those things [...] if you commit to somebody it should be you give yourself really [...] that's very, very different to their approach.

Fredrick and Tim (209a and 209b)

Fredrick is a 36-year-old white man who works in communications and earns a higher than average salary. His partner Tim is a white 33 year-old who works in finance and earns a higher salary. They met seven years ago over the internet, and were 'married' two years ago. After 'going out' together for a couple of months, Tim came out to his mother. Her response was to say 'Go for the weekend and I'll tell [your dad]'. While Fredrick was out to his parents they had really liked his previous boyfriend which made Tim nervous. Fredrick gets on wonderfully with Tim's parents. He hasn't seen his own father for a while now as they never got on. He views Tim's dad as more of a father.

After a year, Tim moved into Fredrick's shared rented accommodation. They wanted a space of their own, and decided to buy a house, but that involved Fredrick commuting for five hours a day. As Tim put it, 'you were depressed and just come home and sleep, and get up and go to work and come home and sleep [...] you didn't have a life'. Fredrick left the job, was unemployed for six months and then started working closer to home. When things were settled he 'proposed' to Tim: 'We'd sort of talked about having a civil partner – or getting married for ages, hadn't we?' This was followed by nine months of organising. They found the perfect place for their wedding which they initially thought was unaffordable, but:

> Fredrick: somehow managed to convince ourselves that, actually, we could double the budget to our wedding [...]

Tim:	(laughs)
Frederik:	And so we went for the big wedding. We hired [the venue].
Tim:	Took out a few more credit cards (laughs).
Frederik:	Took out a few more credit cards.
Tim:	And away we went.

There were about 85 people at the ceremony and 150 at the evening celebrations. As far as they are concerned, it was worth the cost because, as Fredrick puts it: 'traditional weddings are [...] very beautiful occasions [...] And we wanted ours to be similarly beautiful'. As Tim recounts, 'We wanted the wow factor really'. The wedding was a turnaround in terms of unexpected responses from some older members of Tim's family who were initially nervous about going to a same-sex wedding but who, according to Fredrick, 'to this day, say, "Oh, it's the best wedding I've ever been to [...] it was so lovely [...] It was so romantic'. For Tim it was 'a perfect day', for Fredrick 'It was the best day absolutely ever'. Getting married was the 'icing on the cake'. It didn't change how they felt about each other or how they did their relationship, it just 'Felt right, felt like the next step' (Fredrick) and 'it kind of makes it a bit more complete' (Tim). They recount:

Tim:	It's almost like a process you go through (laughs) of kind of getting to know someone, going out with them, and kind of like the final, complete step of that is kind of marriage and [...] I think that's just where we got to, wasn't it?
Frederik:	It's kind of the way society does things, and I think, because of that, you're kind of probably slightly conditioned to expect that your life process is you meet someone, you marry them, you grow old together

In addition, Tim remarks, 'I think there was a little bit in there as well about the equal kind of rights [...] officially now we are next of kin for each other [...] but certainly wasn't a major factor'. Despite one of Fredrick's brothers who has 'inherited' his father's homophobia, he and Tim have had good experiences of being recognised as a couple, especially 'in those situations of being in hospital or doctors or whatever, they've actually always been very, very good. But [...] technically, they could've refused one of us entry to see the other one or something'. Dealing with health professionals is something they have much experience of as Fredrick has epilepsy, and Tim was recently ill and then diagnosed with a degenerative disease. For Tim, dealing with the practicalities of the health issues they've encountered has 'brought us closer together'. He recounts:

> it's almost a bridge you've kind of crossed [...] he had to take me to the toilet and wipe your arse and stuff like that, and you think if somebody's going to stand by me and do that then actually, I haven't got many problems in our relationships because you know if he'll do that for a month to get me back on my feet [...] or [...] if I'll sit with him when he's had a seizure [...] there's a possibility that in five or ten years time I could end up in a wheelchair or something but I don't feel scared by that as much as I would have done if he wasn't around [but it is also] those little things that really do make a difference and just make you feel more secure and more comfortable.

For Fredrick, the key to their relationship is love, unlike his parents' relationship that 'was based around the fact that my dad had got my mum pregnant'. He feels his approach to his relationships 'is different purely because I was lucky and found someone I love [...] Rather than my mum who was forced into it by circumstance'. In contrast, Tim sees his relationship with Fredrick as 'reasonably similar' to his parents', who are open, communicative and couple-focused. He recounts: 'I won't say there's anything majorly different or anything I particularly saw with my parents that I was like "Uh, no mustn't do that or must change that" or anything like that'.

Ordinariness, acceptance and difference

A striking feature of the stories of Hanna and Tammy, Kathryn and Louise and Fredrick and Tim is their confidence in their ordinariness. Hanna and Tammy's story is of an ordinary relationship that is actively embedded in mundane practices linked to mutual family care, local commitments and supports for the couple. Their story is also a fairly ordinary one of romantic and more mundane practices of love. It is an unexceptional story of the dynamic life-contexts in which commitments are lived and develop, including financial constraints, everyday dilemmas and life-crises linked to illness and death. This points to the ways in which partners themselves saw their couple relationships as vital: as central to negotiating the challenges thrown up by day-to-day living. Marriage itself was viewed as a relatively ordinary way of acknowledging this centrality to each other and to close associates, and its continuation into the future (see Chapter 4).

Kathryn and Louise's narratives tell a story that is also inflected by their social and personal circumstances. Like Hanna and Tammy, their story concerns mundane family practices, but is more focused on care, commitments and supports involved in parenting. They place less emphasis on romantic love as a driver in their relationship and more on their shared class and cultural backgrounds, their compatible family values and their practices and plans with respect to parenting. Their narrative of parenting-centred couple commitments is in many senses a common one. While the detail of their becoming parents may still seem exceptional, they also signal the 'ordinary' options that come with middle-class confidence. While they are ambivalent about the language of marriage, they are committed to its ordinary ideals: communication, sharing a life and fully giving yourself to the commitment (see Chapter 3).

Fredrick and Tim's story is of a relationship that is actively supported by Fredrick's mother and Tim's parents. Fredrick's account is a familiar one of good relationships with most family members and more strained relationships with others. The couple's account of the developing commitment involves the tribulations of planning a grand traditional wedding that they could not afford, the day-to-day challenges of home-making, work, commuting, unemployment, and the trials of 'depression' and serious illness. At the heart of their story the couple features as the focus of mutual care and as central to a sense of security for the future. Their wedding, though less modest than Hanna and Tammy's ceremony and more formal than Kathryn and Louise's one, is also portrayed as a family event, where the relationship is validated by family and friends as a form of marriage or as on a par with it.

Like Kathryn and Louise, whose use of the terminology of civil partnership and marriage depends on whom they are interacting with, Fredrick in his interaction with the academic interviewer punctuates his own enthusiastic account of his marriage with a note about being 'slightly conditioned'. This does not make his story or the emotions and commitments that underpin it any less 'real', but it does highlight that these are not scripts that are simply followed but emerge through the vital circumstances of day-to-day interactions in context. This connects to how our partners' confidence in their ordinariness seemed linked to the ways in which the legalisation of civil partnership was seen to potentially alter the day-to-day contexts in which partners lived and did their relationships. As Hailee puts it:

> The civil partnership also made people treat you differently [...] I feel like I work in quite a gay-friendly world anyway but it sort of has got this legitimacy to it which everyone really [accepts].
>
> Hailee (120b)

If what Blasius terms the 'heterosexual panorama' (the way in which it is only heterosexual relationships that are made visible in the culture) was once central to 'compulsory heterosexuality', our young partners' narratives suggested that this could be disrupted in fairly mundane ways by civil partnership or same-sex 'marriage'. Not only are gay marriages represented in the media, but same-sex relationships are also more routinely visible in day-day living:

Peter (216a)   When you look around and you see things now, like you go into shops and it's got, you know, there are civil partnership cards and all this kind of stuff. And you see it in day to day, you know, when you fill forms in it'll have, 'single', 'married', 'civil partnership', and when you go to click something online, it used to be you had to select married and it would go, 'you can't be married because it's two males'. And now they all have civil [partnership] as an option.

Nathan (220b):   I've just bought a new car and [...] they asked who Eric was [...] They have to tick a box so they tick this little [married/civil] partnership box. And because it's written in front of them they accept it and like I said most everybody does, most people do.

Eric (220a):   We've never come across anybody's who's caused a stink or caused a problem or hasn't been able to cope with it.

Thus, even for younger generations of sexual minorities, the changing circumstances in which same-sex relationships can be lived are noticeable. For those at the older end of the age spectrum of our interviewees, a long distance has been travelled in a short time. As Cori (115a) put it:

I don't even think that was something that even occurred to me as being an option really [...] I was fifteen [...] sixteen years ago it was like there weren't really openly gay people on TV, no one ever talked about it where I was from [...] all of that stuff is completely different [...] just a million miles away from where things were when I was a kid.

It would be easy to see new stories of the shift from the 'heterosexual assumption' (Weeks et al., 2001) to 'assumed acceptance' of sexual difference as evidence of a lack of self-conscious recognition of the reality of continuing prejudice. It may well be the case that in publically narrating their stories some couples emphasise the positive over the negative. However, adopting this view as an overarching frame for understanding narratives of increasing acceptance would undermine the links between people's experiences and the stories they tell about these. Also, as we shall see in the following chapters of the book, partners could be brutally honest about the less than positive aspects of their lives and relationships (see Chapters 5 and 6). There is another way to view these stories of acceptance: as *one* expression of the diverse possibilities for contemporary non-heterosexual lives and same-sex relationships. In the not too distant past, the predominant story told about sexual-minority lives was one of systematic marginalisation, familial estrangement, social hostility and pathologisation. Yet, beneath the headline story there were also less often heard accounts of continuing connectedness, acceptance, and resistance. Nowadays, and certainly among our participants, more-or-less 'full' acceptance by family, personal communities and broader networks is becoming an increasingly audible story about sexual-minority lives. Yet, beneath this headline story there are also stories of estrangement, hostility and marginalisation. These latter stories do not necessarily undermine or invalidate the former, but throw into sharp relief differences *within* sexual-minority experience.

The differences within sexual-minority experiences raises the issue of how claims to ordinariness and relational options more generally are linked to situated personal circumstances, and how these in turn are linked to socio-cultural location. It is worth discussing these in more detail and in terms of the more established and newer axes of 'difference' that sociologists tend to be concerned with: class, gender, race and ethnicity, religion and disability. At the outset, it is important to note that while young same-sex partners' relationship stories were inflected with specific situating details in terms of these axes, they were not *uniformly structured* by socio-cultural location in these respects. Put another way, women and men – irrespective of their different locations – could narrate similar stories of ordinariness, acceptance, estrangement, hostility and marginalisation. Our concern here is with the ways in which socio-cultural location could feature as a critical interpretive frame for understanding 'personal' relational possibilities.

Few partners explicitly linked the constraints they encountered in 'being in' or 'doing' same-sex relationships to institutionalised prejudice. Of those who did, Maria (104b) told a story of the intense stresses that living a non-heterosexual life as a mixed-race family could entail. For Maria, being black and in a same-sex biracial parenting relationship promoted a sense of distance from what she termed 'traditional black families', 'traditional gay couples', and 'traditional straight relationships'. She and her family's distinctive position minimised the supports that were available for the relationship and led to a strong sense of marginalisation. As a black and white same-sex partnership that was parenting a black child, her family was viewed as strange by her and her partner's own families of origin, other black families, and by straight and gay couples (who for the most part did not have children). As well as the institutionalised prejudice they encountered as a same-sex couple and as a mixed race couple, the fact that they were same-sex parents meant that the 'system' wasn't set up to deal with them and that they were marked as 'different' by other (heterosexual) parents. For Maria, black families, straight relationships and lesbian and gay communities had distinctive values, norms and practices that were at odds with hers. Discussing lesbian and gay relationships, she recounted:

> In the gay community, if a relationship doesn't work then you just leave and that's that and it's not that simple, we don't have enough money for starters to just leave.

While Maria emphasised the limited supports for her relationship, in terms of black, white, heterosexual and gay cultures of relating, in the above quotation she also refers to financial resources required to live in accordance with cultural ideals. In this respect she highlights how economic resources represent a limit to what Giddens (1992) terms the 'pure' relationship where equality and satisfaction in relationships is premised on the power of partners to leave it. The constraints that diminished financial resources place on the doing of relationships also featured highly in other partners' stories, most notably those who were from the most disadvantaged class backgrounds. Economic constraints and struggles featured highly in Mark (203a) and Callum's (203b) and Hanna (108a) and Tammy's (108b) accounts of their own relationships and of their strong connections to their families. Both couples recounted how the very possibilities of getting married and living independently as married couples were constrained by financial resources. Money worries were a shadow against which they narrated their relationships. However, they recount how tackling this shadow together has made their relationships stronger. For Hanna and Maria, this is part of a wider family project, where economic constraints imply a strong sense of mutual responsibility for family care. Economic constraints are not only linked to class, but also to other factors like disability and illness. In this respect, access to relational citizenship in the form of marriage could exacerbate these constraints. As Kurt (217b), a disabled man, recounts:

> It sounds terrible. I've actually said this before, it's an awful thing to say but [...] if they didn't have [...] equality for [...] gay couple[s] then Henry and I would be [...] a lot better off than we are [...] because we'd be classed as two single men [for benefits] and we'd have everything [...] the fact is that because we have equal rights, and I agree with having equal rights, but in Henry and my situation it means that we are incredibly near the breadline and struggling incredibly.

Others pointed to how their religious family and cultural backgrounds, Christian and Muslim, enforced gendered and heterosexual 'norms' (see also Yip, 2008). In one exceptional case, a partner discussed how because of familial and cultural expectations it was impossible to be open about her same-sex 'marriage' to family members, and how this would inevitably shape her life:

> My parents will expect me to marry [a man]. At some point I will get married. And that will be my life [...] If things were different, if my parents knew of this relationship and were accepting of it, then this would be my proper life. But because that's not the situation, and because of all these restrictions, I know it's not realistic to continue this. And so this is just something that is for now. But later I'm probably going to get married again [to a man].
>
> Josha (101b)

Josha's narrative emphasised the difficulties of being open about her sexuality and relationship in the context of her Muslim family and community background. The stigma and shame this would imply was not simply hers, but also her broader family's. Intensely religious backgrounds were mostly associated with highly heteronormative assumptions and expectations. Those who were most likely to struggle with their sexualities and same-sex desires, and were inclined to experience coming out as personally and relationally problematic, were from these backgrounds. Nevertheless, despite residual guilt, most partners claimed to have more-or-less overcome the obstacles that religion placed in being openly in same-sex relationships, and to have achieved a degree of parental and familial tolerance. Who knows how things will turn out for Josha? Despite the pressures, the fact that she has 'married' a woman indicates that she has not wholly succumbed to these. What about the gendering of same-sex marriage stories?

As Mansfield and Collard (1988: 42) suggest, in their discussion of the class backgrounds of the newly-wed partners they studied, a marriage cannot be reduced to a social class. Developing this they recount that 'social class did not appear to account for the main differences we observed in the experiences of the newly-wed marriages: in practice gender proved to be a more influential divisor'. In fact, much of the research on heterosexual relationships in the decades before and after Mansfield and Collard's work has emphasised this point (Benjamin and Sullivan, 1996; Duncombe and Marsden, 1999, Jackson, 1996; Jamieson, 1998, Van Every, 1995). In reviewing the British research on the gendered nature of domestic labour from the 1970s to 1990s, Dunne (1997) noted that in the majority of heterosexual partnerships women take responsibility for and perform the bulk of domestic tasks. This is the case where both partners are full-time waged, are without children, where women have higher occupational status than men, and even where couples see themselves as 'fully' sharing. Van Every (1995) also noted the difficulties that arise in challenging gendered assumptions in self-consciously non-sexist living arrangements. Duncombe and Marsden (1999) noted the gender divisions of emotional labour in relation to love and intimacy. And as noted earlier, Mansfield and Collard suggested that married men and women operate as 'intimate strangers'. Building on this, Delphy and Leonard argued the following:

> The hierarchy within the family household [... is] not something chosen by some heterosexual couples and refused by others. Many seem to find this particularly difficult to see. What they notice is that nowadays some husbands and wives interchange tasks and spend a lot of time together, that their interactions seem informal rather than governed by etiquette, and that they love each other. This leads them to suggest that marriage has changed 'from being an institution to companionship', and to the claim it is now 'symmetrical': that it exists between people who have different responsibilities and do different things but who are equal and complimentary human beings. Or, alternatively, they suggest that women can avoid whatever residual male domination there may be by having children on their own or by having their intimate relationships with other women.
>
> Delphy and Leonard (1992: 266)

For Delphy and Leonard, the point is that 'marriage is a relationship between men and women who because they are men and women do different things; who because they do different things are unequal; and who because they are unequal are seen as different sorts of human being (one more human than the other)' (ibid). Also, neither single mothers nor lesbians fully escape the gender order. Because of diminished economic resources, or stigma related to being a single parent or lesbian, they 'are constantly reminded they are abnormal' and in the case of lesbians can be 'downright ostracised or physically attacked'.

However, given that in same-sex partnerships couples do not set out with the assumption that partners are innately different or that they will do different things on the basis of their gender, and that the majority of our female partners (like male partners) recounted the everyday acceptance of their sexualities, relationships and 'marriages', we might well ask if their stories undermine the universalising tenor of arguments like Delphy and Leonard's. While such stories may not wholly negate such arguments, and gender still clearly matters in a range of contexts, they certainly trouble them. The overarching stories that emerge from male and female partners' narratives of same-sex marriage are more similar than they are different. As we shall see in the following chapter, partners' stories of the marriages they grew up with, their biographical circumstances, their relational aspirations, choices and constraints, and practices are not reducible to gender in any overarching and fundamental way (but see Chapters 5–7 for significant gendered nuances). The point is partly that analyses like Delphy and Leonard's are of their historical time. Even then, grounded as they are in static institutional and structural frames, they cannot adequately account for situated, diverse and dynamic marriages as they are experienced and lived on the ground today. This becomes clear in the following chapters where we consider the situated, diverse and dynamic qualities of self-defined same-sex 'marriages'.

3
Relational Biographies

As discussed in Chapter 1, one strong sociological narrative that has emerged from previous studies of same-sex relationships is that partners must 'invent' their relationships from scratch. This has been linked to the lack of cultural guidelines and social supports for lesbian and gay identities and relationships, and implies the possibility (or even necessity) of undoing deeply habituated practices of the self and relating. This narrative suggests that how same-sex relationships are 'done' is linked to a more-or-less complete break from inherited mores, values and practices and a more-or-less complete reworking of the self and relating orientations. This involves a kind of radical self and relational reflexivity that stems from a social distancing from families and communities of origin that is often focused on creating alternative family forms (Heaphy, 2008). A rather different story emerged from our own study of young same-sex couples and partners: of enduring as well as disrupted practices of the self and relating; of connections to, as well as breaks from, inherited mores, values and practices of relating; of continuities in relating orientations as well as their reworking; and of self and relational reflexivity that can be as focused on maintaining 'given' personal bonds as it is on creating alternatives.

This latter story is partly linked to the biographical approach we adopted in the individual interviews, which was focused on generating relational biographies (see Appendix 1), but also to the specific generational contexts in which these biographies emerged and were narrated. This chapter discusses same-sex partners' relational biographies in three ways: by focusing on the relationships and marriages they grew up with (their parents'); the implications that coming out had (or did not have) for an altered sense of connectedness to their familial and personal networks; and the part that friendships played as a biographical anchor. As we shall see, young partners were as likely to emphasise the continuities between their own and their parents' relationships as they were the differences. They shared the marriage ideals of their parents' generation, but believed they were better placed to achieve them in practice. They were more critically reflexive than previous cohorts of heterosexual married partners about their parents' 'failures' to fully meet marriage ideals. However, their critical reflexivity seemed relatively uninfluenced by an engagement with feminist or sexual critical communities. Rather, it was deployed to suggest the need to work hard at making relationships and marriages successful. Along with this, young couples recounted very limited involvements with alternative, chosen or friendship families. While socialising with friends was valued, the couple was almost universally seen as the most important relationship, with parents' supports generally valued over friendship supports. This is partly linked to the ways coming out tended *not* to fundamentally disrupt 'given' relationships with kin, and the ways in which same-sex relational ideals and practices were embedded in relational biographies. This highlights one of the ways in which younger same-sex partners' life experiences were distinctive compared to previous generations: their identities and relationships did not always and automatically imply a distancing from their families of origin or from the relational ideals and practices they grew up with. Because of this, they did not necessarily see themselves or their relationships as intrinsically different to their heterosexual generational peers. At the same time, it is also clear that their distinctive positioning *as* sexual minorities was not wholly erased.

From the outset, we were interested in the links between our study participants' relationships and their biographies. By focusing on these we sought to explore how partners 'relating selves', and their ideals, practices and 'orientations', developed over time. Biographies, like self-identities, are narratives that people tell to themselves and others. They are fundamentally relational in that they are formed, rehearsed and reshaped in interactions with (real and imagined) others over time. Their form and content is shaped by the contexts in which they are narrated, and they can be examined for the part they play in the life of the person, relationships and the social order (for discussion of different approaches, see Atkinson and Delamont, 2006; Gubrium and Holstein, 2009; Plummer, 1995; Riessman, 2008). By focusing on relational biographies, our aim was to avoid conflating relating selves with social identities: we sought not to assume an automatic link between people's approaches to relating and their gender or sexual identity. Such an assumption would risk falling foul of the 'hazards of rigidifying aspects of identity into a misleading categorical entity' (Somers, 1994: 606). Put another way, by focusing on relational biographies and relating selves, we sought to avoid the temptation to assume a straightforward link between the gender or sexuality of partners and their relating practices. As Somers (1994: 606) argues, the focus on relationality can be categorically destabilising. For us, it brings personal and social connectedness to the fore in a way that analyses of relationships that foreground social *identities* (linked to class, gender, sexuality and so on) can sometimes lose sight of. At the same time, the focus on relational biographies also troubles the idea that individualised selves are disconnected from the socio-cultural contexts and from the families, communities and relational conventions in which they were formed. By adopting a relational view of biographies, we aimed to forego the idea that society today should be seen as 'a society of individuals' and that the individual has superseded families, close relationships and communities as the unit of social reproduction. Our approach shows how young same-sex partners' relating orientations and practices remain connected to the contexts in which they were formed and developed, even if they are not determined by them.

The marriages we grew up with

One striking aspect of our participants' relational biographies was the extent to which their *parents'* approaches to relating and marriages featured as central influences. For example, Daniel (202a) linked his previous 'abusive' relating tendencies to his father's; Robert (202b) articulated his need to be in a relationship as one he had 'inherited' from his mother; and Callum (203b) linked the 'active' role he adopts in his relationship to a female tradition in his family. Hanna (108a) recounted that she shared the same relational values and practices as her parents; and Mark (203a) recounted the similarities between his relationship and his parents'. Meanwhile, Fredrick (209a) compared his loving relationship to his parents' duty-based one; Louise (105b) contrasted her sharing relationship to her parents' non-communicative one that was entered into out of necessity; and Kathryn (105a) wanted a partnership that, unlike her parents', was not based on two different 'roles'. Maria (104b) recounted how her relationship was based on a degree of free choice, unlike her mother's that was based on force. Overall, these stories indicate how relational biographies – and by extension personal narratives of same-sex marriage – are often anchored in experiences and memories of the relationships and marriages that people are most familiar with: their parents'. This is unsurprising. As Mansfield and Collard recount:

> Although young men and women may not explicitly follow the marriage styles of their parents, yet the experience of having lived alongside their marriages is bound to have profound effects on their own behaviour and attitudes as married men and women.
>
> Mansfield and Collard (1988: 14–15)

However, the issue of how relational biographies and practices are anchored in experiences and memories of parents' relationships is more complex than Mansfield and Collard seem to suggest. First, the matter of influence – of cause and effect – is a tricky one, especially when we consider that, despite growing up in a heterosexual family context, same-sex couples do not go along with the heterosexual assumption. Second, the narration of biographies – to oneself and others – depends on the tricky ways in which memory works. Third, and linked to the last point, the context in which biographies are narrated shapes the life-stories that are told. Overall, by their very nature, relational biographies are not 'objective', 'neutral' and 'full' accounts of selves and relationships. While they can be explored for the part they play in lives and relationships, and treated with caution they can reveal historical truths (Weeks et al., 2001), they can also be read as claims about selves and relationships. Thus they may be explored for the marriages and relationships that people 'live by' (Gillis, 1996) as opposed to the 'real' relationships and marriages that people grew up with. Some partners were highly attuned to the ways in which their relational biographies were based on a partial view of events:

> the perception of family life that I have is that of being a child, but I'd imagine that my parents probably didn't lead particularly different lives than what Jan and I do today.
>
> Diego (208b)

> I don't even know if they'd ever had a partner before each other. They met on a blind date, so quite a traditional [...] they both lived at home, both only children, met on a blind date, got together, got married, lived together, with my dad's mum, she died, then they moved [...] so quite a traditional.
>
> Kathryn (105a)

At the same time, it seemed that some relational biographies could be based on deep observation of parents' relationships and an almost forensic analysis of relating selves. This was most commonly the case where partners felt they had grown up in especially troubled and personally damaging relationships. In such cases, partners recounted their intensive monitoring of their parents' and their own relationships in an effort to learn from past mistakes. This points to the ways in which there is ongoing conversation between the relationships people grew up with, live with and live by (Gillis, 1996). As Frazer (215a) puts it:

> You watch your parents [you] grow up and you watch your parents interact and you take that on board [...]. I look at my parents and my step-parents how their relationships work out now, and how my parents worked out before they got divorced, and see where they went wrong [...] also I take into consideration Todd's family [...] how they interact with one another, and [...] I think together we ensure that we don't have the same [...] pitfalls as what they do. We make sure we talk about those pitfalls and try and clear them up before they happen. So I think it is the foundation of what we do.

The actual influences of parental marriages on partners' own relating practices and orientations is, we would argue, impossible to measure. As the stories detailed above indicate, such influence does not work in any straightforward or unidirectional ways. For those who narrated direct similarities between their parents' and their own approaches to relating, there are equal numbers who emphasised the differences. For those who seem to have 'gone along' with their parents' ways of doing things, there are equal numbers who have rejected them. However, even those who rejected their parents' marriage as a model could acknowledge the continuing influence of their 'inheritance'. This was a strong theme in partners' stories of unintentionally repeating their parents' approaches to relating. It seems to be an anxiety that underpins Frazer's account of his intensive monitoring of his parents' *and* his own relationship. It is also one that underpins Rebecca's (109b) anxiety about her parenting practices:

> Dad had a lot of influence in our family [...] it was quite strict my childhood growing up which might be some of the issues that come into our own parenting [...]. I don't think I am strict but it makes us wonder am I strict 'cause that's the type of childhood I had [...]. I do try and explore that but I try to do the best I can.

One important common feature of relational biographies that works against the measuring of parental influences, is that they weave together accounts of circumstance, choice and chance. While early life circumstances are influential, they do not *determine* relational orientations and practices. In this respect, participants like Kathryn, Louise and Fredrick (see Chapter 2) emphasised the decisions and efforts they made not to relate as their parents' did. Similarly, partners like Hanna and Tammy (see Chapter 2) emphasised how they actively embraced their parents' ways of relating, while Tim (see Chapter 2) saw nothing to reject. At the same time, most acknowledged that they were constrained in their choices. For example, Rebecca (quoted above) suggested that one could never be sure that inherited relating orientations were wholly undone. In Kathryn and Louise's case there was also some tension between being drawn together on the basis of their shared middle-class upbringings and values, and at the same time rejecting the relating values of their parents who had 'transmitted' these values. While Maria (quoted in Chapter 2) rejected the cultural expectations about marriage that she had grown up with, she also recounted how her relating choices were constrained by heterosexism combined with racism. In Hanna and Tammy's case, the emphasis was placed on different kinds of constraints linked to material resources and associated with class. Also, while some of these accounts stressed family continuities, there was a sense that such continuities implied familial expectations that actively constrained their choices.

As we shall see in the followings sections, relational circumstances and choices are not the opposite of each other. They operate in conversation, but also in tension, to influence the course that relationships and marriages take. Partners make choices in the context of these circumstances and such choices act back on their circumstances even if they did not wholly undo them. At the same time, personal choices were influenced by personal histories, which were in turn linked to partners' socio-cultural locations. On the one hand, this latter point has been underacknowledged in discussions of the self and intimate relationships in theories of individualisation, where the emphasis is on the freedom to choose within relationships. On the other hand, it has been overemphasised in some discussions of the extent to which social location linked to class, gender, race and ethnicity and other factors more-or-less wholly determine relational choices (see Chapter 2). If the latter were true, relationships would be more-or-less wholly predictable. However, the ordinary vitality of same-sex relationships and marriages is linked to the ways in which this is not the case. In this respect we agree with Thomson (2009) who, on the basis of a ten-year longitudinal qualitative study of 100 young people between 1996 and 2006 in the UK (that in theory could have included our participants or their generational peers), argues that it is impossible to predict the route that a person's life will take, even though in retrospect we may think we 'see a logic – even a sense of inevitability' (2009: 2).

Relating circumstances and ideals

One of the key themes to emerge in relational biographies is the dynamic nature of the circumstances in which partners relate and 'do' their relationships and marriages (see Chapter 2). Relational biographies also contained stories of how parents' relationships and marriages had changed over time. Escalating conflict, abuse, alcoholism, affairs and the like could lead to divorce. Growing discontent could lead to ongoing hostility or to married parents living together as strangers. Illness, bereavement and similar experiences could bring parents closer together or further drive them apart. A history of doing things together, developing routines and mutual respect could allow the relationship to grow. Despite this, in reflecting on their parents' relationships, partners tended to 'fix' them in accordance with three kinds of marriage: the 'good' marriage, the 'unhappy' marriage and the 'ambivalent' one. The good parental marriage most closely approximated that which Hanna described (see Chapter 2). It was based on love, and involved trying to work things out, being in it for the long run and standing by each other through thick and thin. Above all, it entailed mutual respect, communication and a high degree of stability. As Ellen (114a) recounts:

> what I think I have inherited or brought from seeing them is a big thing about respect and communication. And that they're both very important in the sense that my parents had a great deal of respect for each other, and that means that you take the time to understand the other person's opinion [...] my parents relationship was largely very stable

In contrast to the good marriage, the unhappy parental marriage, which most closely approximates the one that Kathryn described (see Chapter 2), was one that was not entered into for love but for the 'wrong reasons'. Commonly, it involved little mutual respect and communication and limited sharing. It involved partners who had not 'fully' given themselves to the relationship, and was inherently unstable. As Garry (227a) recounts:

> [T]hey [...] may have formed their relationship [...] over things which weren't necessarily perfect. And so because of that, I think they developed, certainly on the part of my father, some resentment [...] they argued, they fought all the time [...]. My father was incredibly nasty to my mother and shouted at her all the time and I think it was because, certainly from his side and maybe too an element of her side, the relationship was initially founded on something which wasn't necessarily love.

The ambivalent marriage, contained many characteristics of the unhappy marriage. It closely approximated the one that Fredrick described (see Chapter 2), and its primary foundation was not love but duty. It was distinct from the unhappy marriage in that couples tried to make the best of their lot and do the best they could. It was stable, but short on communication. As Todd (215b) puts it:

> I haven't tried to emulate their relationship (laughs) any way, shape or form and nor will I ever want to. I think my mother and father have struggled on and you know duty bound [...] tried to work things out. It's quite obvious that they, they probably need to [...] or should separate and they'd probably lead happier lives, so that duty, that sense of duty [keeps them together]

While it might be unsurprising that partners held critical as well as positive views of their parents' marriages, their stories are quite different to those recounted in previous studies of heterosexual marriage. In the 1980s, Mansfield and Collard's study asked newly-weds to look back and recall any impressions they had of their parents' marriages. In response, the majority 'looked blank'. Most said that when growing up they had never thought about their parents as a married couple. A small minority who had experienced their parents' divorce or the death of a parent 'were most likely to have considered the marital experiences of their own parents' (1988: 15). When their interviewees did reflect on their parents' marriages, their comments 'were positive though usually unspecific. Such marriages were considered 'good' because they had been secure and stable and had provided a good setting in which the children had grown up' (ibid). They also note that very few newly-weds were able to articulate any specific aspects of marriage which they viewed as model. Those who could referred to 'sharing and companionship and their fathers having shown respect for their wives' (1988: 16). This raises four issues.

First, there are notable continuities in what is defined as a 'good' marriage. As we have seen, sharing and respect were key themes in our partners' accounts of a good marriage. These were core benchmarks for assessing the success of a marriage. Among our partners, communication was seen as crucial to a sharing and respectful marriage, although it is notable that Mansfield and Collard do not specifically mention this. However, on the basis of their study, they do note that because of different gendered ways of relating, newly-weds often fairly soon ended up as 'intimate strangers'. This resonates strongly with the 'unhappy' and 'ambivalent' parental marriages that many of our partners recounted.

Second, same-sex married partners seem to be more critical and self-reflexive with respect to parental marriages than Mansfield and Collard's newly-weds: they present a far less uniformly rosy picture of parents' marriages as the bedrock of family stability. What underpins this critical consciousness? Mansfield and Collard's observation that the minority who had previously reflected on their parents' marriages were those who had experienced their parents' divorce or death provides a clue to this. Divorce and death can be viewed as moments of 'biographical disruption' (cf. Bury, 1997) which raise existential anxiety and in turn imply that what was taken for granted has to be revisited and rethought anew. Such disruption and its consequences for a critical take on the order of things and heightened self-reflexivity have been discussed in a number of contexts (see Adam and Sears, 1996 on temporal reorientation; Berger, 1990 on marginal situations; Giddens, 1991 on fateful moments; Heaphy, 2001 on self-disruption; and Thomson et al., 2002 on critical moments). Developing this point we might ask if the perceived realities of the unhappy and ambivalent parental marriages that many partners grew up with are so deeply at odds with 'taken-for-granted' cultural stories about what contemporary marriages *should* be like (based on communication, sharing, respect, equality, love and the like) that they can promote a heightened sense of narrative disjuncture and *chronic* critical reflexivity with respect to relationships. This would partly explain stories of the intensive monitoring of parents' relationships and one's own relationship that the earlier quotation from Frazer described as the 'foundation' of his relationship.

Third, the newly-weds whom Mansfield and Collard studied were the generational peers of many of our interviewees' parents, and the marriages of intimate strangers they describe are closely akin to our interviewees' descriptions of unhappy and ambivalent parental marriages. In describing these, our partners explicitly deployed the language of generation, along with 'tradition', to account for the differences between their own 'good' marriages and their parents' ones. The following quotations from female partners, for example, indicate how, while heterosexually gendered differences and expectations were clearly the subtext underpinning accounts of parents' unhappy and ambivalent marriages, such differences and expectations were rarely explicitly named *as* gender or heterosexuality as such. Rather, the interpretative emphasis was placed on 'generation' and 'tradition':

> I think my parents' generation and my parents in particular just took the idea that you get married and you're in a relationship and that's it [...] I think they just lived in the same house and also they had very clear definite defined roles, mother does the cooking, cleaning, child care, father earns the money [...] I think also my parents' generation saw ending a relationship as a disaster.
>
> Maria (104b)

> They got married in a totally different era [...] it was much more an expected thing for them [...] and I think that my mum she had decided that she was giving up things to get married. She never went to university although she was more than capable of getting there [...]. She kind of moulded her life round my father's.
>
> Pam (119b)

> because of the way they were raised, you know, you marry somebody and you stay married and that's just the way it is, so it's almost like they just took it for granted that they would be together [...] they just do things the way they do and the way they always have.
>
> Theresa (110b)

> I remember, Dad being in a temper [...] he was married to someone he didn't love, but I guess it's a different generation isn't it and that generation when they're not in touch with your thoughts and feelings actually, that became everybody else's problem as opposed to his problem to deal with.
>
> Louise (105b)

By implication, these accounts link the opportunities for 'good' marriages to changing historical circumstances. They suggest that traditional demands, expectations, norms and sanctions that led to 'unhappy' and 'ambivalent' marriages no longer hold the sway they once did. This leaves the door wide open for *mutual* marriages that partners can work at as equals. This has clear resonances with arguments about detraditionalised 'pure relationships' that are entered into on the basis of mutuality and dialogical intimacy, and that are unsullied by socio-cultural constraints and power (Giddens, 1991; 1992). In other words, it could be argued that partners were recounting the possibilities for 'post-emancipatory' marriages and relationships. However, it is worth interrogating the critical interpretative frames that our partners deployed. What is especially striking in the above quotations, as was noted earlier, is how tradition and generation are deployed to account for the gendering of parents' marriages and relationships. In narrating their parents' marriages, partners' very often referred to their mothers' and fathers' different relational power, as the following examples illustrate:

> I think it was quite a traditional, sort of stereotypical relationship in that he, you know, my Dad made the decisions I mean he probably would discuss them with her but ultimately he'd make the decision I think.
>
> Theresa (110b)

> I think my dad was like kind of patriarch [...] worked a lot, never home but at the end of it, he decided the important things my mum was just a house [wife] look after the kids, she worked as well but it was not fairly balanced.
>
> Victor (216b)

> I just knew that the situation in the family was sometimes really bad [...] there was lots of alcohol involved [...]. And patronising. I know my mum, she wasn't happy in the relationship. I believe if she had a chance she would have run away. [...] If she didn't have us. She had responsibilities of three children. She couldn't just run away. She had to stay there and get along with all the bullying and harassment she got.
>
> Radinka (103a)

This raises the fourth point. While stories about parents' marriages were embedded in narratives of generational and traditional circumstances, and while parents' different relational 'roles' and power were very often referred to, partners rarely deployed a critical discourse of *gender, heterosexuality and power* in an explicit way. This is worth noting, because it contrasts sharply with the findings of previous studies of same-sex relationships, where personal narratives and relational biographies seemed much more *explicitly* grounded in critical interpretations of gender and its links to heteronormativity (Dunne, 1997; Weeks et al., 2001). In this respect, our partners' narratives suggest one new direction in how same-sex partners' critical relational reflexivity is being framed: in terms of tradition and generation and away from gendered heterosexuality.

Changing circumstances

In contrast to the ideals of love, care and acceptance often associated with 'the family', feminist and queer critics have since the 1960s high-lighted its 'dark side'. As Voller has suggested, 'Nowhere has the hostility to homosexuality been more frightening to large numbers of gay men and lesbians than in their own families, forcing them to feel like a minority in their own homes' (cited in Muller, 1987: 140). Little wonder then that a strong narrative of lesbian and gay life has been about the extent to which coming out entails estrangement from given family and distancing from the heterosexual relational contexts in which lesbians and gay men grow up in. There is a wealth of work on the links between emotional estrangement and geographical distancing. Moving away from the family and community contexts they grew up with has, for many lesbians and gay men, been central to creating a sense of same-sex relational possibilities (Cant, 1997; Chauncey, 1994; Coyle, 1991; Cruickshank, 1992; Davies, 1992; Weston, 1995).

'Coming out' has been linked to expanding the historical and personal possibilities open to lesbians and gay men for self and relational invention – for transforming the givens of the self and relationships. For Blasius, coming out is more than as an initial realisation: it is a lifelong process, 'the continuous process of individual and collective empowerment in the historical context of heterosexist domination and homophobic subjection [...] the creation of an ethos' (1994: 211). Blasius sees this as involving an ethics of self-invention in the contexts of affective communities and erotic friendships, which is fundamentally challenging to gendered-heterosexual ideologies of incompleteness that shape heterosexual ways of relating and living:

> With this [heterosexual] truth regime displaced as the foundation of erotic relationships, the possibility of a new relational ethic emerges: reciprocity [...] lesbians and gay men need not look for the 'other half' to complete themselves.
>
> Blasius (1994: 211)

At the heart of Blasius's argument is that coming out involves an estrangement from the heterosexual relational contexts that people grow up in. It involves social relocation and the accessing of resources – friendship networks, support groups, self-help materials, virtual or face-to-face connections, fiction, art and so on – that provide supports for a new and empowered sense of self and how it is possible to relate.

However, our own study suggests that the contemporary contexts in which many members of same-sex relationships imagine and articulate their sexualities make the issue of coming out more complex than Blasius suggests. One of the most notable features of the young partners' relational biographies was the extent to which, compared to earlier generations, coming out was not a universally pivotal feature of personal histories. In narrating their relational biographies, roughly one-third of the women and half of the men made little – and in some cases no – reference to their initial coming out as a critically significant moment in their lives. Indeed, it is striking that Hanna and Tammy's and Kathryn and Louise's relational biographies were for the most part devoid of stories about the struggles of 'coming out' (see Chapter 2). Theirs were fairly straightforward stories of 'just' being gay (a term often used by women and men) and of having relationships on that basis. In narratives like these, minority sexual identities seemed to have very little to do with the 'ups and downs' and 'ins and outs' of their relationships with others. These are stories about sexual identities and same-sex relationships that did not seem to require explanation or justification, and appeared to have been more-or-less straightforwardly accepted by family of origin and personal communities.

About one-third of the women and a quarter of the men talked about initially coming out in a way that suggested they had assumed and experienced it to be unproblematic. For some, more often women than men, same-sex relationships were spoken about as if they were an unproblematic matter of personal choice in the context of meeting the 'right' person:

> I never really had [...] this kind of big realisation that I'm gay, or discussions with people [...] I don't see it as an issue [...] I hadn't really thought too much about what I wanted or anything and then when I met Stacy I knew that that's what I wanted.
>
> Theresa (110b)

Finally, about a third of women and a quarter of men *had* experienced coming out as difficult or as problematic. Some women and men had been sure of their 'orientation' from a very young age and had struggled to be open about it. This could be linked to a fear of rejection, humiliation and prejudice. Some did not want to be 'gay', and others said they did not know how to go about coming out or meeting others like themselves. Some partners, like Nancy quoted below, saw this as a 'personal' problem, while others, like Veronica and Jeremy quoted below, linked it to the circumstances in which they had grown up and the limited choices these presented for coming out.

> I've never been confident like in coming out [...] even though my mum was really fine and my dad he's fine as well [...] he's like 'whatever makes you happy' [...] he hasn't appeared fazed at all and my mum's really supportive of everything I do.
>
> Nancy (106b)

> I've known I was gay for just as long as I can remember pretty much. When I was about twelve I got involved in a church group at school at around the same time – [I had] a bit of a difficult time with that – it took me a long time to get over feelings of guilt about my sexuality because of all this baggage associated with, with Christianity.
>
> Veronica (107b)

> I got the job managing the pub next to where my parents live. That's where I met Stewart and things just sort of went from there really but, I mean beforehand it wasn't something that I ever dreamt was possible [...] I didn't think that I could ever, in my wildest dreams, come out in [Place] [...]. I don't think I actually existed really, until I came out to my parents [...]. That was quite hard, for a lot of my years growing up.
>
> Jeremy (206a)

While many young women and men were supported in their coming out by their family or origin, friends and networks, others experienced less than positive initial responses in the form of shock, hostility or disappointment. However, irrespective of how they came out and initial responses to this, the majority of partners told positive stories of (eventual) acceptance by family of origin and their close and wider social circles. As Iris (122b) puts it:

> [A]s soon as I kind of actually admitted it to myself that I thought [...] I'm gay it just [...] all this sort of flood of emotion and excitement about actually being able to talk to people about it, but scary at

the same time because I wasn't sure, you know I had lots of friends that know me as being straight [...] and it was a bit scary, I felt like they wouldn't accept me for who I was now. But [...] generally on the whole everybody was really good about it, especially my family, my family were much better than I expected them to be.

Despite the changes that have taken place with respect to the visibility and apparent acceptance of sexual diversity, it is clear that at the time of their coming out many younger women and men had experienced and/or internalised the stigma associated with sexual-minority identities and same-sex relationships. This is not surprising as many of our participants would have been coming out in the late 1980s and 1990s, and as a general rule the more recently partners had come out the more positive initial reactions were likely to have been. However, irrespective of when partners came out or how intensely difficult this was or the negative nature of initial responses, partners only rarely made straightforward links between coming out and the *enduringly* radical disruption of their family of origin and close relationships.

It is clear from young partners' narratives that we cannot assume coming out to be a 'shared' or 'common' experience as Blasius does. The specific historical and relational contexts in which people come to know themselves as lesbian, gay, bisexual or queer matter. For many of our partners, like Jeremy, 'assumed heterosexuality' and the 'heterosexual panorama' still mattered in constraining their imaginaries of non-heterosexual living and relating. For others, like Theresa, the weakening of these assumptions and panorama opened up considerable opportunities and choices. However, the point is that in a new context of relative acceptance among heterosexual family, friends and personal communities the sense of radical self and relational disruption is lessened. This can imply less of a perceived need or desire for social relocation, and less perceived need or desire to become a wholly 'different' person. Instead of the sense of estrangement that previous generations tended to associate with coming out, for young generations coming out could be experienced as relatively uncompromising for a sense of connectedness to 'given' family and close relationships.

In such contexts, the need to form or turn to critical communities could also be lessened. Only a very few participants indicated that they had been involved in LGB community activities other than commercial scenes, or that they had sought out the resources and supports that such communities might provide. If partners referred to sexual communities, they tended to use 'gay community' to refer to commercial scenes and to (physical and virtual) spaces where friendships and relationships might be formed. There was little evidence that such scenes were the focus of self-reinvention or a self-consciously politicised sense of self. While they were often cast as spaces where identities and relational practices could be tested and experimented with, they were most often cast as transitional spaces en route to 'mature' couple relationships. Where gay scenes were explicitly linked to specific relational ethics, this tended to be framed in less than wholly positive terms:

> My experiences on the gay scene and things like that were very different from what was right for me [...] what I would class as sort of stereotypical, sort of gay bars and things like that where there's a lot of people who weren't sort of similar to me, they were [...] extremely sort of masculine women and things like that. [I was] thinking well 'I know I'm gay and I like women but I'm not like that so what am I?' It felt like I was another breed.
>
> Louise (106b)

> everybody else that I'd gone out with had spent probably years going out on the gay scene and their life revolved around the scene, or gay people that were on the scene, they were all a bit messed up in some way you know. I think it's probably different now because it's so much more accepted but I think my generation and people older than me [...] I mean I did when I first came out as well, I just suddenly became very gay you know, I mean if you went out you went to a gay place or, and your friends were gay people [...] and they had a little bit of being messed up, and I think without exception I've cheated on every one.
>
> Fiona (122a)

> the gay scene was always, it was kind of a means to an end, it was where you found gay men. It wasn't somewhere you went, 'cause "oh isn't that cool", it was cool 'cause there's lots of gay men there. It's mate finding. And once you've found the mate you kind of don't need it anymore, is my personal reading of it.
>
> Fredrick (209a)

> the gay scene [here] is very bitchy, you will always get the younger ones [who] are worse than the older ones, you'll get the newly, well what we call the new people that have just come out, that have to be perfect, that bitch people, that put people down that has to ruin

people's relationships, you know, they've got a stereotypical view of a gay man and that's how they are, they know that a gay man should be bitchy and this that and the other and loved by all and that's what they're trying do and they don't care who they hurt in the process.

Callum (203b)

Friendships and the couple ethos

On the basis of their study of same-sex intimacies in the 1990s, Weeks et al. (2001: 50) noted (as did numerous other studies) that friendship 'is key to understanding non-heterosexual ways of life'. It was the most important recurring theme among the 98 narrators in their study (of whom at least 70 were partnered) and was central to non-heterosexual relational experiments and practices of care, commitment and trust. They note that in the context of lesbian and gay lives, friendships were especially significant as the basis of what Nardi (1999) terms 'invincible communities'. For sexual minorities, friendships have been at the core of chosen families (Weston, 1991), and at the heart of critical sexual communities where 'friendships [...] often become de facto families' (Altman, 1982: 90). As Weeks et al. (2001: 52) put it:

> Friendships particularly flourish when overarching identities are fragmented in periods of rapid social change, or at turning points in people's lives, or when lives are lived at odds with social norms [...] they can allow individuals who are uprooted or marginalised to feel constantly confirmed in who and what they are [...]. They offer the possibility of developing new patterns of intimacy and commitment [...] these features give a special meaning and intensity to friendship in the lives of those who live on the fringes of sexual conformity [...] provid[ing] both emotional and material support [...] affirm[ing] identity and belonging.

The quotation above implies that the more marginalised are sexual minorities, the more friendships are likely to be important (see also Rubin, 1992). Elsewhere, Giddens (1991) has argued that it is primarily individualisation that makes friendship especially important as an exemplar of the pure relationship in late modernity, where adult relationships are more egalitarian because they can be ended by either party as a matter of choice. The difference between these analyses is that whereas Weeks et al. (2001) see non-heterosexual friendships as central to an enduringly embedded sense of relational connectedness, Giddens sees them as indicative of relatively free-floating individual choices. Weeks et al. make a different point: 'Friends may change; new people may enter the circle. But friendship networks seem permanent [...] In contrast to the vagaries of one-to-one [couple] relationships, friends [...] are the focus of long-standing engagement, trust and commitment' (2001: 61). They argue: 'Friendships are most important when they have been embedded in 'taken-for-granted' assumptions and patterns, when you are accepted for who you are' (2001: 60). For marginalised lesbians and gay men, friendships can be an additional, or the only, source of emotional, social and material supports and of recognition and validation. Even where family of origin are accepting, friendships can provide affirmation of the 'real' self that family may not see.

In light of this, we were somewhat surprised by the extent to which our young partners' accounts of their biographies, current lives and preferred sources of social support suggested friendships to be transitional relationships and friendship networks to be less important than the couple or family of origin. As we shall discuss in more detail below, friendships were a regular feature of our partners' previous single lives. While some partners deemed their current friendships to be as important as family, and many couples and partners valued socialising with friends, couple and family relationships mostly trumped friendships when it came to current intimate and caring commitments or the preferred source of emotional, social and material supports at critical life moments (see Chapter 7). The general tendency was to see 'mature' couple commitments and family commitments as enduring ties, and friendships and friendship networks as more transitional bonds. Before considering this, and other notable features of the young partners' friendships, we look at how friends and friendship networks were valued in relational biographies. Frazer (215a) implied that his search for a partner was partly influenced by his personal inability to make friends:

> before the relationship I was probably very insular, very insecure, quite quiet person, I didn't meet people very easily, I was very insecure of who I was and who I should be. So I didn't make friends or meet people very well [...]. But I knew what I wanted. I can say that much. I knew what I wanted in life and in a relationship, and I didn't know how I was gonna go about getting it.

Those who described their lives before their current relationships as less than satisfying often mentioned the absence of friendships as much as they did partners. It is therefore unsurprising that friendships figured highly in biographical accounts of more satisfying single lives:

> I'd been single for ages, living in [Place], living in a shared house, you know nice group of friends quite a lot of lesbian friends, and just kind of having a good time [...] so I was quite happy, I was quite settled.
>
> Juliet (107a)

> I was in university, wanted to meet somebody, a girl [...] I wasn't very confident with who I was really, certainly the first two years of university, and then in my third year I met some really good friends and we started going gay clubbing and we started socialising together, outside of gay clubs as well so it wasn't all, sort of, loud music and alcohol related.
>
> Andrea (118a)

> I had quite a close small group of friends that I used to be out with quite a lot [...] probably most weekends and sort of stay round their houses that sort of thing, and 'cause a couple of them had their own places, I was sort of chatting to guys and stuff on the internet, met a few guys [...] relatively short-term relationships but nothing overly significant.
>
> Tim (209b)

> I think mostly I went out and I had a very, very active social life in terms of going out with friends for dinner and drinks and trying to meet people and trying to meet women.
>
> [Edith, 112b]

In these quotations, friendship is linked to feelings of happiness, developing a sense of self-confidence, being settled, socialising, companionship and connectedness. Erotic friendships, as discussed by Blasius, are also hinted at in Tim and Edith's quotations where meeting 'guys' or 'women' referred to casual sexual relationships. Overall, friendships played a crucial part in most participants' lives before their current relationships. In some cases, friendships continued to be strong after the participant entered a partnership. These included friendships that were seen *as* family or as 'better than' family. In discussing their *current* relational lives, 10 out of 100 partners referred to friendship in this way:

> my friends have always been the substitute family I've had. My family is quite fucked up.
>
> Robert (202b)

as I said before you know I'm very close to my friends [...] I classify so many of my friends as my adopted family.

Ian (218a)

I class my friends, I'm close [to], my friends are my family.

Phil (212b)

we've both through our lives and our experiences have got very good friends and we find the support that we have from our friends [...] supersedes the support we have from our family, really to be honest.

Kathryn (105a)

my friends are the most stable thing. I have friends from high school we're all really close and that [...] my family life, it's not bad it just hasn't been consistently stable.

Nancy (106b)

I think it, friends are probably more important to me I think than my, than my family.

Veronica (107b)

Support, comfort, stability and continuity – many of the ideals associated with 'family' that given families fail to live up to – can be provided by friends. In addition to these explicit accounts that linked friendship and family, in four cases couples used the language of 'family and friends' consistently in a way that suggested that they were reluctant to make a distinction. This points to how friends and family could be highly suffused relationships: where in practice friends could provide the 'goods' associated with family, and where family could provide the goods associated with friendships (Pahl and Spencer, 2004). Partners themselves represented the most suffused relationships of all: they were spouses, family and also 'best friends'. Among 10 female and 12 male couples, friends were a regular feature in their accounts of their relationships and lives, but not to the degree that they suggested 'families of choice' or highly suffused relation-ships. These were often socialising and couple friends and less often 'close' friends. Among eight female couples and seven male couples, friends were mentioned but not in any significant detail. Friends were clearly significant to many, but in only in 18 out of one 100 cases did they seem to be as centrally significant as suggested by studies of previous generations of lesbians, gay men and bisexuals. This we suggest is in large part due to the dominance of the couple as a relational ideal, and to the extent to which most partners were invested in the couple at the point in their lives when we interviewed them (see Chapter 4).

One feature of young partners' current and past friendships, which distinguishes them from previous generations, was the mixed nature of their networks in terms of gender and sexuality. Commenting on their study of same-sex intimacies in the 1990s, Weeks et al. note:

> One significant feature of our interviewees is the tendency for close friendships to be homosocial, or single sex, though this is by no means universal [...]. A number of gay men who we interviewed claimed to not know many lesbian and vice versa [...] to an important extent lesbians and gay men inhabit different social worlds. Many lesbians and gay men do mix together in networks, but for others there is a barrier which separates them.
>
> Weeks et al. (2001: 61)

In contrast, among our participants, both women and men tended to have friendships with heterosexual and non-heterosexual women and men. None had only single-gender friendships, and several had mostly heterosexual friends. As Eric (220a) put it, besides a couple of gay friends 'all of our other friends are just normal heterosexual couples'. Eric's comment raises three issues. First, among young partners the barriers to friendships that cut across gender and sexuality were rare, if not non-existent. Some women made a point of noting that they had friendships with mostly heterosexual and gay men, while some men also made a point of noting their friendships with heterosexual men and lesbians. The fact that they highlighted these suggests an awareness that these friendships might be seen to be surprising. Second, by emphasising that their friends included 'just normal heterosexuals', young partners often underscored their own claims to ordinariness. In doing so, they refused reductionist assumptions about their ways of life based on their sexuality or same-sex relationship. Third, like Eric, many young partners' accounts of their friendships emphasised 'couple' friends. While some partners did maintain independent relationships with friends, couples tended to talk about their mutual friends. Also, while couples did maintain friendships with people who were not in relationships, they tended to value friendships with other couples. In these respects, their friends were people like themselves who, irrespective of their gender and sexuality, shared their relational values and were often also married:

> for me it's nice that a same-sex relationship has this potential to be able to view each other as husbands and married, and it's been quite wonderful that the support of friends and people that have said to us, 'Wow, I really admire the commitment' it's so great, you know, sign of the times that we are the first sort of revolutionary era in terms of same-sex relationships that this is possible.
>
> OJ (225b)

For the hegemonic voices of previous generations of sexual minorities, marriage and husbands were obstacles in the way of the gender and sexual revolution. Nowadays, for people like OJ, claims to marriage and the 'right' to be a same-sex husband is a revolutionary claim. This reflects a shift in the kinds of communities that young same-sex partners' relational imaginaries tend to be embedded in.

Reconfiguring connectedness

As discussed earlier, in previous studies of lesbian and gay selves and relationships, 'coming out' has been linked to radical biographical disruption and reconstruction. For example, Davies (1992) argues that coming out involves social relocation: different places, different social networks, and different social and sexual contexts. He argues that through coming out the person becomes 'in a real sense, a different person' (1992: 76). Others have argued that coming out implies 'coming into' lesbian and gay communities which provide the cultural and social resources for reimaging how it is possible to live and relate. Such communities become the basis for a new self and new ways of living as a lesbian or gay man. Building on this, and as also discussed in Chapter 1, a number of theorists and researchers have suggested that lesbian and gay selves and relationships are underpinned by a distinctive ethos of relating: one that is rooted in an ethics of friendship (Blasius, 1994; Nardi, 1999; Weeks et al., 2001; Weston, 1991). Indeed, Weeks et al. (2001) in their mid-1990s study of same-sex intimacies, found that their participants' life stories echoed these theoretical accounts. Coming out was linked to radical self-reinvention and often implied a radical break from the relational ideals and practices that participants had grown up with. Lesbian and gay communities and friendship networks provided cultural and social resources for alternative selves and relating practices.

They also appeared to promote critical reflexivity with respect to hetero-sexually gendered ways of relating. Weeks et al.'s participants were often disconnected from the families they grew up with, and friendships were at the heart of their 'chosen families'. They were frequently critical of gendered-heterosexual relating norms and sought to structure and do their relationships in unconventional ways.

As detailed in this chapter, our interviewees' relational biographies suggest that a generational shift is occurring in some contexts with respect to the possibilities for same-sex relationships. For some, it now seems possible to be in a same-sex relationship without experiencing the sense of estrangement – and the need to reinvent oneself – that previous generations of openly same-sex partners did. This has enabled some, like most of our participants, to maintain their connections with their families of origin, and to recognise their 'inherited' relational mores, values and practices (whether they embrace them, are antagonistic towards them or are ambivalent about them). On the one hand, there are clear gains that come with this, not least in terms of not having to bear the costs incurred by previous generations who had to live with the material, emotional and social burdens of marginalisation. There might also be said to be gains in not having to bear the costs (material, emotional and social) of having to engage in the labour of intensive self-invention and relational innovation. On the other hand, it is clear that these generational developments could equally be associated with loss: of what some see as the radical creative potential of same-sex and queer relationships for undoing oppressive relational and social orders. However, for the moment, we put the issues of losses and gains to one side, so as to explore in more depth the implications of these new gener-ational developments for how people create and do their relationships. We will return to them in the Conclusion of the book.

4
Forming and Formalising Relationships

Given the emphasis that many of our couples placed on the ordinary, and the enduring nature of the relating ideals and values that they had grown up with, as discussed in Chapter 3, it is perhaps unsurprising that they should choose to 'marry'. However, while the majority of partners saw their entry into civil partnership as an expression of their free choice, a minority felt that they had little choice but to formalise their relationship so as to protect it. At the heart of couple and individual narratives of marriage are stories about romance, love, mutual care and commitment that attest to the enduring centrality of the couple to the relational imaginary. These are stories about self and relational investments in couple projects and of the affirmative power of formalising commitments. They are also stories of convention and its disruption. While the majority deployed some of the conventions of marriage in ceremonialising their relationship, the fact that they were same-sex couples could also disrupt such conventions in practice. Same-sex unions could trouble the heterosexual relational landscape and at the same time bolster the couple as the 'natural' focus of adult relational life.

This chapter focuses on the formation and development of commitments that lead to 'marriage', and on the ceremonialism that surrounds the formalisation of relationships. In line with romantic notions of love, many couples linked the formation of their relationships to chance and fate while others emphasised reason. In practice, romance *and* reason were often intertwined when it came to 'finding' the right partner to commit to. Decisions to marry were most often cast in the language of love and confirming commitments, even where legal 'rights' seemed a primary motivator. Generally, relational rights were presented as a secondary, and in some cases a relatively insignificant, consideration. While most couples emphasised that they married to confirm their

mature commitments to each other, ceremonies themselves often represented a critical moment where familial and personal community inclusion and the reality of the marriage were mostly affirmed but sometimes
negated. Given the emphasis that young partners placed on love, we
begin the chapter by discussing the links that sociologists have made
between love, power and the broader social order.

Love, power and order

In their classic essay on marriage in modern Western societies, Berger
and Kellner (1964) link marriage to ontological or biographical order,
stating that it creates for the individual a 'sort of order' in which
they 'can experience his life as making sense' (1964: 1). They suggest
that individuals invest in the 'private world' because of their sense of
agency in shaping it in contrast to the 'powerful alien world' of public
institutions. They argue that this sense of agency stems from ongoing
'conversations' between partners through which they redefine themselves and the 'little world' around them and construct a shared vision
of the future (ibid). Berger and Kellner also acknowledge that agency is
socially framed, noting that people 'choose' marriage from 'within similar socio-economic backgrounds' (1964: 20) and the range of ideological supports that legitimate marriage as an obvious and natural choice:
'familialism, romantic love, sexual expression, maturity and social
adjustment, with the pervasive psychologistic anthropology that under-
lies them all' (1964: 18). They suggest that such supports ensure that
'[t]he marital adventure can be relied upon to absorb a large amount
of energy that might otherwise be expended more dangerously' (ibid).
Thus they link marriage to the broader social order. While marriage in
Western societies is no longer the unproblematic focus of lifelong commitment as Berger and Kellner assumed it to be in the 1960s, some of
their core arguments are still relevant to understanding contemporary
couple-centred relational lives where, as discussed in Chapter 3, the
committed couple is linked to a sense of (ontological) security, where
self and couple projects are enmeshed, and where dialogical intimacy
rules as a relational ideal.

Many commentators have criticised Berger and Kellner's male-
centred version of marriage, and their analysis does not address the
links between marriage, institutional heterosexuality, gender and
power. In terms of these links, some analysts have seen romance, love
and marriage in ideological terms. The feminist philosopher Adrienne
Rich (1983), for example, argued that heterosexuality was a system

imposed on women throughout history that regulated women's experience, history, culture and values which are distinct from the dominant patriarchal heterosexual culture. Romance and marriage were devices through which women were subordinated and ideologies of romantic love led women into unequal relationships with men, naturalised gender roles and unequal labour, and privileged men's pleasure above that of women.

Developing this point, Dunne (1997: 13) and others suggest romantic and gender ideologies are wholly entwined: they construct men and women as unfulfilled opposites that can only be complete through a heterosexual union. Institutional heterosexuality therefore provides 'the logic underpinning marriage [...] as a commonsense "normal adult goal"' (Dunne, 1997: 16). Yet, for many feminist theorists, institutional heterosexuality, and the notion of a reciprocal state of dependency between men and women that underpins it, also 'shapes and is shaped by relations of production' (Dunne, 1997: 16). In this sense, institutional heterosexuality naturalises gendered differences and inequalities in relation to domestic and paid work. Ideologies of sexual difference, especially as they relate to heterosexual romance and family life, constitute men and women as different economic actors, and reinforce men's dominant economic position over women.

Despite these arguments, traces of Berger and Kellner's analysis have come to the fore in 'new' analysis of late modern marriage, albeit with a 'gloss' of economic and feminist thinking. This is especially the case in Giddens's (1992) argument about how marriage is being transformed under the auspices of the 'pure relationship' which he sees as part of a generic restructuring of intimacy. For Giddens, pure relationships are sought and entered into only for what the relationship can bring to the contracting partners. The guiding justification of the pure relationship is that it should survive only as long as the commitment survives, or until a more promising relationship offers itself. For women, this is only truly possible where they are not economically dependent on male partners. Women's economic autonomy in late modernity, he argues, is a key factor in the increased pressure for a wholly equal and reciprocal relationship – as economic independence implies the freedom to leave. This freedom is central to Giddens's notion of confluent love:

> Romantic love has long had an egalitarian strain [...]. However, [it] is skewed in terms of power. For women, dreams of romantic love have all too often led to domestic subjugation. Confluent love presumes equality in emotional give and take, the more so the more

any particular love tie approximates closely to the prototype of the pure relationship. Love here only develops to the degree to which intimacy does, to the degree to which each partner is prepared to reveal concerns and need to the other.

Giddens (1992: 61)

Confluent love and the pure relationship involve a high degree of instability, and a new contingency in personal relationships. Once taken-for-granted roles, behaviours and commitments must be continually negotiated, with couples being explicit about how they want things to be. As each partner is engaged in the process of developing a self, there is a distinct possibility that different agendas will emerge over time – and the relationship cannot be presumed to continue. Hence, partners must constantly assert, reassert, and negotiate their commitment and what they want. In short, Giddens is arguing that intimacy today assumes that the individual is the maker of his or her own life and that there is equality between partners. The drive to find a satisfactory relationship is personal affirmation, and marriage and couple relationships are sustained only for as long as they provide emotional satisfaction through close contact with others, from intimacy (Giddens, 1992). Marriage becomes less of a status transition, more a symbol of commitment, as potent as that which lies at the heart of many other forms of relationship, including non-heterosexual forms.

Part of the attraction of Giddens's analysis is that it seems, on the surface at least, to address feminist concerns by factoring in the real changes in women's economic conditions. Also, it seems to be as applicable to same-sex commitments as it is to heterosexual married *and* unmarried ones. Thus, it appears to incorporate key elements of interactionist analyses of marriage like Berger and Kellner's while simultaneously linking this to larger-scale economic and social changes. However, Giddens's arguments are far from unproblematic and have been the subject of trenchant criticism on the basis of their normative thrust (their vision of how things *should* be) and their lack of empirical support. Berger and Kellner recognised social constraint and convention as well as individual agency, by stating that the while the individual encounters the socially ordered world 'as a ready-made world that is simply *there* for him to go ahead and live in, he modifies it continually in the process of living it' (1964: 4). In contrast, through his emphasis on detraditionalisation and individualisation Giddens effectively uncouples the individual from the ready-made world. In doing so, he argues that individual agency has to a large extent been set free from social constraints, and posits a reflexive 'relating self' that is liberated from its biographical contexts. As we shall see, young same-sex partners' accounts of romance, love, commitments and affirmation suggest a much more complex relationship between choice, constraint and convention when it comes to couple-life and marriage. This becomes clear when we examine young same-sex couples' marriage stories as part of a broader personal and cultural privileging of the couple.

Marriage commitments in context

While Berger and Kellner's idea that marriage is a transition where 'two strangers come together and redefine themselves' may once have seemed unproblematic, today, when it is common for couples to have lived together (often for a relatively long time) before marriage, this statement seems rather antiquated. Marriage nowadays can involve couples who have a substantial knowledge of each other, who have tested their commitment and who are more-or-less fully incorporated into each other's lives. This was certainly the case for many of our couples. Almost all of the couples had lived together before formalising the relationship, and it was the decision to live together (or to buy a property together where this was feasible) that signalled a critical moment of commitment. Given that the length of relationships before 'marriage' ranged from less than a year to over seven years, many had what they considered a deep knowledge of their partner and relationship. It was unsurprising therefore that many expected civil partnership to make relatively little difference to their relationships and lives. As Angela (106a) and Nancy (106b) recount:

Nancy: people keep asking us that and 'if it's any different'
Angela: I didn't really think it would be any different
Nancy: I think we are what we are, I don't think it should change us really
Angela: [...] you don't know what to say 'cause it's just like the same

In cases like this, formalising the relationship was more often about signalling continuity rather than 'transition' or change. The difference that formalising a relationship makes will be discussed in more detail in Chapter 7. We raise it here to signal that in understanding young same-sex marriages, and marriages today more generally, it is less than useful to begin with the notion of marriage as a key life transition, or to begin analyses of marriage by focusing on the decision to marry.

Rather, a more appropriate starting point is the formation of the couple itself. Ultimately, marriage commitments need to be understood in the broader context of the personal histories, relational imaginaries and the perceived choices and constraints that influence couple commitments. One of the striking themes to emerge from our interviews was that while a relationship with a particular partner was seen as a choice, the idea of a committed couple relationship in itself was often not seen as a choice but as a driving desire or even an essential need. This was the case for Linda (117a), who recounted having little choice but to radically disrupt her otherwise complete life so as to meet a partner:

> it was only really from the relationship point of view that I felt maybe really I hadn't got any choice [but to move away from family and friends] because I didn't know how I was gonna find somebody up here.

The fact that participants like Linda were willing to take such drastic action to meet a potential partner attests to the significance that a couple relationship can have for the individual. In Linda's case, the hope of finding 'somebody' made it worth sacrificing the relational goods she associated with living nearby her family and friends. This seemed to be a large cost indeed. Her quotation expresses the arrival at a 'point' in life where the anxiety about not meeting somebody was so unbearable that she was spurred into dramatic action: moving to a new area, getting a new job and making new friendships. Linda clearly sees a non-couple life as a more-or-less incomplete life. While the majority of our interviewees did not tell the kind of dramatic stories that Linda did, many like Fredrick (209a), quoted below, suggested an incomplete or even inauthentic life and self before meeting their partner. Fredrick, recounted the happy – but 'plastic' – single life he had lived while actively searching for a life partner:

> I had my little plastic apple computer and my little plastic smart car and my little plastic life and I was very happy and [...] was sort of just chugging along trying to find Mr Right really.

While the desire for a committed relationship may be partly explained by the enduring 'ideology' of the couple, or by the increasing significance of the couple for a sense of ontological security in an increasingly individualised world, this did not make such desire any less powerful. Indeed, the powerful emotional charge and sense of personal yearning that the quotations above communicate underpinned a push to action and agency. To reduce such desires to ideology risks trivialising personal lives as they are experienced. At the same time, it is the case that participants' accounts displayed little evidence of an engagement with cultural critiques of the primacy of the couple. Rather, partners tended to frame their 'quests' in terms of the natural need for love. This need also featured in the biographical accounts of those who denied that they were on a quest:

> I'm not saying that I was seeking a relationship [...]. But, it was a point that, to be alone, it's not our, [...] Human beings, they need to be, feel that they are loved at some point in their life. And they need to give love to someone.
>
> Radinka (103a)

In this quotation, the 'need' of love is deployed to naturalise the couple as the focus of love. The quest or desire for a *loving partnership* was not conceived as a choice as such, but in a less critically reflexive way as a natural 'drive'. Indeed, choice was also often downplayed in accounts of relationship formation that deployed the romantic tropes of 'fate and destiny':

Nicole (111b): I did at the time, and still do, feel very lucky that we met each other in such kind of random circumstances working in a very small business. And just by chance happened to kind of get to know each other and kind of found the person that I'm destined to spend the rest of my life with [...] A kind of accident and fate almost.

Barbara (111a): And it's always, for me, seemed like Nicole kind of was there at that – exactly the right time because I was – had gone through a most horrific time in my life and then Nicole was there. And that was sort of destiny and meant to be [...] that was a really crucial [...] point in my life that I realised, you know, she's the one.

It is not necessary to subscribe to Barbara's belief in destiny to agree that it is notable that she met her partner Nicole at a critical point in Barbara's life. Barbara puts this down to the uncanny working of fate with respect to love. Several partners put the formation of their current relationships down to the mysterious workings of love, desire and to their mutual recognition of the 'special' and distinctive qualities of the other. At the same time, it was clear that they were also at a point where they were ready to commit to a relationship with 'someone'.

> I felt that I had had certain experiences that looking back, meant I was kind of ready for if something did happen I think I was ready for a more serious next stage of life.
>
> Edith (112b)

Berger and Kellner suggest that, in deciding to marry, 'individuals have already internalized a degree of readiness to re-define themselves'. Many of our young partners indicated that readiness to commit to a couple relationship was more important than readiness to marry in terms of redefining themselves. As Edith's comments about being ready for a 'more serious stage' of life suggest, many partners associated entering into a committed relationship with a more mature redefinition of themselves. Edith's comments also point to the fact that while sociologists nowadays are reluctant to talk about 'life stages' due to the term's universalising and normalising implications, young partners themselves regularly deployed the notion of stages in reasoning about their readiness for a committed couple relationship. Partners often cast their entry into their current relationship as a critical stage in their progression into maturity. Maturity itself implied self-awareness. While some saw this as something that came naturally, others saw it as entailing work. As Jan (208a) recounts:

> at first there would be the excitement of a new relationship [...] after two weeks you get irritated with them, you don't want them round and you're ignoring their phone calls [...] it wasn't till I sort of explored more and had more counselling it started to hit home [...] I used to try and please a lot of people, I'm a people pleaser.

As Jan's comments suggest, couple commitments could be linked to self-development *through* a relationship. Berger and Kellner suggest that '[i]n the individual's biography marriage brings about a decisive phase [that] has a rather different structure from the earlier ones. There the individual was in the main socialised into already existing patterns. Here he actively collaborates rather than passively accommodates himself' (1964: 13). While we might well challenge this account on the basis of its framing in terms of gender and 'phases', and its assump-tions of passivity in childhood and 'adolescence', we quote it here to underline the self-agency that can be involved in socialisation into the conventions of the couple. This highlights the vital ways in which power works: it is not that partners simply followed social conventions and cultural norms in committing to the couple. Rather, partners like Jan often actively worked towards making themselves 'couple material', and by linking the couple relationships to maturity partners actively invested their self-meanings in the couple. At the heart of accounts that linked the formation of current relationships to maturity was the idea of working towards a future. This was rarely cast as a self-project, but rather as a relational one, and more specifically as a couple project. As Trevor (226b) puts it in discussing his attraction to his partner:

> he was very cute [...] but another thing that attracted me was that also he seemed like a very [...] nice bloke [...] I made several assumptions which turned out to be true that we had a shared [...] we'd gone through [...] some rubbish as well [...] personally. But I knew that we also had a focus and a direction.

As Mansfield and Collard suggest, the idea that modern marriage commitments are first and foremost love matches obscures the extent to which romance *and* reason are both significant motives for couple commitments today. This is highlighted in Trevor's account of his partners' 'special' qualities, but also their shared 'focus' and 'direction'. The point is not that some people formed their relationship on the basis of romance *or* more rational and instrumental reasons, but rather in most cases partners narrated the formation of their relationships in ways that encompassed romance, rationality and instrumentalism. People could be more-or-less reflective about their motivations for entering into their current relationship, but in the main they were rarely critically reflexive about the couple as the primary focus of their relational commitments. This is no doubt partly linked to ways in which their accounts of their relational imaginaries were ordered to 'fit' with their current couple commitment and future plans. At the same time, these current commitments and plans were embedded in experiences of the relationship as it had developed over time, which made it distinctively significant compared to other personal relationships. The entry into civil partnership was often an acknowledgement of this.

Implicit in Berger and Kellner's account of marriage commitments is the idea that people feel they have more agency in the 'private world' than they do in the 'alien world of public institutions'. The distinction between 'public' and 'private' is problematic here – public life does not stop at the front door, and neither does personal life stay at home. The point is that while contemporary couple commitments may be partly symptomatic of an entrenchment from an increasingly alien 'public' world or a 'retreat to intimacy' (cf. Noys, 2008), they can also be the basis of new kinds of engagement with it. In this sense, many partners described the couple relationship as strengthening their sense of self, confidence in themselves and being supported in their engagements with others and institutions. They variously linked this to trust and relating skills built over time, the rebalancing of work and family commitments, support for their public performance as a parent, unexpected acceptance for who they were, shared ethics, solidity and stability and to material and emotional supports. They emphasised the mutual supports that exited for realising future plans, but above all emphasised the couple as the focus of caring supports:

> I found Radinka, after some time I found Radinka quite caring and considering of others. Also I think that was during the time that my father was diagnosed with cancer, and Radinka was quite understanding towards this and very supportive, so I think that's what really helped me a lot to make a decision that, okay, maybe I can maybe progress with this relationship.
>
> Kamilia (103b)

The point is that accounts of developing relationships entailed highly emotional, rational and pragmatic reasons for committing. And these are the backdrop against which young same-sex couples' choices to formalise their relationships need to be understood.

Choosing to marry?

Most partners had not imagined entering into a formalised same-sex relationship or marriage before their current relationship. While several women had had previous committed couple relationships with men, and some had children in this context, only one had married a man in the past. Neil recounted that he had once dreamt of a life with a 'wife and two kids and a nice house and a car', but instead ended up with a 'husband and two dogs'. Emily (125a), quoted below, who 'always wanted' to get married, had become accustomed to the reality she had grown up with – that marriage was only for heterosexual couples:

> I never thought I would ever get married because I just thought there was no chance. I'm gay, I'm not gonna get married.

Irrespective of legal limitations or possibilities, some partners had not seen themselves as the marrying type, often on the basis of their family experiences. As Robert (202b) puts it: '[i]n my family, divorce is quite rampant. It wasn't anything that I ever thought I would become involved in'. However, a few couples, who were together before civil partnership was legalised, had had religious blessings or humanist commitment ceremonies. On the whole, partners had only ever considered formalising a relationship within the context of their current one. This was variously linked to fact that civil partnership had only relatively recently become available, the troubled nature of their previous relationships or simply because they had found a partner who they were prepared to make a 'permanent' commitment to.

About half of the couples (14 female and 13 male) recounted that civil partnership seemed like a natural progression of their relationship. They often described it as the obvious next step in the relationship. The notion of civil partnership as a form a marriage allowed it to quickly become a commonly accepted step in sealing and displaying the couple's commitment. For most, the appeal was enhanced by the fact that this was a civil expression of commitment, and not a religious one. As noted earlier, partners mostly claimed to have entered into civil partnership for love. However, the significance of social recognition was often implied when couples recounted that they did not want to be seen as 'just two guys that live together' or as 'merely' boyfriends and girlfriends. These ways of seeing same-sex partners clearly have adolescent connotations and partners themselves often wanted to be seen as a couple who were willing to take on mature commitments. Frazer (215a) and Todd's (215b) story captures the essence of partners' narratives of progression. They met in their early 20s at a point when both had moved away from home and were working full time. It did not take long before they were living together.

> We wanted to get married because everything was going right for us. We both had pretty decent jobs [...]. I had just got a job with [company name], but I was up to be promoted and stuff like that, and we had been approved a mortgage. Everything was just fitting into place. It was just part of a thing that we should really do because everything was going right for us.
>
> Frazer (215a)

While Giddens argues that marriage is becoming less about status recognition than a symbol of commitment, it does seem to be the case that younger same-sex couples do see marriage as a marker of 'mature' social status. This may well be linked to the ways in which same-sex relationships and non-heterosexual identities have been historically construed as socially and sexually immature. As well as psych-discourse that has historically cast homosexual desires and relationships as stemming from stunted sexual development, discourse about gay men's immature lifestyles (imagined to be focused only on pleasure) casts them as the antithesis of 'responsible' adults. As well as claims to mature status recognition, couples were also subject to seemingly innocuous banter about marriage and commitment, mostly from family or friends who, as Frazer (215a) recounts, kept asking 'when are you guys gonna get married?' For some couples, the slow drip effect of such banter could prompt a sense that the idea of getting married (or not) was something that *should* be entertained, if only to have an answer prepared for others. We will return to the question of why young couples decided to formalise their relationships later in this section. First we consider how a key convention of marriage was adopted and adapted by many same-sex partners: the proposal.

The 'proposal' was a critical feature of many marriage stories, and in some cases it was a critical event for the couple themselves. In this respect, it is worth distinguishing between prenegotiated proposals and surprise ones. In the prenegotiated proposal, couples had clearly signalled to each other their keenness or willingness to formalise the relationship. Explicitly or implicitly, both parties' desire or willingness to enter into civil partnership had been agreed. In these cases, reservations, ambivalences or concerns had been worked through by the couple in advance of the proposal itself. The surprise proposal was a much more risky proposition, as it could potentially reveal one partner's ambivalence about the assumptions that the other had made about future direction of the relationship.

Indeed, some partners who were proposed *to* narrated the event with a notable degree of ambivalence, and explanations of the decision to marry in the form of 'I was asked' or 'being asked helped' suggested they agreed to marry with relatively limited enthusiasm. On the one hand, such responses bear a striking resemblance to the aloofness that men show about marriage in heterosexual relationships when they claim to 'do it for their' wives (Lewis, 2001; Mansfield and Collard, 1988). On the other hand, in same-sex relationships (like many heterosexual relationships nowadays), ambivalence about 'marriage' can have many roots, both personal and political. In this context the surprise proposal could be a powerful act, as to reject it could have threatened to disrupt or even end the assumed shared reality of the couple. While some proposers were sensitive to this, the partner who was proposed to often seemed under pressure to accept. The following extract from Moreen (119a) and Pam's (119b) interview illustrates this. Moreen had intended to propose to Pam on a holiday, but 'disaster' broke out:

Pam: We were talking about marriage and I declared that I didn't believe in it and Moreen burst into tears because she was going to propose to me [...] in a very romantic fashion [laughing].

Moreen: I had the rings. I'd been saving up [...] to buy this ring 'cause it's like made of recycled gold with an ethical stone [....] and I knew that Pam would like it and I'd kind of snuck out a ring and I'd got it measured and [it took] them ages to make it and then it had come and I finally had this ring so I [...] had it planned out and then we're sitting on the train and she just announces this and I was just like 'Oh!' and I was so upset [...] I think it's the biggest spectacle I've ever made of myself in public [...] just tears with embarrassment.

This couple did decide to marry a couple of months after this event. The part that Moreen's efforts and devastation played in Pam's overcoming of her objections to marriage are unclear. In the absence of obvious gender differences the subtleties of power involved in the proposal cannot be reduced to institutionalised gender power as such. But it would be naïve to think that the absence of obvious gender differences meant that the interactions and decision-making within couple relationships are power-free. Proposal stories and proposals themselves were often handled with playful humour where partners teased each other about 'playing hard to get' and 'winning over'. Humour could also involve the 'play' of power:

Hanna (108a):   She cried when I asked her.
Tammy (108b):   Oh, shut up [laughter].
Hanna: I'm proud of that moment.
Tammy: I finally gave into you [laughter].

While the surprise proposal had the power to put the suspecting partner on the spot, the playfully rehearsed proposal was deployed as defence against the powerful implications of a rejection:

Olga (126b):   Well, I think the first time you say it as a joke to protect yourself, just in case the other person is like, 'Ha ha ha, how ridiculous'.

Mandy (126a):	[laughs]
Olga:	Um, but then when the other person goes, 'Oh, okay,' then it becomes just, 'Oh well, why not?'

Others, who did not have the right to stay in the UK because of their immigration status, were in a less structurally powerful position in relation to the proposal and in relation to the decision of if, and when, to formalise the relationship. Their commitments were also vulnerable to distrust and to public scrutiny and suspicion. Compromised immigration status could compromise the future of relationships, and this was the case for eight of our couples, three of whom met abroad and five of whom met in the UK when the non-European partner was on a work or study visit. Stacy (110a) and Theresa (110b), who met abroad, spent the first six years of their relationship living in two countries. The financial and emotional costs of this were not viable in the long term. Caroline (112a) and Edith (112b), who met in the UK, lived under the constant threat of being separated. While this caused a degree of emotional strain, their decision to enter into civil partnership caused a different kind of strain: their relationships became the subject of 'public' evaluation. On one occasion, Caroline was taken aside by her work supervisor. She rehearsed their conversation:

Supervisor:	'I believe congratulations are in order.'
Caroline:	'Thank you very much.'
Supervisor:	'You're not just doing this for immigration though are you?'
Caroline:	'Well kind of yes, but you know, I love her too.'
Supervisor:	'Just making sure.'

While couples in this situation were prepared for questions that might be raised by immigration authorities, they were less prepared for the questioning and evaluation from well-meaning friends, family members or colleagues. Caroline, like the other partners in her situation, became attuned to the need to explain and validate their relationships with recourse to love. This was evident in the interviews we conducted with other couples in a similar situation, when partners like Jeremy (206b) explained their reasons for marrying:

It [his immigration status] wasn't the only reason 'cause I mean obviously, you know, we love each other.

Trust and suspicion can came to the fore in relationships where marrying has a clear advantage for one partner. This made it impossible for the non-European partner to suggest marriage as a solution to their own insecure immigration status. Andrew (204a), for example, met Graham (204b) when his visa was due to expire in six months. While the relationship was getting serious, Andrew was hesitant to tell Graham about his immigration status. He eventually told him, but did not discuss it any further at this point. Graham told his friends who generally advised him to be careful. Graham did not share their suspicions, and knew Andrew would not propose:

> I just knew that Andrew was never going to mention civil partnership because I knew that he would think that this is all about him staying in the country. So by Christmas I'd made a decision in my mind that I was going to raise civil partnership in January when we got back home, because I knew Andrew was never going to do it, so I knew it had to come from me.
>
> Graham

The threat of being separated prompted partners like Andrew and Graham to enter into civil partnership before they would have done so otherwise, and two couples stated that they would not have done so if there were other ways of securing a partner's immigration status.

While public debates about same-sex marriage are centred around the right to access couple and family 'rights', they presume love – the most intangible thing – to be the measure of an authentic relationship. This marks a shift in the ideology of 'good' marriages as being based in socio-economic compatibility to emotional compatibility. Yet, compatible socio-economic status is still a significant feature of marriage choices, and this was the case for our younger same-sex couples. Partners' incomes (or in the case of students, their earning potential) were often broadly similar (for details and variances see Chapter 5), and while money is a complicated matter in relationships (see Chapter 5), financial security rarely featured as an explicit reason to formalise the relationship. However, the fact that about half the men and a much greater proportion of the women did not to enter into committed relationships with people who earned (or had the potential to earn) significantly less or more than them suggests that similar earnings and occupational status could contribute to the sense of a 'good match' (see Chapter 5). This is consistent with findings about heterosexual marriages that suggest partners are most likely to come from similar socio-economic backgrounds, although women still generally earn less than men.

In one exceptional case, the financial benefit to one partner explicitly influenced the decision to marry. In Amina (101a) and Josha's (101b) case, civil partnership had a clear financial incentive for Amina, whose work permit restricted the areas in which she could work and thus her earning potential. After a long and sustained campaign by Amina to get Josha to agree to a civil partnership, Josha eventually capitulated. As Josha puts it:

> I agreed because, [...] I mean if that wasn't the case I suppose we wouldn't have got married, because I didn't feel there was a need to set it in stone. Especially since I knew it was going to be temporary.

When Josha completes her studies, her family expects her to marry a man. However, from the story that she and Amina told, it is clear that she felt that she had little option but to agree to Amina's proposal in the face of Amina's persistent demands. Josha linked her own willingness to go along with Amina's demands to the gendered expectations she (Josha) has of relationships: that having taken the more 'feminine role' she had little choice but to eventually go along with Amina's plans. She may also fear that Amina will expose their secret life. The point is that Josha reluctantly entered into the civil partnership, and her circumstances certainly challenge the idea of marriage as a joint project, serving the needs of two partners (Giddens, 1992). Josha and Amina's case provides a rather extreme example of power imbalances within same-sex relationships. For the vast majority of young same-sex partners, power relationships were far more subtle and dynamic (see Chapters 5–6), as may well be the case in young heterosexual ones.

Parenting also played a significant role in prompting some couples to formalise their relationship. Of the eight female couples who had children in their care, five formalised their relationship with parenting in mind. None of the male couples had children in their care, but Chung (224a) and Warren (224b) believed that marriage would improve their chances of being considered as adoptive parents. For female parents, the position of the non-biological parent was a primary concern. This was sometimes linked to the hostility of biological fathers, refusals to acknowledge non-biological parents as legitimate family members, or refusals by family members to acknowledge non-biologically related children as 'their own'. Kathryn (105a) and Louise (105b), who have one child and are expecting another, voiced fears about their parents' possible claims over their children should one of them die. As Louise explains:

> All of a sudden our families, which seemed supportive [could] suddenly start making decisions about 'Oh I don't know anymore, whether I'm quite so supportive, and actually that's my Grandchild, not yours' sort of, those sorts of scenarios we just wanted to tie [...] belts and braces [around] the situation.

Despite the extent to which families of origin tended to accept same-sex parenting relationships, fears about the risks that given kin presented when it would matter most could still run deep. Same-sex partners are clearly not immune to the pressures of marrying for the sake of children. While some indicated they were happy to do so, their narratives suggested that the choice to enter into civil partnership was not a wholly free choice as such – they saw it as a necessity if they were to be fully recognised and 'protected' as parents and as a legitimate family.

Making it real

Berger and Kellner (1964: 9) note that in marrying, partners embark 'on the often difficult task of constructing for themselves the little world in which they will live'. The fact that most of the younger same-sex partners had already begun this task before entry into civil partnership in part undermines the 'cataclysmic connotation' (ibid) that marriage may have once had for those embarking on it. Nevertheless, marriage still has such connotations in the popular imagination which 'is underlined as well as psychologically assuaged by the ceremonialism that surrounds the event' (ibid).

Nearly half of the couples (22) celebrated with what they termed a 'wedding' or 'wedding reception'. These partners tended to be on good terms with their families of origin. While weddings were sometimes seen as uniting two different families, parental involvement in planning the wedding did not seem to be important to the partners. The input from parents did not approximate that which might be associated with heterosexual weddings. Help was not necessarily volunteered or wanted, and the planning was very often a couple project. The weddings could be large and expensive and take months of preparation. Frederick (209a) and Tim (209b) went for a 'big white wedding'.

Tim: It was all planned to the last millisecond.
Frederik: Every detail, every little

Tim: 'cause you have to have everything different. Everything
            has to match [...]
Frederik: Tim, you're a sort of [...] control freak in one way and I'm
            a control freak in a different way. So you put two control
            freaks on something like a wedding, it becomes like a
            military operation.

While weddings were an opportunity to affirm and display the couple's
commitment, they were also an opportunity to affirm and display the
couple's tastes and social aspirations. Here are Tim and Frederik again:

Tim: 'cause you're all the arty and the way it looks and what-
            ever, and I'm more, right, so it must go to time and what
            are we gonna do and
Frederik: so we actually – I really enjoyed all the planning part,
            actually.
Tim: Yeah, yeah.
Frederik: And dealing with all the suppliers. And I did all the design [...]
            side for the wedding and built the website and so on
            and so forth. We were very specific about the food. We
            wouldn't go with their stock food, sort of their standard
            menu. We went to every wedding place we'd been able
            to find, pulled all their menus together and we spent one
            Sunday going through every item on every menu.

Like heterosexual weddings today, same-sex weddings were 'life-
styled'. By this we mean that they said as much about tastes and styles
associated with socio-cultural location and aspirations as they did about
sexuality. Some couples, like Mandy (126a) and Olga (126b), adopted
what they termed an 'organic' approach but struggled to decide how to
celebrate. Initially they opted for a 'do-it-yourself thing' whereby friends
would bring the food and they would take care of the decorations themselves: 'very Guardian' style as they described it. A few months later
these ideas were put to rest when Mandy's father encouraged them to
do it 'properly'. He also offered the means to make this happen. They
ended up with a wedding in a 'beautifully converted barn out in the
country', with 'amazing food' and over 70 guests. In this case, the wedding said as much about Mandy's family and their economic and social
standing as it did about the couple.

As well as those who opted for weddings, some partners self-consciously
chose celebrations that were less like weddings: that did not include

a formal sit-down meal, speeches or religious symbolism. Some celebrations were based on small guestlists or were present-free. Scaling down the guestlist proved problematic for some. Fiona (122a) and Iris (122b) worried that they would upset people as neither wanted a 'big fuss'. In the end, they decided to limit it to those who were 'completely hundred per cent behind' the formalising of their relationship, who would affirm the authenticity of their commitment. Others still wanted a less expensive way of marking the event whereby guests would pay for their own meal or bring a dish. Some opted for a unique venue, on a train or on a ship, others choose an unusual timing such as at Christmas. As well as personal taste, the nature and style of the wedding or celebration were often dictated by economic circumstances and the size of personal networks, with some partners opting for a 'small and intimate' affair (10 couples), a 'party' (8 couples) or no celebration at all (4 couples).

For those who opted for a wedding, the absence of a clearly defined gendered wedding script meant that endless decisions had to be made. The dilemmas encountered included: Do we have a hen weekend? Who gives the bride away? Who will be paying? Most people welcomed opportunities to create their own ceremonies, but for some, like Andrew (204a), the lack of clear directions made their celebration feel 'inauthentic.'

> There was nothing traditional about it, it felt like [...] we felt we were making it all up made it almost feel like a charade, or like a sham or like we were acting rather than it was a real thing, but on the other hand, the fact that we, that we did make it all up made it very personal.

In many respects, same-sex couples' dilemmas about how to ceremonialise, celebrate or mark the formalisation of their relationship are not so different to those faced by many heterosexual couples that stem from a sense of expanded choices in terms of 'style', and the sense that the wedding should be an authentic expression of the couples' (or at least the bride's) individuality. Dawn (120a) and Hailee (120b), who struggled with the decision about what to wear on the day, wanted to avoid the 'tragic matching suits' that they thought defined lesbian weddings:

> You see lots of photos on the news, on the TV, of like two lesbians getting married and they always, they often have sort of like really tragic matching suits and stuff, and we were just like we don't want that [laughs].
>
> Hailee

We were surprised by the extent to which the partners, like Dawn and Hailee, were disparaging of what they termed 'gay weddings', and that this was a 'style' that they self-consciously sought to avoid. 'Gay weddings' were thought to be silly and described as 'a circus' or as 'ridiculous'. OJ (225b) recounted how a 'gay wedding' would obstruct the 'real' message of becoming a family.

> We wanted an austere wedding, it would have been way too easy in our minds for that ceremony to become a sort of pantomime, 'Sex in the City, Gay Wedding', which is hell in both of our aesthetic visions [...] I didn't want it to be distracting in terms of the fun of the ceremony, the craziness, then you wake up the next day and go, 'Shit, what have I done?' I wanted it, the ceremony, to sort of represent, Herman phrased it very well at the time, to be about becoming family [...] it was a serious event and I think both of us were very keen that the way the event was organised would show that to us. There wouldn't be any sort of silly distractions.

Despite the various reasons for formalising the relationship, the majority of participants emphasised that first and foremost they entered into civil partnerships 'for themselves': as an expression of their love and already existing commitment. At the same time, familial, personal community and broader affirmation were clearly important, although it was less often explicitly mentioned. The critical nature of the event was reflected in many partners' descriptions of their ceremonies as 'special', or their wedding days as the 'best day' of their lives. Many also described the ways in which others (and especially older and more distant family members who might be assumed to be disapproving) had deemed it special or 'the best' wedding they had attended. In this way, entry into civil partnership and the ceremonialism that surrounded it involved the objectification of a social relationship, part of a process 'by which subjectively experienced meaning becomes objective to the individual and, in interaction with others, become common property and thereby massively objective' (Berger and Kellner, 1964: 9). Put another way, civil partnership as a form of marriage *confirms* the couple's reality, and the wedding itself can be indicative of the ways in which 'the groups with which the couple associates are called upon to assist in co-defining this [...] reality' (ibid). In this respect, family, friends and personal communities were not simply called upon to witness the couples' expression of their commitment, but to be actively involved in objectivation of the relationship and in codefining the reality of the marriage. This partly explains the aversion to 'gay weddings'. These potentially undermined the seriousness of the event because they risked mocking it. This was at odds with the significance of the event for most partners, which was linked to making the relationship visible and 'real' in terms that could be understood by significant others, and involving these others in the co-construction of their reality.

For the most part, the young couples' marriages were positively affirmed by friends, families and parents. However, in some cases, significant others refused to affirm the commitment as worthy of celebration. This was the case for Radinka (103a) and Kamilia (103b), who noted that when they presented the news of the impending civil partnership over the phone to their families there was no 'Wow', not even 'congratulations':

Kamilia: I was a bit disappointed that none of them really made the effort to come to the civil partnership [...] That was one of the really disappointing things wasn't it, really?

Radinka: Yeah, and my father, I actually told my father [about my sexuality] just before our marriage.

Kamilia: I can't be cross with them, but it really makes you think a bit. I can't say with certainty, but I think if I was about to marry a man, then they would definitely come. Especially if it was an English man, they would go, 'Oh, well, our daughter's [getting married]' and the whole village would know about it.

Garry's (227a) experience of his father's refusal to confirm the authenticity and value of his partnership was a more explicitly brutal one. His relationship with his father had been very strained for some time, but Garry hoped that he would still attend the wedding; however he did not. Things took a more negative turn. A few days after the wedding, Garry was banned from seeing his mother who had suffered from a chronic condition for a long time. His father had always blamed Garry for his mother's illness and the wedding had apparently made her condition worse. Garry does not know if he will see his mother again. He explained:

I'd be happy to [see my mother]. I'm not sure if I'll be able [...]. I would very much like to. I don't know how it would be possible. Unless my father changes his mind at some point in the future, I have absolutely no idea how I could do it without basically laying myself open to accusations of trying to go and make her, trying to go and kill her faster.

At a symbolic level, weddings provided the opportunity to confirm or affirm the connection between same-sex couples' little worlds and the worlds of their families and personal communities, and to involve same-sex couples and their personal communities in co-constructing a world together. However, they could also involve symbolic violence, as in Garry's case, where a powerfully significant other could refuse to affirm the legitimacy of the relationship.

Marriage as a political act

Given that civil partnership was a relatively new possibility when our young partners entered into it, in principle there is no reason why it should be automatically seen as marriage or as a form of marriage. The fact that most of our interviewees saw it in this way, and entered into it in this spirit, suggests that it is not simply that civil unions and marriages themselves potentially 'normalise' younger generations' same-sex relationships, but rather that firmly embedded meanings and practices associated with the couple as the 'inevitable' focus of mature adult relationships make the legal privileging of the couple seem natural. Most of the young same-sex couples that we studied did not fundamentally trouble this view, and in this sense it seems that they are indeed 'ordinary' relationships (but see Chapter 6). However, it is also the case that, while most couples tended to frame their decisions to marry as a 'free' choice that was based on love, there were also those who were prompted to marry so as to protect their couple and parenting relationships, and for more instrumental reasons. In this latter respect, new generations of same-sex relationships are not so completely different to previous generations' heterosexual relationships, where romance and reason are factors that influence decisions to marry (cf. Mansfield and Collard, 1988). As well as this, our same-sex partners' decisions to marry were often, like previous generations' heterosexual marriages, linked to a sense of maturity and enhanced social status.

While we, as sociologists, may now be more sceptical than we once were of the notions of 'life stages' and key 'life events' that are linked to social status, partly because of their universalising connotations, it is clear that these notions hold sway in everyday lives. Previous generations' same-sex relationships have been excluded from mainstream markers of maturity, life-stage progression, and key life events. They have been associated with denigrated, as opposed to enhanced, social status. In this respect, it is perhaps unsurprising that some members of new generations should so enthusiastically embrace the new options and opportunities they are offered. Formalising relationships provides some partners with the opportunity to invite the others they care about to become involved in the co-creation of their world. By the same token it symbolises a willingness among many of those others to take up this invitation. At the same time, where significant others refuse this invitation, the enduring nature of conceptions of same-sex relationships as 'immature', 'inauthentic' and 'troubling' is underscored. Whether we view it in negative or positive ways, the invitation to others to co-create same-sex relational realties (whether it is taken up or refused) can be seen as a two-sided political act: in that it shores up the idea of the couple as a naturally privileged relational from, while at the same time disrupting the heterosexual relational imaginary.

5
Money, Couples and the Self

A key part of our enquiry into the lives of young same-sex couples focused on the question of money management. In this chapter we explore whether practices and meanings of money appear to be different to understandings derived from studies of heterosexual relationships. The question of money management has been a significant one in studies of heterosexual relationships for some time (Nyman and Dema, 2007). Money and how it is handled between men and women, especially in marriage, became a foundational framework for explorations of gender inequalities hidden within the private sphere. Money was and is associated with power in heterosexual couples (Burgoyne, 1990; Vogler, 1998; Vogler and Pahl, 1994). Here we explore whether money and power can be equated in the same way for same-sex couples and consider whether other meanings can be derived from the practices they engage in.

Money in relationships

An important strand of research on heterosexual money management was pioneered by Jan Pahl in Britain, who began a series of projects starting in the 1980s and continuing into the 2000s (Pahl, 1980; 1989; 1990). A core element to Pahl's approach was the development of typologies of money management in which she identified different systems that couples would adopt once married. For example, she identified the housekeeping model in which a husband as sole earner would give his wife a set amount each week or month to enable her to run the household. He could regard the money he kept back as his own to spend as he wished, whereas the wife would have to ask him for spending money for personal consumption such as for new clothes for herself. Pahl also identified a pooling system which was not the dominant model when she started her research, but which became more extensive over time. Here, couples would open a joint bank account where all wages or salaries would be put, thus allowing both (more) equal access to shared financial resources. As Pahl's work became increasingly sophisticated and as social, economic and political conditions changed, she added new elements to her studies. She (and others) started to include more complex models (e.g. partial pooling), new forms of money (e.g. credit cards, pensions), decisions on spending (e.g. who really chooses the purchases) and finally the impact of children (e.g. discovering that mothers spend more of their money on the children). As more studies have been carried out, they have also explored how different constituencies of people arrange their financial affairs: for example, couples who have been previously married, young cohabitees and same-sex couples (see Burgoyne and Morison, 1997; Burgoyne et al., 2006; Vogler, 2005; Vogler et al., 2006).

The legacy of this trajectory of research has been that money (and how it is managed) has become a virtual index of inequality within heterosexual couples. Thus, the woman who leaves all financial management to her husband, who only has a vague knowledge of what he earns, or who has to show receipts for everything she buys from the 'joint' account is axiomatically seen as being in a position of relative powerlessness and vulnerability. We would not necessarily dissent from this conclusion, but here we suggest that it is problematic always and only to read the meaning of money in this way. One important issue for this study is that if we import this specific understanding of money into our analysis of same-sex relationships, then we may fail to identify other possible 'readings' of everyday practices. We may also find ourselves engaged in the unrewarding task of trying to assess whether same-sex relationships are more equal than heterosexual relationships. We are therefore reticent about following this well-trodden path. Instead of taking these established findings and analyses as our starting point, we shelve them initially, but return to them at a later point having first explored our own data through a different lens.

Our own approach prioritises the social meanings of money and recognises that money is a complex emotional and cultural currency which has both different meanings for different individuals and different relationships, and which can change its meanings over time as well. This is an approach adopted by Stocks et al. (2007) and which builds on sociological traditions initiated by Simmel (1990) but is also centred on a more social interactionist approach (Nyman, 2003; Zelizer, 1994).

Stocks et al. argue that money (its management, its exchange, its meanings) is both part of doing gender and also entwined with the doing of and becoming a couple. This approach coincides with anthropological work on the cultural significance of material possessions which has reinvigorated understandings of the ways that meanings are invested in material objects (Miller, 1998; 2001). Thus, how we collect, exchange, cherish or disregard material possessions is firmly understood to be part of a process of identity production (Dupuis and Thorns, 1998; Smart, 2007).

We begin by providing an overview of the incomes of our couples at the time of the interviews. This will form the foundation for the following discussion of the significance of money for our young couples. We consider how money can be part of a story of becoming a couple, in particular how money is part of a process of bonding. We also explore the significance of the ways in which these individuals tell stories of their families of origin in relation to money. We will go on to investigate examples of respondents telling redemption stories of misspent youth, money and rescue, and how these narratives also reflected the ways in which managing money is part of a story of becoming responsible and hence a matter of identity production (Sonnenberg, 2008). Finally, as noted above, we will return to the issue of money, gender and power in the conclusion.

Table 5.1 shows the income levels of the young men in the study. It shows that the most frequently occurring individual salary fell between £24,000 and £36,999 per annum (14 out of 50 individuals) while a further 13 young men earned above this level. The only couples (as opposed to individuals) on very low joint incomes were Henry (217a) and Kurt (217b), Edwin (211a) and Ivan (211b), and Miguel (223a) and Robin (223b). However, among the individual low-earners, Jan (208a), Henry (217a), Leroy (219b) and Wayne (226b) were all self-defined as students and so their low incomes were likely to be temporary. Ivan and Edwin, who were a low-earning couple, were struggling to be actors and this inevitably meant their incomes were patchy. Other individual low-earners could benefit from the fact that their partners brought in a considerably higher salary and this group of male couples is notable in that just over half (N = 13) had quite large income differences of at least £12,000 p.a. Because we asked partners to put themselves in an income band, we cannot see their exact salary levels, however, and so differences may be even greater than this where one individual is at the bottom of one band while his partner is at the top of another band.

Table 5.1 Income levels for men

	£1–3,999	4,000–7,999	8,000–11,999	12,000–16,999	17,000–23,999	24,000–36,999	37,000–49,999	50,000–99,999	100,000+
202								Daniel	
203						Robert			
204				Mark & Callum					
205				Andrew				Graham	
206					Stewart	Jorge	Kevin		
208		Jan				Jeremy			
209						Diego	Fredrik	Tim	
210						Oliver			Ben
211		Ivan	Edwin						
212				Phil		Otto			
213					Felix			Cameron	
214					Albert	Duncan			
215					Frazer		Todd		
216						Peter		Victor	
217	Henry & Kurt								
218					Ian	Neil			
219	Leroy							Benjamin	
220					Nathan	Theo	Eric		
221						Hayden	Lucas		
222			Eugene						
223			Miguel & Robin						
224					Warren	Chung			
225					Herman & OJ				
226			Wayne			Trevor		Garry	
227						Umberto			

Table 5.2 Income levels for women

	£1–3,999	4,000–7,999	8,000–11,999	12,000–16,999	17,000–23,999	24,000–36,999	37,000–49,999	50,000–99,999	100,000+
101		Josha					Amina		
103				Radinka	Kamilla				
104			Maria	Doris					
105				Kathryn			Louise		
106				Angela & Nancy					
107						Veronica	Juliet		
108			Hanna		Tammy				
109		Rebecca	Zoe						
110					Stacy & Theresa				
111								Barbara & Nicole	
112						Edith	Caroline		
113						Olivia	Fay		
114				Holly	Ellen				
115						Gillian		Cori	
116				Isabel & Sam					
117					Linda & Natalie				
118			Helen	Andrea					
119						Moreen & Pam	Dawn & Hailee		
121						Brooklyn	Sara		
122							Fiona & Iris		
123			Jasmine	Kenzie		Phoebe			
124					Annabel				
125					Emily & Gail				
126						Mandy & Olga			

The levels of annual income for women are shown in Table 5.2. Unlike the men, they are more evenly spread across the different income bands with 10 individuals in each band from £12,000, £17,000, £24,000 and £37,000. This meant that very few individuals earned less than £12,000 and only three earned more than £50,000 p.a. It was also more unusual for one individual in the couples to earn much more than the other. In only four cases was the differential more than £12,000 p.a. and in 10 cases the women put themselves into the same income band. In strictly economic terms, therefore, the female couples were more equally matched than the male couples in terms of their individual income levels, and as couples the men appeared to be better off and to have more disposable income than the women. Moreover, because eight of the female couples were raising children, it seems likely that the women's personal spending was further constrained.

Among the women with lower incomes there were four students (Josha, 101b; Andrea, 118a; Helen, 118b; and Jasmine, 123a) and, as with the male students, it is likely that their earnings would increase in time. However, a couple like Zoe (109a) and Rebecca (109b) had low incomes because both had low-paid, part-time jobs which had to fit around child-care responsibilities.

Discussing money

Some empirical researchers have noted that getting respondents to talk about money can be difficult because money (in the form of income and wealth) is often deemed a private matter and, in the UK at least, discussing money issues in public is not 'the done thing'. There is a coyness over wage or salary levels and in this study our awareness of this potential source of embarrassment led us to provide respondents with a list of income bands on which they merely had to tick the broad category of personal income which approximated most closely to their own. In other words, partners did not have to speak (publicly) of actual income or wealth. Yet when we began to talk about money management and their own relationship to money we found that almost everyone had a great deal to say. There was no reserve at all. Indeed, their narratives took off into quite reflexive onto-logical accounts of the self and it almost seemed as if in enquiring about relationships with money we were able to tap into strong biographical storylines remarkably easily. Moreover, relationships with money could often appear as defining features of the couple relationship (as exempli-fied by the appropriateness of sameness of approach or, paradoxically, as exemplified by the satisfactoriness of completely different approaches).

Most notably, almost every partner, when it came to the money section of the schedule, laughed when they were asked the first question which was simply 'Can you tell me about your relationship with money?' We cannot be sure what the laughter meant for everyone of course. It was possibly slight embarrassment, but as people then usually moved with enthusiasm into their story it seemed as if it was more like a kind of shared cultural knowingness about the territory they were entering. Respondents seemed to be remarkably open about their relationships with money even if a few were cagey or vague about how many accounts they might have, or even in a few instances about the number of properties they might own.

We began to feel that asking people about their relationships with money was a direct (but unsuspected) route into asking them about the kind of person they were and how they managed going about their relationships in and with the world more generally (Sonnenberg, 2008). Here are two typical responses:

Interviewer: How would you describe your personal approach to money and finances?

Louise (105b):   Fairly sensible financially. I think, probably fairly – I know I spend over my means and, but it, I know this sounds silly but despite doing that it's a fairly, it's fairly sensible as I generally [...], you know I'd never get myself into ridiculous debt and I understand how finances work and generally quite good at shifting money around to sort of make it, make life feel fairly, fairly stable. I've always had to, well since I was eighteen, I've looked after myself financially and, have needed to, [...] to give myself a secure home life and any times, and there are times I've had to borrow money off my dad but when you get a loan off my dad it's not like any other normal parent, if you get a loan off my dad, you also get a legal document saying when you'll pay it back and how you'll pay it back and with what so and so, so it's never, money's never just been, sort of handed to me, I've always had to work very hard for what I've got.

Interviewer: How would you describe your personal approach to money and finances?

Ivan (211b):   Okay I've not got a very sensible approach to money and finances [laughter] although I think I'm getting a handle on it as the years go by. I've never been motivated by earning money and I suppose that's due to the fact that although I was sort of, wasn't spoiled as a child at all I never, options were never closed off to me, as I was growing up so, you know, my parents could afford to send me to university which was great, I mean I went to university before we had, you had to pay for fees and that sort of thing so I was lucky there, but yes, so university was a possibility and so I think what I'm trying to say is I'm, I've been relatively privileged growing up but also knowing the fact that my parents don't earn vast amounts of money and compared to friends' parents, so I know that, so I've known that they'd had to be sensible and be frugal but Dad's quite tight as well so, so that's good. So I've, I think basically, had I grown up and sort of been completely spoilt, or had I grown up and been underprivileged entirely, I might have been more motivated to either sustain the lifestyle I'd become accustomed to or to do complete reversal and actually make some money, I don't know.

We will explore these two quotations in more detail below, but we highlight them here to demonstrate how our respondents would typically move quickly into a dense story about themselves, their family backgrounds, their current relationships and also accounts of personal change and struggle. These responses took us instantly onto the terrain of emotions, morality and complex personal/familial and cultural meanings of money. Hardly anyone gave us a 'factual' kind of response to this question or, where their stories were anchored by factual detail (e.g. keeping spreadsheets or checking receipts), the descriptions of these activities were laced with moral evaluations (e.g. 'I'm not totally anal') or with explanations about why such practices had developed. We came quickly to the conclusion that is already evident in studies of material culture, that money, like possessions or the home, speaks volumes about how people manage relationships and identities.

Money and the making of the couple

As discussed in Chapter 4, almost all of couples had lived together before formalising their relationships, and some saw their entry into civil partnerships as signalling the 'mature' nature of the couple commitment.

Thus civil partnership could provide couples with the opportunity to review their financial affairs with a mind to ordering them in a 'responsible' manner. For the majority of our couples, meshing finances was something which was still a relatively new experience. Many had not settled on a preferred arrangement before their entry into civil partnerships, and several had not done so at the time of the interview. Because for many of the couples this was the first time that they had attempted legally to mesh their affairs, they were driven more by ideals, hopes and a desire to bond than by experience or caution. Almost none had gone through experiences of a legal separation from a previous long-term partner, and so they were not guarded about how they might manage their financial affairs in their current relationships (Burgoyne and Morison, 1997). Also, few seemed governed by strong principles about how money in couple relationships 'should' be organised. Expressly feminist concerns about the need to keep a degree of financial independence hardly surfaced at all in these narratives, and although some couples expressed the view that marriage should herald a specific form of money management and sharing, the majority seemed to adopt an entirely pragmatic approach. One of the small minority of couples who spoke of their civil partnership as signalling a particular financial arrangement was Annabel (124a), who felt it was wrong to have separate bank accounts:

> I just, I don't get it. If [...] you're married, especially if you're married then [...] you're both earning for each other it's not mine and yours, it's together.

The theme of joint money (or 'our' money) was a common one, but it coexisted with a dizzying range of actual practices from a pooling system, where couples put everything into one joint account, to systems where there was a joint account with various separate accounts, and onto situations where there was no meshing of accounts at all but more an everyday virtual commitment to jointness combined with haphazard practices.

Entering into a civil partnership did seem to be a platform for combining aspects of couples' finances, but it did not dictate precisely the form that this should take (Burgoyne et al., 2011). The most common arrangement was one where couples created a joint account to pay for utility bills, joint purchases and the rent or mortgage, while keeping separate accounts for personal spending and even for personal savings at times. This model appears to be becoming the most popular in the

UK (50 per cent of heterosexual couples use this; see Vogler and Pahl, 1994) and it does also seem to be an arrangement which is chosen by younger heterosexual couples (Vogler et al., 2006). This option is therefore not peculiar to same-sex couples but could be said to be an emergent norm for couple relationships of all sorts. That stated, a lot of couples did avoid financial jointness but not for purely principled reasons. What we discovered was that external circumstances rather than 'choice' often dictated the kind of arrangement couples entered into on marriage. The main external constraining factor for couples was debt.

Debt was a dominant framing reference for how our young couples regarded money, their relationship with it, and the practicalities of their financial arrangements. Because so many of the partner had accumulated debts (16 men and 20 women) prior to their civil partnership, it was this burden which tended to determine how they proceeded as a couple. But even where there were no actual debts (except mortgages) at the time of the interview, couples also framed debt as being the one thing which must be avoided. Talk of debt infused their narratives.

In some instances the debts had been incurred by 'reckless' spending on credit cards prior to finding a stable relationship (and we say more about this below), but in other cases debt came about through student loans (11 cases) and student living more generally. In instances where one person had all the debt, the other was reluctant to create a joint account because their income or savings would disappear into the black hole of the debt. In a few cases, individuals were advised strongly not to have a joint account and certainly not to have a joint credit card as the person with a good credit rating would lose their creditworthy status. Money management for these young couples was therefore shaped by the existence of prior debt in ways which, we suspect, would have been much more of a rarity for previous generations of couples:

> I think partly, I mean due to the fact that I am in a good amount of debt and when we first met, I was in even more, because of that I've never really wanted to combine our finances just because that would mean that outgoings would, that I, I mean I don't want him to be paying for my, for my debts at all so we've not ever combined finances in the way that [other couples do].
>
> Ivan (211b)

Debt is important to these relationships in another way because the existence of the financial burden, and in some cases just the memory of past debt, shaped how couples together would manage their finances on a day-to-day level. Put simply, the person who incurred the debt often gave up control of their financial affairs to the partner who had avoided debt. This tendency cut across issues of gender because the men who had debts were just as likely to relinquish control of their finances as the women. Equally, on the other side of the equation, women were just as likely as men to take control of their partners' spending and saving practices where there had been debt. The existence of debt provides a very different lens through which to understand questions of equality in these relationships. For example, it might, at a superficial level, appear that 'old' gender roles re-assert themselves in these marriages because of the frequency with which one partner takes control over financial matters. However, putting debt and poor credit ratings into the equation creates a different picture, and points to the more complex and vital nature of power. These forms of 'lost' money have the potential to shift the operations of power (if we accept for the sake of argument that the person in control exercises more power) away from gender as a determining factor towards an appreciation that financial and loan systems created beyond the reach of couples can be highly deterministic. Put simply, the person carrying the debt into the relationship is in a weaker or potentially more vulnerable position when it comes to negotiating over money and how it should be managed.

However, this does raise the question of whether the debt carrier or the finance manager in the couple relationship has more power in their couple interactions. The situation is a complex one because the spectre of debt could be felt differently by different people. Relevant here, of course, was the level of resources a couple might have. However, it was not only the couples on low incomes who experienced debt. Among the men, Daniel (202a), Graham (204b), Cameron (213b), and Lucas (221a) and Todd (215b) were among the highest earners yet all experienced debt. Among the women, Juliet (107a), Caroline (112a), Fay (113a), Haliee (120b), Sara (121b) and Iris (122b) – who earned between £37,000 and £49,999 – all had debts. Acquiring or having debts was not related directly to social class position or income, but it seems likely that being able to resolve the problem of debt was experienced differently by low-earners, especially where the debt was caused by illness or unemployment.

It was clear that some of those who confessed eagerly to being, or wanting to be, in control of the money in their relationship were the ones who were most worried by debt and by the failure to pay bills and credit card charges. These were people who had been brought up to avoid debt at all costs or who, having experienced the terror of being in debt, were determined never to go back there. By contrast, some of those who relinquished control of financial matters could appear to be liberated by the arrangement. They were freed from the grind of consulting spreadsheets, checking receipts and moving money around to meet variable demands. As Stewart (205b) puts it:

> I've got no head for figures at all which is quite funny with the type of job I do but I don't; I don't get involved in the finances, Jeremy takes care, takes care of the finances. [...] I don't really, I don't really get involved with it at all, and there's, I just don't want to get involved with it, it you know, there's not much left over at the end of the month so it makes me sort of angry because I really want, we want to buy more things for the house and spend more money on us, and going out for dinner more or doing things that will make us feel better but, you know it frustrates me a little bit sometimes. But that's, I think that's probably why I don't even want to hear about the finances, I'll just ask him, let's go, can we afford this, can we afford that? And that's about it, and that's, that's where it stops for me, I don't want to hear anything about it anymore, I don't want to get involved with him doing the finances or the paperwork at all, yeah.

Interestingly, in his interview, Stewart's partner Jeremy (205a) said that if they were starting over again he would want to keep their finances separate. But this couple do demonstrate how hard it is to read off from actual arrangements to the nature of power relationships in same-sex couples. Pahl (1989) has argued in relation to heterosexual relationships that the control of money becomes a burden where there is very little of it to go round and where men can foist the responsibility of avoiding debt and keeping the household afloat onto women. However, this was not a discernible pattern among our couples. Jeremy and Stewart, for example, were both in full-time employment and Jeremy's salary was equivalent to the average annual salary (around £28,000 p.a. for men in 2010; http://www.statistics.gov.uk/cci/nugget.asp?id=285) while Stewart earned slightly less than this. In other words, they were not poor and the burden that being in control of their joint finances generated for Jeremy was to do with the fact that Stewart absolved himself of all responsibility while wanting the pleasure of spending. This context reveals the importance of the meanings that individuals place on money and not just simply the quantity of money available. For example, we found very similar arrangements with the female couples, where one partner simply relinquished control over the finances and only wanted to be told what she could spend. But we also found instances where this arrangement was defined as an unpleasant form of dependency rather than a release from responsibility. Jasmine (123a) and Phoebe (123b), for example, had just such an arrangement with Phoebe taking control of their finances. However, Jasmine (who was a postgraduate student at the time) fell seriously ill and could not contribute to the joint account for several months. Her parents helped out, but suddenly finding herself in the situation of being more dependent on Phoebe's income was uncomfortable for her. Jasmine recounts:

Jasmine (123a):	Yeah, it felt a bit, yeah, it did feel a bit, it was a bit stressful for, I mean, both of us really, but for Phoebe in terms of the fact that all of a sudden her income was effectively halved. But I don't think she cared, other than the fact that it made things a bit more difficult for us. But yeah, it did, it felt a bit weird for me, because, just because I wanted to be contributing and, yeah, I wanted to just say, 'Oh, you know, it's cold tonight, leave on the heating, it's fine'. But I didn't, sometimes I sort of thought, you know, 'Oh, we should be saving money', um, stuff like that.
Interviewer:	And therefore you didn't put the heating on?
Jasmine:	Well [laughs], yeah. For as long as I could bear it, yeah. So yeah, it's kind of strange not contributing. [...] And even now I don't have, like I don't contribute half and half really. Um, but I don't feel so bad about that. I mean, I don't really feel bad about that at all, because, um, because Phoebe earns more than me but that's fine, because I'm, you know [studying].

Jasmine's comments reveal that control and dependency are separate dimensions of financial arrangements between couples. It is important to note in this context that very few of the respondents were financially dependent upon their partners. As we have noted above, none of the men in the study had any parental responsibilities and there were only two instances (Jan [208a] and Diego [208b], and Benjamin [219a] and Leroy [219b]) where couples had huge differences of income levels (e.g. £25,000–£50,000). Typically if one was poor, both were poor. This latter point holds for the women too, but it is here that child-care responsibilities make an important difference. As noted, eight of the 25 female couples were raising children together necessitating reduced working hours for one (and sometimes both) mothers. Two women were, in addition, pregnant and anticipating a reduced income for at least a period of time. A further nine women had plans to adopt children or to get pregnant through donor insemination. This made these relationships quite different in character to the men's relationships because either there had been a period of financial dependency or there was likely to be one. Moreover, a dependent child (or sometimes more than one) was part of the household and so financial management and spending regimes were influenced by this additional responsibility. We are not suggesting that motherhood necessarily creates financial dependency in women's relationships, but it has the potential to do so where one parent is able to strengthen their position in employment while the other parent's position weakens. This potential problem could, however, be overcome by decisions to alternate pregnancies, and it is clear that where feasible mothers had done this or were planning to do so. This is discussed in greater detail in Chapter 7; however, it should be noted here that none of the mothers suggested alternating motherhood for economic reasons even though the impact of such decisions would have financial consequences for the couple.

Debt and redemption

As suggested above, debt and debt management were crucial practical elements in the lives of these recently 'married' couples. Also, debt can shape future practices and has the power to distort aspects of relationships. Debt, of course, has strong moral connotations in cultures that are still influenced by a Protestant ethic and distaste for all forms of financial indebtedness except for mortgages. Although there appear to be generational changes occurring in this cultural attitude, especially with the ubiquitousness of credit card debt, debt still has an element of opprobrium surrounding it. It is this quality, which can in turn attach itself to persons, that we explore here. It is our argument that debt is not just a practical issue but also a site of conflicting values and moral worth in relationships.

We noted above that debt for our young couples was mainly acquired through processes of being a student or through 'reckless' spending at a specific time in the past. Of course, these two things could overlap, but the person who acquires a debt in pursuit of education in a climate where it is almost impossible to avoid loans and overdrafts is subject to less opprobrium than the spender who is deemed to be reckless. In addition to this moral calculus pertaining to how debts are accumulated, there is the issue of how debts are or have been managed. So the person who has had a student loan (and hence debt) but who gets organised to pay it back is in a different position to the person who goes on accumulating debt or who lives as if there is no debt. It was clear, too, from many of the stories of living with debts, that very few people did not care about indebtedness – but this did not mean that they could find a way out of debt and some spoke of simply not being able to cope with the enormity of it.

Given this backdrop, debt can be seen to bring emotional baggage into relationships as well as potential value judgements, and these features can also contribute to how couples relate to one another. In particular, a theme which became very apparent among those who had racked up debts in the past was what we refer to as the redemption story. Those who had debts framed their relationships with their partners as ones based on redemption: they were once lost but now are saved through the good housekeeping of a more stable or sensible partner. There was a narrative of both being saved and being grateful, sometimes combined with accounts of becoming a different (i.e. better) person through the guidance of the more mature partner. These stories were not gendered in the sense that both men and women would rehearse this same narrative, but there was a strong sense of seeing their partner as saviour, protector or even parent when it came to money matters:

[Laughs] Money – I'm one of these people that, you get people that save and have investments and bonds and everything like that and I just, I just like if you've got the money now then spend it now. I know that – part of me, a little bit of my head niggles and says 'Oh I should really think about a rainy day and think of the future' but right now we're – we are kind of struggling for money at the moment but I'm not at work. I'm still on, I'm on additional maternity leave so get paid so – Annabel tends to do all the money things. She does take that role on doesn't she, the protector?

Kenzie (124b)

And I was in a hell of a lot of debt that caused me and Neil you know no amount of torture; Neil just thinking I was just being a moody, depressive bastard, and me knowing deep down that I just wasn't coping. Em, so money to me is this terrible thing that you apparently have to have to get through life. Fortunately, Neil's incredibly good with money so it's not such an issue for us as a couple because there's somebody [laughs] who's sensible.

Ian (218a)

Escaping from debt, starting to budget, and even beginning to save money were seen by the majority of our respondents as part of 'settling down' or at least becoming mature and starting to live a more sensible life. Much of this narrative drift reflects the 'stage' that young partners perceived themselves to have reached where they mostly felt that they had gone through an immature single phase and were now, with the help of a grounded partner, entering into a less frenetic or less worrying period. As discussed in Chapter 4, these respondents did tend to reflect on their lives in terms of stages and, as part of this, the way in which money came to be disciplined formed part of their critical transition. Becoming a person who could manage money, or at least one who could see their own limitations with money, marked a transition of the self which was brought about through their relationship. The idea of redemption sits uneasily with the formal principles of an equal relationship, however, and it is not clear whether the potential imbalance created would always be easily managed.

Money, self and family stories

Blokland (2005) has argued that it is helpful to understand identity not as a fixed achievement by which one arrives at a place where one knows the kind of person one is forever after, but as a process which has no real end point and which is not linear (i.e. from a weak person to a strong one) but which goes through different identities in different contexts and at different times. This flexible process of 'identifications' (as she calls it) does not necessarily sit easily with how people speak about themselves and how they project an image of themselves into social interactions. This is not to dispute Blokland's thesis, but it is to recognise that the contemporary drive of narratives about one's self – given that narratives are provided at one moment in time (viz. the interview) – tend to fix identity at the moment of speaking. In this narrative. there is an appreciation that change may have occurred (e.g. I was that kind of a person then), but typically the person speaking tends to assume they have arrived at the sort of person they will remain at the time of speaking (e.g. I am now this kind of person and will remain so). To suggest in a narrative that one is a different kind of person in different contexts, or even that one will be different again soon, could imply a kind of inauthenticity or a shallowness of character even if this is all entirely probable.

Speaking of money seems, par excellence, to be a moment when people fix their identity. But our interviews revealed more than a process of fixing the individual because so many of our young couples explained their identity vis-à-vis money in the context of their family of origin. So, talking of money also led quickly to what are referred to as 'family stories' which are also a part of the process of fixing identity. John Gillis (1996; 2004) has pointed to the significance of family stories as a kind of cultural and personal currency which families generate as ways of both bonding together and as ways of reflecting themselves outwardly to others (Smart, 2007). These may be stories of special events or holidays, or they may be stories about particular 'characters' in families who show the kind of calibre of the family members. Family stories do not have to be stories of goodness or heroism but they encapsulate aspects of families which can be passed down to next generations or can be used to explain different family members' attitudes and practices. Family stories can take material form in such things as family photograph albums which can be brought out on special occasions – often when a new partner is introduced into the family. Or they can take a ritual form, for example in the shape of ways of celebrating birthdays, religious festivals, and summer holidays and so on. Sharing family stories is also part of becoming friends with a new person or becoming a couple, where people swap such stories as ways of indicating in a short-hand way, some of the facets of a person's character.

These are not new insights, of course; however, we did not anticipate in starting our study of young same-sex couples that the focus on money and money management would also reveal a rich seam of these family stories. As we note above, our first question to respondents was to ask about their relationship to money, but very often what followed was a narrative about families of origin. In the first quotations we reproduce above, Louise and Ivan both segue rapidly into thumbnail sketches of their fathers. Louise says that to borrow money from her dad virtually entailed signing a legal document, while Ivan refers to his dad as 'quite tight'. The incorporation of snippets of family stories into explanations about their own relationships with money is fascinating because they say as much about the person speaking as they do about the person interpolated in the narrative. Louise uses her story about her father to substantiate her claim to being sensible about money, and she regards her father's practice not as admirable in itself, but as giving rise to a good outcome in terms of how she had to react to him. Ivan's account is more complicated because he is bemoaning the fact that his family was rather middling, which is to say neither rich enough to spoil him nor poor enough to let him endure hardship. He feels that this very averageness has robbed him of motivation to earn money, but the one good thing in the story is the fact that his dad is tight with money. His account contains apparent inconsistencies, but this is not as important as the fact that, like Louise's, his character as it relates to money can be laid at the door of his family of origin. This facet of identity was formed in the milieu of parental practice and familial culture.

Other accounts we received stressed the existence of bridges across generations in terms of attitudes towards money. Hence, one person might account for their poor money management skills by explaining that their mother had been hopeless too. Equally, another might say they were good with managing money because their mother had been so hopeless with it. These narratives are not sources of literal truths about why people come to be (or come to see themselves as) competent or incompetent with money, rather they are tropes. By this we mean that bringing in the family story or snippet into an explanation is a metaphorical way of invoking all that needs to be known about a person's circumstances. Thus, invoking the scrooge-like father, the debt-ridden mother, the anal household, the lavish childhood – all culturally familial characters and settings – works to explain 'everything' in just a few words. Thus, talk about money appears to be a very parsimonious way of identifying one's self comprehensively to others. What was also interesting in the ways in which individuals spoke was that when asked why their approach to money might be the same or different to their partners', most would reach for exactly the same tropes. So respondents were not only explaining themselves to us in these terms, it is clear that they explained themselves to their partners in these terms, too, and their partners could recite the very same family stories on their behalf. In the account below, Maria (104b) meshes accounts of her family with accounts of Doris's (104a) family to explain the kind of combination they make, and also the kinds of difficulties they can find themselves in:

> Yeah, I think she's just, they, she's never been aware of her family wanting for money certainly not until she was an adult, and so I think she's much more relaxed about it and I think she's more securely middle class in that sense, whereas I come from a background which was working class. I was the first person in two generations of my family, so about sixty people, to go to university, so I kind of, yeah, come from a different place and I always still feel it now, that kind of I'm never sure how I would be classified, whether it's middle class or working class and sometimes you get caught between the two with trying to do more than, really you can afford.

This short account is packed with meanings and also emotions, as well as comparisons and evaluations. Maria seeks to explain their different attitudes to money through the trope of family background. It is as if, at the point that individuals have to negotiate over money management, their entire extended families (sometimes several generations) enter into the negotiations with them. Doris is not just dealing with Maria but also with Maria's mum and dad, possibly a few aunts and uncles and also even grandparents.

Of course, a complicating factor can be that once mothers and fathers are introduced into the process, it becomes clear that parents themselves have conflicting approaches to money. The following quotation from Olga (125b) is interesting in this regard because although she talks about her 'family' as having a particular approach to money, it is clear that the approach she admires is that of her father while her mother is something of an irritant.

> My parents have very opposite attitudes to money. My father won't buy anything unless it's a house, and my mum buys stuff. She has stuff everywhere. It drives me crazy. I couldn't live with her. Her house is just full of things. And this house has quite a lot of material possessions in it, but it does get very firmly scrutinised very often as to which ones are necessary, whereas I prefer to save my money and spend it on things like Apple computers, but I don't tend to buy a lot of junk [...]. So I think we're both quite similar in that respect. I think our families are both savers and risk moderators in terms of money. Neither of us comes from families where credit cards are an acceptable way to pay for things that you can't afford – and both of them are very strong work ethic or view, pay your bills before you go out and have fun and this sort of thing.

Later in the interview, Olga expresses distaste for the way in which her father required her mother to produce receipts for everything she buys, including the food shopping. This she regards as a prehistoric way of organising their finances, and she reflects upon the importance of women having jobs and thus some financial independence. She therefore wants herself and her partner to have both joint money and independent money which they can spend on themselves without consulting. The significance of this is that in Olga's story she holds up her family as a beacon of probity with money (e.g. the Protestant ethic) while at the same time rejecting the terms on which her parents actually negotiated (if that is the appropriate term) their money management between themselves.

Seen in this light, it becomes possible to see a different direction of travel between early childhood experiences and later attitudes towards and practices with money. These stories reveal the extent to which people can reach back into the past to select family stories (or memories) which explain current events and choices rather than providing factual accounts of family relationships (Misztal, 2003; Radstone, 2000).

Money management therefore was far more than a simple or practical arrangement between cohabitees in a household. It was also far more than an objective index on equality, even though the management of money has important links with how equality works in practice. Rather, we found that in talking about money, these young people spoke about their ontological positioning and sense of self in relation to significant others. Tracing money was less a way of summarising a dyadic relationship which is played out in the present, and more a way of comprehending the workings of past and present biographical relatedness formed in kinship and friendship networks.

Money, gender and power revisited

It is tempting to read the working of power into these relationships based on the arrangements the couples made for their financial affairs. For example, one female couple had an arrangement where the flat they lived in was in just one person's name and where the incoming partner also paid her wages into an account which was solely in her partner's name. Another couple had an arrangement where one paid the mortgage and utility bills while she paid for the daily consumables. Such an arrangement could seriously jeopardise her financial status later on if they were to separate. We have also already referred above to numerous instances where one partner entirely conceded all responsibility for money management to their partner. From a gender (and indeed a simple legal) perspective, all of these patterns would be seen as dangerously disempowering. Yet of course, they were not seen as such by the parties themselves.

What is at stake in the interpretation of these negotiations between couples around money is how power is theorised. A classic structuralist approach might look at the relative income and employment status of the individuals in the relationship. Exploring access to social and cultural capital might reveal differential positioning, meaning that one partner could be both more influential and also more safeguarded against risk. Adopting a more interactionist approach, the exercise of power in small daily exchanges might reveal that the person who takes responsibility for financial management is the most burdened rather than most privileged partner. But as we also note above, the gendered sameness of the couples means that understanding how these things work cannot be read from a template which presumes that one partner is already more vulnerable than the other because of their gender.

We have noted that the typical arrangement for both male and female couples was to have a joint account for joint costs, combined with separate current accounts which allowed a degree of independent spending. But some individuals volunteered that they also had separate personal *savings* accounts which were treated as if they were something separate from everyday conjoined finances. It was also the case that a tiny number of the men (2) and women (2) expressed a desire for totally separate financial arrangements notwithstanding their civil partnership:

> It's separate. And I think that's probably a hangover from, you know, the years of our relationship when Robert felt he was dependent and, you know, he knows my PIN numbers, you know, if he ever needs any money, I'll just give him money or whatever. But, you know, there's independence there, so he has things in his name. The bills are sort of in individual names, separate bank accounts.
>
> Daniel (202a)

> We have separate accounts but we, we have separate accounts and because everything was already set up, mainly because this is my house and was my house and even when [former partner] and I were here together, it was all just in my name because I came up here first and moved up here, so that's just remained the same. So everything just goes out of my account and Linda just puts some money into my account.
>
> Natalie (117b)

Many couples spoke of the importance of an ideal of independence, but Daniel and Robert, and Natalie and Linda were the exceptions because very few actually carried this ideal through into keeping their financial affairs entirely separate. Moreover, even where the system of joint accounts with separate personal accounts was the norm, this did not stop partners criticising each other for 'inappropriate' spending, nor did it mean that partners felt they could just spend as they wished even from their own accounts. As Ashby and Burgoyne (2008) have pointed out, what people feel about money and how they manage it is immensely complicated and it is essential to go behind the actual arrangements in order to understand the purposes a couple may have for organising money they way they do. But we would also add that it is not enough to focus on the couple alone because, as we suggest above, individuals import into their relationships experiences of how their own parents managed money. More than this, the individual's sense of self is bound up with money and its moral connotations. For our couples, this was brought strongly into perspective because of the significance of debt. Over half (56 per cent) of all our couples were dealing with debt (excluding mortgages) in some way or another, and this meant that an individual's moral calibre could be under intensive scrutiny. The existence of the debt could also mean that plans had to be postponed and it was impossible for couples to move their relationship forwards by, for instance, buying a property or moving to a new area.

Money was therefore about far more than understanding the workings of gender and power because our focus on how individuals and couples related to money opened up a more panoramic vision of everyday relationships and also treated money as an embedded emotional currency (Nyman and Dema, 2007). Of equal importance, tracing money sheds light on the ways in which individuals became couples because the sharing of money also shows how trust works, how caring can operate, and how a merging of material possessions can be achieved. It is at the very heart of how people can both become a couple and yet retain a sense of (independent) self. We disagree with Burgoyne et al. (2011: 703), however, when they suggest that non-heterosexuals seem 'able to both write and enact their own financial "scripts"' because, even allowing for the caveats they provide, we did not find scope for this kind of freedom from cultural, social or biographical constraint.

6
Sex and Security

As discussed in Chapter 3, young formalised same-sex relationships need to be understood within the context of the enduring privileging of the couple as an adult relational ideal. Also, as noted in Chapter 2, partners viewed stability as central to a 'good' and fulfilling relationship or marriage. In this chapter we consider how the privileging of the couple as the focus for stability promoted commitments to sexual monogamy. In contrast to findings about previous generations of same-sex relationships, the majority of our young couples were sexually monogamous. In modelling their relationships on the ordinary, most couples assumed that their relationships would be monogamous from the moment of commitment.

In addition to exploring couples' narratives of (non-)monogamy in some detail, the chapter also situates their sexual commitments in terms of the changing meanings that partners give to sex over time. We also consider the ways sexual practices and their meanings are linked to the temporal rhythms of couples' day-to-day lives. Some partners could experience sex as a problematic issue, and the ways in which this undermined a sense of relational security goes some way to explaining why couples were so invested in sexual monogamy. Overall, the chapter illuminates the links that partners make between sexual monogamy and a sense of a 'mature stability'.

Sexual meanings and assumptions

The young partners we interviewed invested sex with diverse meanings: it was important as a source of pleasure, linked to the 'connection of souls and bodies', an expression of love, and an aspect of intimacy and closeness. In some cases the quantity and/or quality of sex was seen as a measure of how the relationship was progressing. At the same time, sex could be a source of anxiety and worry. It was sometimes the focus of arguments, tensions and intense discussion, and could be linked to a sense of self and relational vulnerability. For a few men, sex and love were separate entities and this could facilitate a sexually non-monogamous relationship. For the majority of our interviewees, both male and female, sex was relatively important to the relationship, but it was never *the* most important aspect. Most partners believed their relationship could survive without sex as it was not an *essential* aspect of intimacy and closeness. The significance and importance of sex changed as the relationship progressed. While sex could be (but was not always) key to the formation of the relationship, many thought it was natural for sex to become less important over time. As Duncan (214b) puts it:

> I think in any marriage or any partnership there is an old saying 'save a penny in the jar for the first year' [...] I think as you do grow older a little bit, sex is fine and sex is good, but sometimes you just want a pair of slippers and watch the television. So on that side, it is a case of 'yes sex is good' but it just depends on the mood.

Prior to meeting their current partners, our interviewees had diverse experiences of sexual relationships. Forty-one women and 43 men had had previous same-sex experience before entering into their current relationship. Fifteen women had had sexual relations with men in the past, and seven men had had sexual relations with women. Participants tended to describe their previous approaches to sexual relationships as 'mostly serial monogamy', 'mostly casual' or 'promiscuous'. In reality, the boundaries between these categories were blurred. As Robert (202b) puts it:

> I'd like to say that I was a serial monogamist but then that would imply that I was being monogamous at those times [laughs] but I suppose in the pattern probably did follow [serial relationships].

As Robert indicates, sex in practice did not always match up neatly with the terms used to describe approaches to sexual relationships. Similarly, sexual ideals and desires could not simply be read off sexual practice. Fredrick (209a) recounts:

> I – had meant to try playing the field because I'd never tried playing the field, never had a one-night stand, any of things you're meant to do as a gay man, and I ended up just being a serial monogamist.

While Fredrick puts his approach to sexual relationships down to chance, others, like Maria (104b) who also described her approach to sex as serial monogamy, clarified the two different phases of serial monogamy she had had. In the first phase the emphasis was on sex, and in the second phase the emphasis was on friendship before sex. She recounts:

> when I met Doris I was in a totally different phase of my life, I was no longer interested in being young and out on the scene it just didn't interest me at all and I had, before I met her, made a decision that [if] I did date again I was going to be friends with the person first in terms of have a good relationship because [...] previous to the that [...] I was on the scene so I was the only black lesbian around which meant lots and lots of attention but it was just vacuous.

Men were more likely than women to have had a history of casual sex, and as the earlier quotation from Fredrick suggests they tended to see casual sex as a fairly ordinary aspect of single life for gay men. Very few men viewed casual sex negatively, although several recounted that it was not something they had been interested in. While it was the case that several women had enjoyed casual sex in the past, women on the whole were more likely to express a range of views about casual sex. Tammy (108b), for example, was at pains to clarify that, while she had had sexual experiences before her current relationship, she had *not* had casual sex, implying that that would have undermined her moral character:

> I had one other relationship before like we met, which had ended about three months before I met Hanna, I think that lasted on and off for about a year, I hadn't had like any casual sex or anything.

While Hanna (108a), Tammy's partner, had experienced (and presumably enjoyed) casual sex in the past, the way in which she contextualised this in terms of her previous 'immaturity' suggested a degree of shame:

> I'm not proud of it but I used to have like quite a few one-night stands and that and I had like a few relationships and I was quite I would say more immature.

While a few women and more men used 'promiscuous' to describe or clarify their approaches to sex before their current relationship, women were more likely than men to use the term in a pejorative way. Fay (113a), for example, clarified that her previous casual relationships should not be read as indicative of her promiscuity:

> Not by any stage promiscuous [...] but yeah probably in four years of studying, five or six different people, [a] couple may have been for a couple of months, others may have been casual really.

Graham (204b) gave more of a detailed description of his own 'promiscuity', while at the same time challenging the moral implications of the term:

> I suppose most people would say quite promiscuous really, but that's a very subjective thing, certainly my mother would describe my life before I met Andrew as quite promiscuous but then I'd never discuss anything like that with my mum anyway, but to other gay friends you know I just lived the life of a single gay man and I probably had casual encounters or different sexual partners, at least one different partner every couple of weeks [...]. And sometimes I'd see people more than once. I had a small number of what you would call fuck buddies [...] I viewed it as safer, to have regular sex with a small number of guys rather than you know meeting a stranger every single time.

Irrespective of individuals' sexual histories, the overwhelming majority (45 couples) described their current relationship as sexually monogamous or exclusive. The remaining five (one female and four male couples) defined their relationships as non-monogamous or open. Since the 1970s, studies have reported the prominence of non-monogamous practices among gay men, and some have implied that sexual exclusivity may be an exception rather a rule (Blasband and Peplau, 1985; Blumstein and Schwartz, 1983; McWhirter and Mattison, 1984; Peplau and Cochran, 1981; Peplau and Gordon, 1983; Sahir and Robins, 1973). More recent studies have focused on how non-monogamous relationships operate (see for instance Heaphy et al., 2004; Klesse, 2006, 2007, Yip, 1997). Attention is less often given to monogamous same-sex relationships, the assumption being that the meaning and significance of monogamy for the couple is obvious. One of the 'obvious' political meanings afforded monogamy in the literature on queer relationships is that it is linked to heteronomative ideologies. This understanding of monogamy has underpinned some criticisms of political campaigns for same-sex marriage. In an overview of such criticisms, Hull (2006: 79–84) notes that some critics have argued that such campaigns risk 'reinforc-ing the romantic/sexual couple' as the single model for intimate life (Waters, 2001), while others suggest that they betray the promise of gay liberation and radical feminism by glorying 'the monogamous dyad' (Card, 1996; Polikoff, 1993). Others still have argued that same-sex mar-riage makes gay sexuality 'less threatening to the straight world' (Hull, 2006: 83; Warner, 2000). While Bersani (2010) recognises the legitimacy of homosexual couples' demands for legal rights and benefits that are similar to those enjoyed by heterosexual married couples, he comments that what is surprising in the current 'conjugal fervor' is how:

> [A] community that has been at times notorious in its embrace of sexual promiscuity has [...] made an unprecedented attempt to persuade what is curiously called the general population of the gay commitment to the ideal of the monogamous couple.
>
> Bersani (2010: 85)

For many critics, the risk inherent in claiming the 'right' to marriage or marriage-like legal arrangements is that it endorses the monogamous couple as the only legitimate focus of sexuality and redraws – as opposed to fundamentally challenges – sexual hierarchies. In this respect, marriage (be it heterosexual or same-sex) potentially tames queer sexualities, and more radical approaches to sex and relationships (e.g. non-monogamy and polyamory) could be further marginalised and the relational imagi-nary further restricted. Thus, same-sex marriage risks neutralising the potential that same-sex relationships have previously been thought to have for challenging the norms, values and power associated with disci-plined sexualities. The belief in such potential was linked to theoretical possibilities that living outside of heterosexual norms offered for more easily separating love and sex, seeing sex as a source of mutual pleasure and for negotiating the interpersonal significance of sex. This was sup-ported by empirical work, such as that referenced above, that suggested that same-sex partners (and especially gay male partners) often success-fully negotiated non-monogamy and in some cases polyamory.

In terms of the meanings our young partners attributed to monog-amy, in describing their relationship as monogamous they mostly but did not always mean that they only engaged in sex with their couple partner. Some couples did engage in threesomes and still regarded their relationship as monogamous (see also Heaphy et al., 2004). The majority of our partners had *assumed* their relationship would be monogamous by the time they committed to each other, although nine couples had explicitly discussed or negotiated this. As most partners had never had an explicit conversation about sexual exclusivity, many seemed surprised when we asked them about how the monogamous commitment had come about. Our question seemed to catch them off guard, and at times they were unsure if they understood our question correctly. The following exchange illustrates this:

Interviewer:	Is this a monogamous relationship?
Annabel (124a):	Yeah absolutely.
Interviewer:	Yeah, how did that come about?
Annabel:	What being monogamous?
Interviewer:	Yes.
Annabel:	Er [long pause] I don't know. Monogamous is just the two of us isn't it?
Interviewer:	Yes.
Annabel:	Yes sorry [laughing]. 'Cause I'm thinking about that I'm just; I wouldn't have it any other way.
Interviewer:	Hmm.
Annabel:	I just don't think, especially in a marriage, I don't think there's any other any other way for it. There's no room for anybody else.

Where there was confusion, as in Annabel's case, the question about how monogamy came about troubled the assumed to be 'self-evident' links between being a committed couple and sexual exclusivity. Annabel's partner Kenzie (124b) seemed equally bewildered:

Interviewer:	Would you describe your relationship as monogamous?
Kenzie:	Oh yeah definitely.
Interviewer:	Hmm. How did that come about?
Kenzie:	How did that come about?
Interviewer:	Yeah.
Kenzie:	We're using the right words aren't we?
Interviewer:	Yes.
Kenzie:	I think that's just a given. It's always been a given since the very start yeah.

In Kenzie's case, the assumption about the sexually exclusive nature of her relationship dated back to her and Annabel's 'first kiss'. Our young partners' assumptions about sexual monogamy contrast sharply to Weeks et al.'s (2001) and Heaphy et al.'s (2004) findings about previous generations' same-sex relationships, where monogamy tended not to be assumed and was almost always explicitly discussed at some point or other. Such assumptions are more in keeping with findings about heterosexual relationships where sex outside the relationship is cast as cheating (Allan, 2004). In our own study, assumptions about sexual exclusivity tended to be linked to particular milestones in becoming a couple: when the partners first slept together, when partners started 'going steady', when love was first mentioned, when one or both partners expressed a desire to commit or the couple had moved in together. Among women and men who had a history of serial monogamy, partners saw sexual exclusivity as carrying on as they 'had always done'. Two men linked this to their upbringing, which they said resulted in a 'straight view' of the world. Generally, partners believed that there was little reason to discuss sexual exclusivity with their partner because they were not interested in anyone else. They assumed that this was the case for their partners as well.

Negotiating sexual arrangements

Three female couples did discuss sexual exclusivity at the beginning of their relationship. These couples' sexual negotiations were generally lighthearted, and often took the form of 'teasing' or making playful statements about unacceptable behaviours. As Ellen (114a) recounted:

> I love Holly and I jokingly say, 'I'm very jealous I don't want to share her with anyone else', I just wouldn't want to do it.

Her partner Holly (114b) recalled a similar discussion.

> I guess we have teased each other [...]. The idea has come up in joking about whether we'd be with somebody else at any point. And Ellen's made it very clear that she would not like to see me with anybody else, and I know that I wouldn't like to see her with anybody else. And so I guess from that I've concluded that it is a monogamous relationship.

Another couple, Emily (125a) and Gail (125b), recalled a similarly playful conversation when Emily attempted to set the ground rules. She explained:

> I think I probably said something like, 'That means you can't be snogging any teenagers or anything like that'.

Zoe (109a) and Rebecca (109b), in contrast, had different recollections of how they reached their agreement about monogamy. While Rebecca has no previous sexual experience with women, Zoe is both older and more sexually experienced. Rebecca recounted:

> The only time we sort of discussed it is, we hadn't actually said that we were in a proper relationship or anything. We were dating each other and like I wasn't seeing anybody else and I was hoping Zoe wasn't and as far as I was aware she wasn't. We were spending all the time together and, I think we were driving back from somewhere [...] and I'd said, 'what is our relationship, are we in a relationship or?' 'cause I thought I needed to find out just to make sure 'cause I wasn't sure how things went and we agreed then.

Zoe's version was quite different.

> It wasn't far into the relationship and we said well, Rebecca said 'have you been with anybody else' and I said 'no, I've never been with anybody since being with you and I think I want to keep it that way' and I said 'have you' and she went 'no'. I said 'so it's an exclusive thing then' and she went 'yeah' and then that's it. Since then I've never been with anybody else.

While Rebecca remembers that the conversation was about 'being in a relationship', Zoe remembers it as being explicitly about sexual exclusivity. Thus, the narratives about sexual commitments, like any other aspect of the relationship, are subject to the vagaries of memory but also scripted from the perspectives of different relating selves; in this case Rebecca presents herself as needing to clarify if they were in 'a relationship', while Zoe presents Rebecca as clarifying the exclusive nature of the sexual commitment. Of course, Rebecca may have assumed that being in a relationship implied sexual exclusivity, and both her and Zoe's version of the conversation may well have captured its spirit.

More men than women *explicitly* agreed to sexual exclusivity at the onset of the relationship, and their conversations had a more serious undertone. This seriousness reflected the ways in which different approaches to sexual commitments were perceived to be more common among men than women. Those men who had assumed their relationship to be monogamous often seemed to have done so on the basis that if the partner had wanted an open relationship they would have made that clear. In terms of explicit negotiations, Henry (217a) describes the 'thirty second conversation' he and his partner had: 'Kurt said "I'm looking for exclusive [relationship]". I said "me too"'.

Other men had more detailed conversations about what they expected from the relationship, such as Edwin (211a) and Ivan (211b). When their conversation took place, Ivan was about to leave the country and they had agreed to meet in Rome before he returned to his home country. Edwin had explained to us that he is someone who needs to 'talk everything through'. So, in an orderly manner, they had agreed on being 'boyfriends' and Edwin instigated a conversation the following day about the terms and conditions. He explained:

> I wanted to sit down and have a chat about what exactly he imagined a boyfriend to be and about what I imagined it to be, to make sure we were on the same page.

Ivan elaborated on this in his interview.

> We talked about how we saw relationships and what was important to us, and it came up with both of us that being in a monogamous relationship was what we both wanted and it certainly still is for me.

Trevor (226a) and Wayne (226b) recalled a similar conversation. When asked how the sexual exclusive relationship had come about, Trevor explained:

> [W]ithin a couple of weeks we'd sort of sat down and said is this going somewhere and if it is, what are the rules of engagement really [...] and Wayne was like, 'I do monogamy, it's all or nothing, so either it's an exclusive relationship or it is just a brief fling [...] I say 'yes' [...]. We actually did have a chat about, what does monogamy mean to you, what does it mean to me, what does it mean to us if this continues to go somewhere, so no it was a very clear conversation.

On the basis of their accounts of agreed monogamy, these relationships seem to epitomise the negotiation that Giddens (1992) associates with contemporary intimacy. He argues that because it cannot be simply assumed that people's approaches to sexuality and relationships will follow a given path, partners have no choice but to make explicit the nature of their commitment. Together with the five couple accounts of agreed non-monogamy that will be considered in due course, the nine couple accounts of agreed monogamy suggest that it would be mistaken to equate formalised same-sex relationships with an unthinking retreat to convention. The fact that a total of 26 out of 100 interviewees had explicitly discussed the nature of their sexual commitment (one non-monogamous couple did not have an explicit discussion as such) illustrates that young same-sex partners do not always follow convention in an unthinking way. At the same time, the extent to which sexual exclusivity was agreed *and* assumed by younger same-sex partners underlines the continuing salience of the conventional links between sexual exclusivity and commitment, even if couples were aware of the alternative possibilities.

As noted, five of our couples described their relationship as non-monogamous. The point where this was first discussed and agreed between partners varied. Three couples organised their relationship in this way from the start, and in two cases non-monogamy was instigated further into their relationship. Of those who set out as non-monogamous, in two couples one of the partners was already seeing someone else. The third couple, Otto (212a) and Phil (212b), simply carried on with their established sexual practices, which included casual encounters. Phil explained:

> We've just never really discussed it [having an open relationship]; it's come up in conversation with other people, when I'm just having a conversation and Otto has never said to me 'that's not what I want, I want a monogamous relationship'.

The absence of explicit negotiation is notable in the case. Here, both partners assumed non-exclusivity, presumably on the basis of their matched relating histories. The only female couple that had an open relationship, Juliet (107a) and Veronica (107b), highlighted the importance of choosing your sexual partners wisely. As Veronica puts it:

> There are people who we know who are highly strung, complicated in relationships with other people where it could potentially backfire massively and cause huge problems, lesbian drama, within the community and within the group of friends we know.

Just after Veronica and Juliet met, Veronica had a brief 'fling' with a visiting business partner. Veronica and Juliet both knew this was 'nothing serious' as the business partner lived abroad which meant that this woman 'wasn´t taking anything away from the relationship' as Juliet explained. A few years later, Veronica met another woman. This time around, she was more concerned, partly because they had no ground rules in place and also because this woman lived locally. Juliet was worried that Veronica would leave her. As it turned out, Juliet was not the only one who needed some kind of reassurance. Sue, the potential sexual partner, was not convinced that Juliet was happy with this arrangement so she arranged to meet Juliet to find out for herself. Veronica recalls:

> I was like, 'oh my god, oh my god, that's such a bizarre situation', 'cause I couldn't do anything about it, 'cause I wasn't there. So I knew that Juliet would be a bit freaked out by this woman just kind of going to talk to her, but I also knew that it was the only way that I could get Sue to believe me that this was actually all fine and, you know, above board. So they had what was probably a bizarre conversation.

Veronica's account illustrates how highly contractual arrangements around non-monogamy could be. Sexual contracts were often more straightforward for men who, like Felix (213a) and Cameron (213b), tended to be involved in more casual 'hook ups'. Two couples – Frazer (215a) and Todd (215b), and Neil (218a) and Ian (218b) – explicitly discussed non-monogamy some time after the relationship had been formed as a result of a partner having had sex outside the assumed to be monogamous relationship. Frazer, explained that for many years their relationship had remained monogamous, but one day, 'temptation' came his way. This was still clearly upsetting for Todd and when we asked him about his arrangement with Frazer he responded: 'To be honest, it's a question I don´t really want to talk about'. The agreement now is that sex outside the relationship is acceptable as long as neither partner is explicitly told about it.

Although Ian (218a) and Neil's (218b) arrangement was provoked by similar circumstances, the outcome was dramatically different. Neil had sex with a work colleague and decided to tell Ian immediately.

> [Ian] was quite angry but then after half an hour he basically was quite interested to hear how it actually developed and what happened and I suppose that actually opened a door shall we say to experiences outside of our relationship.

> Neil (218b)

Unlike Todd and Frazer, Ian and Neil now explicitly agree that their sexual 'needs' differ and have agreed to inform each other whenever they have sex with someone else.

In total, seven partners (five male and two female) had sex outside of their assumed monogamous relationships, which they then disclosed to their partners. Young same-sex partners' accounts of these events and disclosures are notably different from those reported in research on heterosexual affairs (Allan, 2004; Buunk and Djkstra, 2004). The partner who had not had sex outside the relationship tended *not* to use morally charged words like 'cheating' or being 'unfaithful'. Instead, these events tended to be framed by the couple as a 'mishap'. For example, Benjamin (219a) and Leroy (219b) had been together for almost 10 years when they 'married'. They recounted that they had always been communicative with each other, but the stress of long-distance commuting started to take its toll on Benjamin. Their communication 'broke down' and Benjamin made what he termed a 'mistake' (i.e. he had casual sex outside the relationship). He told us what had happened when he 'came clean' to his partner and revealed all the details. What upset Leroy the most was not necessarily the 'act' itself, but the fact that Benjamin had left it for months to tell him. Benjamin reflected:

> He won't forget that. But the relationship's based on trust and honesty and one of the things he said is, 'Do you want this to be an open relationship?' I'm like, 'No.' And that was just a stupid mistake and, 'no, I want it to be exclusive'.

A non-negotiated sexual affair, or the betrayal of trust associated with it, could be painful and confusing for the 'betrayed' partner, but it could also open up the opportunity for renegotiation of the nature of sexual commitment. Interestingly, few partners took up this opportunity. In a similar way to Benjamin, Victor (216b) had what his partner described as an 'accident', a term that refuses the position of being the 'victim' of an affair (see Allan, 2004). Despite his partner's understanding response, Victor himself could not put the issue aside. He recounted worrying constantly that he might make a habit out of it, or worse, that he would become like his father who was consistently 'unfaithful' to his mother:

> It's not something that we really talk about – it's not something that I am comfortable talking about [...] it's something that I think was a shocking betrayal and, I tortured myself for it and I'm probably – only about now that – I'm comfortable I've not caused long-term damage but a part of the problem I had was I it made me think 'what have I done here.'

What is interesting here is the effect that the 'betrayal' has for the 'perpetrator' and that it is Victor's own sense of ontological security that seems threatened. The incident clearly cast a shadow over the relationship to the extent that it troubled Victor's perception of his own 'relating self'. In light of the insecurity that this prompted for Victor, it is perhaps not so surprising that he did not seize the opportunity to discuss or renegotiate the nature of the commitment anew. Both partners viewed Victor's non-negotiated sex outside the relationship as a test of the couple commitment, and it was this commitment that 'inevitably' won out. Thus, the commitment was not simply given, but 'won'.

As the personal stories considered in this section illustrate, the assumed or agreed ground rules that governed sex or relationships with others could change over time, as could the meaning attached to sexual monogamy. Time was also an important element of other stories about sex within the couple and the meanings attached to it.

Sex and time

The meaning of sex and its significance for the couple were embedded within the routines and practices of day-to-day life, and need to be understood within the context of couples' changing priorities as the relationship developed. As noted earlier, many couples thought it was natural for sex to decline in terms of frequency, if not in terms of its significance, over the life of the relationship. Many couples recounted how, after the initial 'honeymoon phase' of a relationship (which could last from months to years), sex became less important as a desire, as an expression of commitment and as a route to intimacy. How women and men explained this tended to differ. Women more often than men emphasised lack of time and energy, while men more often than women referred to declining sex 'drives'.

Motherhood had notable implications for our female partners' sexual lives. Most mothers, like Maria (104b), saw this as inevitable and self-evident. Maria responded with laughter when asked about the importance of sex to her, and answered 'I have an eight-year old'. The aftermath of pregnancy and childbirth were often linked to a changed body and a different relationship to it. Kathryn (105a) reflected on how childbirth had made it difficult for her and her partner to engage in sex for some time:

> I had to have stitches and I got a wound infection and it all felt a bit odd down there anyway and it all feels a bit vulnerable there so that hasn't particularly encouraged sort of sexual activity really.

Kathryn also struggled with how she saw her body as 'different', especially with the extra weight she gained during pregnancy. These were important issues for most women who had given birth. Olivia (113b), for example, recounted never coming to terms with her changed body after childbirth despite her partner's ongoing compliments. While childbirth was drawn on to explain limited sex or no sex in a relationship, parenting itself left little time for adult relationships. Partners in non-parenting relationships could also struggle to find the time for sex. As Josha (101b) puts it:

> We don't really have sex very often. I think that´s mostly because Amina is always so tired. I do feel guilty sometimes when I'm angry with her because I feel she´s not making the effort. But I know it´s because she's tired and, erm and been at work all day whereas I haven't [...] Not because she doesn't want to, or whatever.

As in Josha's case, it was not uncommon for partners to link their different 'levels' of interest in sex to the different lives they lived. Despite this understanding, a declining interest in sex could promote a sense of anxiety, which was often most acutely felt by the partner who was less interested in sex. Hanna (108a) and Tammy's (108b) story highlights this. In their case, Tammy is more often tired and less often 'in the mood' but is the one who needs constant reassurance that this will not destabilise the relationship. She and Hanna have recurring discussions about the situation. To complicate matters further, Hanna is not wholly convinced that Tammy misses sex all that much, but feels she *should* miss it.

> I think partly she does miss it, but I think 'cause she reads in all these magazines about if you don't have sex then your relationship is doomed and, it's just crap.
>
> Hanna

Sex was never an important part of Mandy (126a) and Olga's (126b) relationship. In fact, Olga recounted rarely having experienced sex without 'a hidden agenda'. She explained:

> You're either doing it to prove that you can, or you're doing it to say sorry for something, or you're doing it to try and make the person stay with you, even though you don't want to.

With such an outlook, it's perhaps not surprising that Olga and Mandy hardly ever have sex. To Olga, intimacy is more important. She continued:

> Physical intimacies and making sure that you always say goodnight to each other, that you always kiss each other before you go to work and, you know, you pay attention to that. You don't do that kind of fifties wife left at home, husband going off to work peck on the cheek, 'see you at six o'clock, dear'.

Men tended to explain limited sex differently. Like the women discussed above, Robert (202b) recounted that his sex life often suffered because he and his partner were tired. However, the men's discussions were more usually framed in terms of their sex 'drives'. Overall, 18 out of the 25 male couples mentioned sex drive as factor that influenced partners' different emphasis on sex in the relationship. Victor (216b) gave a common explanation:

> I accept people for who they are and human nature. I accept that I, I have a very strong sex drive, I think stronger than Peter does.

Umberto similarly recounted that he and his partner Garry (227a) had different sex drives. Umberto struggled to strike the right balance between pursuing sex and 'pestering' Garry as he phrased it, which often resulted in him questioning whether he had done something wrong. Other male couples also recounted different levels of sex 'drive', but did not rate sex as the most centrally significant aspect of the relationship. Edwin (211a) said:

> I'm usually up for it all the time whereas I don't know if he is, but I also don't think it's the pinnacle, be all and end all of a relationship. I think it's just one aspect of a relationship.

While it appeared relatively easy for a male partner to claim that they had a stronger sex drive or to suggest that their partner had a weaker one, to be the one with the 'weaker' sex drive or the one who had lost his libido was a different story. Instead of embracing the identity of the one who wanted less sex, Ivan (211b), for instance, explained his limited sexual desire in biologistic terms by noting that he had never had a 'particularly high sex drive'. Oliver (210a) saw his diminished sex drive as a more complex biological, medical and emotional matter. He had been on medication for a long time which, he recounted, had affected his libido. This was combined with his unease about openly acknowledging the significance sex has for him:

> I do enjoy sex with Ben and I do like it because it's not just sex; there is a love to it as well and it's very tender and passionate. But part of me finds it very hard to acknowledge that openly and with ease, [...] and that was coupled with my [condition which] cut my sex drive to zero. My testosterone levels went down to nothing.

In addition, Oliver suggested that his depleted sex drive might be related to how long he and his partner had been together, just over five years. Being the one with the higher sex drive could also have its problems, not least because it carries an additional pressure of never having the option to say no to sex. Jeremy (206a), who claimed to have a higher sex drive than his partner Stewart (206b), described this dilemma well.

> I feel sometimes that when he wants to have sex and I perhaps don't, that I do because I know that that's less frequent than when I would like to have sex with him.

This is complicated by Jeremy's need to be reassured that Stewart wants to sleep with him but 'not anyone else'. From Stewart's perspective, sex is 'not everything' or a reason to end the relationship, but at one stage he felt he was not giving Jeremy what he wanted in a relationship. So he suggested that they should involve someone else in their sexual relationship. Yet it became quite clear that neither felt they would be able to cope with the emotional fall-out of this in practice.

Sexual insecurities

Some theorists have linked the anxieties that sex can generate to technologies of governance in late modern societies. For example, Gail Hawkes argues that contemporary discourse on sexuality consistently presents one's sex life as in need of constant attention. To be 'good' at sex is presented as the individual's responsibility. Hawkes (1999) argues that the encouragement to see oneself as a primarily sexual being involves the production of anxieties about how good the individual is at sex. This incites people to become sexual consumers as a means of dealing with these anxieties (1999: 51). In our study, when sex was identified as a source of anxiety it was often linked to a partner's belief that they had 'a problem' with sex (wanting too much or too little). The tendency was for this partner to struggle with a sense of blame for introducing an element of insecurity into the relationship, whereas the other partner's usual response was to say that sex was not the most central aspect of a relationship and to emphasise the value of companionship instead. Linda (117a) and Natalie (117b) are an example of this. We first interviewed Linda, who seemed to downplay the importance of sex:

> I'd say it was quite important, I guess in the sense that a lot of those things that we've talked about like, it's been the sort of the companion side of it as well. Obviously there's, you know, that side of it, the fact that we get on so well and we love being together and that we love each other is all, you know, is more important.

But when we interviewed her partner, Natalie, the picture looked very different. She initially struggled to discuss the sexual aspect of her relationship with Linda. The interviewer asked how important sex is to her, at which point, 'the problem' started to unfold:

Natalie: Yeah, this is going to be difficult, not necessarily to talk about [...]. But a difficult subject for me I think.
Interviewer: Is it?
Natalie: It used to be absolutely vital and it isn't so much now, I've kind of lost my, I've lost my way with it a bit really, so, I want it to be very important 'cause I know that it is important in a relationship but I just am not, I don't really have a great sex drive anymore but I used to and I used to be terrible, meaning that I used to, used to be, just have a very high sex drive and my relationships were, a lot of them were based on sex. Maybe that's why.

At this point, the interviewer asked if this was that something that Natalie had experienced within the context of this relationship or before it. She replied:

> It's kind of happened in this relationship as well but that's, it's me, it's to do with me. It's not, this is, it's not Linda, it's happened before for different reasons, it's happened before in a previous relationship because I just did not want to. I didn't feel attracted to the person anymore. And, also wasn't great, was on medication etcetera, and just, it wasn't happening and I just – I don't know I've just got issues with it [...] I just seem to just lose, I just seem to lose my sex drive

really. And then it'll come back. But it's, it's a bit of a problem really, I'm not happy about it.

While this quotation is full of meaning, we use it here to illustrate the ways in which the 'loss' of sexual desire can be experienced as deeply troubling for a partner, but also the way it is seen to potentially destabilise the relationship itself. It seems that Natalie is less concerned about the meaning that her partner may attribute to Natalie's loss of sex 'drive', but more the unclear meaning of this for Natalie herself. She 'knows' that sex is important in a relationship and in light of her love and commitment to her partner cannot understand her own 'lack' of sexual desire. Underneath narratives like Natalie's, there seemed to us to be an anxiety that such 'lack' might signify desires that were beyond partners' articulation: to no longer have sex with their current partners. Henry (217a) and Kurt (217b) told a story that was similar to Natalie's and Linda's. Although Henry downplays the importance of sex and says he loves being with Kurt and how safe this makes him feel, Kurt's version of their story is very different. Like Natalie, Kurt seems uninterested in sex, and this is not new. In fact, his interest in sex has also declined in all of his previous relationships. He said:

I've never been [sexually active], I don't know why. So, I think the word is [...] active, it's sort of been [laughing], I don't know what the word would be that I had to describe it, it's not that I don't care if nothing happens, that's not true, I just don't [...] I mean the amount of drugs I'm on suppress a lot of things and I do know that because I've been off them before and it does change the way I am but I sort of quite happily go to bed and just sleep and wake up in the morning and do the next day as it comes and then go back to bed and sleep [...] it does worry me and upset me a little bit because I know Henry's different to that and I wish sometimes it wasn't the way it is.

Kurt genuinely believes that Henry does not reveal his frustrations with their sexual life, but on Henry's birthday he (Henry) joked about getting himself 'a prostitute', which alarmed Kurt. He is convinced that the sexual aspect of the relationship is not enough for Henry. They have never actually discussed this and all Kurt wants is for the problem to be 'fixed'. He commented:

Kurt: I just hope deep down inside there's enough between Henry and myself to keep us together.

Interviewer: Don't you think that Henry would understand?
Kurt: Yeah but it doesn't stop his it wouldn't stop his frustra-
                tions or his needs or stuff as well.

What is interesting about Kurt's response to Henry's 'joke', is how similar it is to other partners' responses (like Benjamin's quoted earlier) when sex outside the monogamous relationship had led to an opportunity to renegotiate the nature of the couple's sexual commitment: a heightened sense of anxiety, the desire not to discuss the issue further *and* an active refusal to engage with the non-monogamous option. Also among those who had internalised their 'weaker' levels of sexual desire as a personal problem (like Natalie quoted earlier), non-monogamy was rarely seen as a possible solution. Rather, the tendency was to live with the anxiety it generated and rarely to discuss it. In this sense, and in assuming non-monogamy from the outset, the partners mostly (but by no means always) refused the opportunity to negotiate a sexually open relationship. In doing so, they refused to be at what some see as the 'vanguard' of relational innovation and experimentation.

Refusing innovation

It would be trite to see young same-sex couples' refusals to innovate with respect to sexual commitments simply as an illustration of how they mimic heterosexuality. Nevertheless, couples' and partners' investments in the link between commitment and sexual monogamy were clearly influenced by a sense of what mature committed relationships *should* be like. Even in the most secular cultural contexts sexuality has not been wholly disembedded from morality: how you do your sexuality can still be interpreted as saying much about the kind of person you are. As our partners wanted to be, and wanted to be seen to be, legitimate couples, it is unsurprising that they would model their sexual lives on monogamy. However, given that their monogamous couple commitments provided a certain kind of ontological order, it is also unsurprising that they were reluctant to move beyond the boundaries of the monogamous couple. The risks this presented for the 'little world' that partners had constructed (with the help of their significant others) could be considerable (cf. Berger and Kellner, 1964, see Chapter 5). In the following chapter we explore the issue of innovation further.

7
Couple Worlds

In this chapter we explore how young same-sex relationships develop and change following civil partnership. There is a cultural expectation that love relationships will change once a couple have entered into a marriage, but such expectations are based on what is known about heterosexual couples. It is not at all clear that such expectations should be carried over wholesale into understandings of same-sex marriages. Mansfield and Collard (1988), for example, note that for their young heterosexual couples there was an intense period of adjustment following marriage. For them, just about everything changed. Two-thirds of Mansfield and Collard's grooms and three-quarters of the brides were living at home with their parents until their wedding day. As Mansfield and Collard point out, their couples had no experience of what it might be like to live in a full-time relationship before they married because the period of courtship and dating they went through was far from being a preparation for living together. Indeed, they point to the disappointments that couples often felt because marriage itself was experienced as far less romantic and exciting than the courtship had been. Typically, they found that women discovered their husbands were less interested in hearing all about their daily experiences than they had been when courting. Men, on the other hand, soon found sexual encounters were less thrilling. Their study was, of course, carried out before heterosexual couples began to enter into unmarried or prenuptial cohabitation in large numbers. So it is probable that some of the dramatic transformations that occurred for heterosexual couples in the 1980s are no longer typical (Kiernan, 2002). However, the idea that heterosexual love inevitably changes with marriage remains a strong cultural motif (Giddens, 1992).

Ann Swidler (2003), in a study of heterosexual love in the US, carried out in the early 1980s, addresses the difference between mythic love (which is akin to the romantic love that Mansfield and Collard's couples experienced during courtship) and what she calls prosaic-realistic love, which is the sort of emotion that is the everyday currency of a marriage. Swidler interviewed 39 men and 49 women; they were predominantly middle-class and lived in San Jose, California. They were aged between 20 and 60 and were a mixture of married, divorced and single. Swidler found that people routinely distinguished between mythic and prosaic love. The latter was seen as requiring hard work and commitment, while the former was seen as idealistic, fleeting and magical. However, Swidler also notes that mythic love was not abandoned on becoming settled; rather the 'repertoire' of mythic love existed in a parallel cultural location alongside that of prosaic love. Both mythic and prosaic loves, Swidler argues, are cultural constructs even though one (the prosaic) is expected to surpass and outlast the other (the mythic). As she argues:

> Two cultures of love persist, neither driving out the other, because people employ their understandings of love in two very different contexts. When thinking about the choice of whether to marry or stay married people see love in mythic terms. Love is the choice of one right person whom one will or could marry. Therefore love is all-or-nothing, certain, exclusive, heroic, and enduring. When thinking about maintaining ongoing relationships, however, people mobilise the prosaic-realistic culture of love to understand the varied ways one can manage love relationships. Prosaic love is ambiguous, open-ended, uncertain and fragile.
>
> Swidler (2003: 129)

In her analysis of different cultures of love, Swidler provides an interesting explanation for the kinds of contradictory things people say about love and how they might switch from one sort to the other depending on their situation. In this way she overcomes the idea that mythic love gives way to prosaic love as if it is part of some natural process of maturing. She seeks instead to understand recourse to one or the other as dependent upon one's context and circumstances. She also offers a slightly different definition of prosaic love than might be anticipated because she acknowledges that in the everyday sustaining of relationships things can go wrong and the outcome is never absolutely certain. In her definition, prosaic love is a delicate process not a steady state of being; it is not a safe haven which is reached after the storms of mythic love have passed.

In considering whether some of these insights from studies of heterosexual love and marriage are relevant to contemporary civil partnerships we shall in this chapter explore what our couples had to say about what difference the civil partnership had made to their relationships, what they did together in good and bad times, and what their plans were for building their own families. An overarching question here will also be the extent to which our couples were actually engaged in 'everyday experiments' (Weeks et al., 2001).

Being a couple: Does civil partnership make a difference?

As we noted in Chapter 4, almost all of our couples were living together before they married. The only exceptions arose from the complications of having different nationalities where it was impossible for some couples to live together for long because of immigration legislation. This meant that some had had to return home because visas had expired and the process of prenuptial cohabitation was either truncated or not possible. For most, however, getting married did not entail moving home or even starting a home together as this had been accomplished before the civil partnership ceremony took place. Thus, the question we asked about what difference civil partnership had made to them inevitably focused the couples' attention on the issue of changes to affect rather than on material or behavioural changes.

A common response was to proclaim that the civil partnership made no difference at all to their relationship (see Chapter 4). This response seemed to be a way of establishing that the relationship prior to the civil partnership was already strong, close and loving, and that the civil partnership itself did not alter or improve upon this. Thus, in stating that the civil partnership made no difference, the couples seemed to be affirming that relationships outside 'marriage' could be just as valid and committed as those that were legally recognised. But no one sustained for long the argument that civil partnership had made absolutely no difference and typically they went on to assert that it made them feel more secure. This concept of greater security (sometimes coupled with notions of seriousness, commitment and stability) ran through the majority of replies:

Oliver (210b): Yeah. I mean it did feel a bit different, I did feel you know, afterwards that – that – the way I – I saw my – myself and my relationship with Ben and the way I – we – I saw ourselves – you know, that, that, having done that then it does feel more

Ben (210a): Secure.

Oliver: And serious.
Victor (216b):   I think it feels more secure to me. Um, because it's, you know, it's', we have that legal bond. I think it's given more stability, you know, it's not given more stability, but it's given a sense, a feeling of stability. You know, because it's more formal.
Peter (216a):   For me, none whatsoever; [it] does not make any difference.

The couples often referred to an intangible feeling that they had experienced (Mason, 2008). They suggested that something felt different but they could not put a finger on exactly what it was. This intangibility is not entirely surprising because many of these couples had not been married for long enough to have really concrete evidence that their relationships had become more secure or stable. It is possible to understand these assertions in the light of Swidler's analysis of mythic and prosaic love. Our question about what difference the civil partnership made seemed to provoke responses based on mythic rather than prosaic love; that is to say it seemed to tap into the kind of certainties that attend upon 'knowing' one has made the right choice of partner. There was a magical quality to the 'difference' they identified rather than a mundane or solid element.

A second response to this question was to express pride. This feeling could be based on a loosely political idea that being married is a way of making a stand in a predominantly heterosexual lifeworld (cf. Hull, 2006; Shipman and Smart, 2007). Two couples, one female and one male, were quite fierce about using the terms 'wife' and 'husband' whenever they could. Four male couples and one female couple had opted to take the same surname as a way of publicly proclaiming their married status (and an additional female couple opted for a double-barrelled name). Others wore rings and found themselves drawing attention to them in public.

Umberto (227b): And we get to wear wedding rings [laughter].
Garry (227a):   Yes, which we play with endlessly. [...]
Umberto: But it's nice to wear a wedding ring [laughter].
Garry: I thought, you know, if I was wearing a wedding ring then I'd feel, if people asked me, then I'd feel embarrassed about explaining that I actually, you know, that I share a civil partnership with a man. No, it's the opposite; it makes me feel more confident about the relationship. It makes me feel –

Umberto: More empowered, would you say so?

Garry: Yes, exactly. It's, just because it's a symbol of what we've done, I think the whole getting married aspect was something which does empower you; makes you stronger in expressing the facts in an environment which might be sometimes difficult; expressing the fact that you are in a relationship with someone of the same-sex. [...] I think that feeling of empowerment is somewhat symbolised by the ring.

Others expressed this feeling as getting more respect for their relationship which they also saw in terms of taking a stand (Smart, 2008). As Phoebe (123b) puts it:

And you know in terms of equalities and rights and so on we always feel that in a same-sex relationship you're not given the same level of respect as you were [when] you're in a heterosexual relationship. So it gave a bit of, you know, oh I don't want to say the word standing but you know it.

These accounts reflect the extent to which a civil partnership can be a political act and not solely a matter of personal choice. This is not to say that any of the couples married for political reasons, but having decided to have a civil partnership there could follow moments of clear political consciousness in which couples felt they had a right to demonstrate their equal citizenship.

Finally, among those who felt the civil partnership had made a difference, there was the feeling that it was a signal that they had 'grown up' (see Chapters 4–6). The civil partnership marked a transition for some from being a person who could be impulsive, or who could move on if things were not working out, to becoming a person with responsibilities who needed to start planning a future:

Thinking of more grown up things, now that we're married, and not just because we've got a house but I'm constantly thinking ahead of our future. Where are we going to be in ten years time? We're thinking so much more about our careers now. [...] after the ceremony I remember my mother talking to me about it and saying, 'You're not my little boy any more now, you know you're on your own, you've got your family now'. And that sort of, was quite – what's the word I'm looking for – quite woke me up.

Stewart (206b)

As noted in earlier chapters, the idea of being a 'grown up' also featured in references to life stages which infused so much of the couples' narratives. Weeks et al. (2001: 39) argue that 'there are many strong parallels in the meaning of family practices across the heterosexual–homosexual divide' and we suggest that one such parallel is the way in which young couples construct the biography of their relationship in terms of stages. Within this framework, the civil partnership becomes an acknowledgement that the relationship has moved into a different 'phase' which gives rise to a sense of satisfaction and also an ability to look forward. The couples all felt they had someone to rely upon which in turn meant that plans could be made for living somewhere else, for a new career, for having children and generally moving on. By contrast, staying single was seen as less desirable and a much harder option:

> It's nice to come home to somebody. I certainly wouldn't want to be single, certainly wouldn't want to be gay and single [...] because I don't see it as being really much of a life, do you?
>
> Neil (218b)

The capsule couple

Weeks et al. (2001: 107) argue, on the basis of research with a very different group of lesbian, gay and bisexually identified women and men in the 1990s, that same-sex relationships contained the potential for creativity and choice. This argument was founded upon the core idea that same-sex relationships had no institutional framework and thus gay and lesbian couples had a freedom to take their relationships into uncharted areas. The couples in our study, however, did have something of an institutional framework based on vows of commitment, legal obligations, and state recognition. This does not mean that our couples necessarily felt these frameworks to be constraining and a few of the couples in our study felt they could still be 'unconventional'. One example was Trevor (2226a) and Wayne (226b):

> Trevor: And actually one of the nicest things about being a lesbian couple or a gay couple is that you can make it [overlapping]
> Wayne: You can make it up as you go along –
> Trevor: – as you go along.

In this passage, Trevor and Wayne were talking about the choice of whether to double-barrel a surname on getting married, or whether to defy convention by opting for the surname of one partner in the couple. So for them, the unconventional choice of adopting a 'family name' was understood to be a freedom of expression which still had the power to shock. Such actions alert us to the importance of active meaning-making in everyday life, because although in a heterosexual context the convention is of 'man and wife' taking one surname (his), for same-sex couples the practice is not a passive acceptance of convention but an assertion of a new sexual citizenship.

The couples in our study did seem to have different priorities to those in the Weeks et al. study, however, and few seemed to be committed to the idea that their lives were an experiment. This can be explained by the fact that the two research projects took place in different eras, in which the cultural and political contexts for the formation of same-sex relationships were different (Weeks, 2007, see Chapter 1). Moreover, our couples were, by definition, in favour of legal recognition for their relationship while there was a more mixed and often more reluctant view among the earlier sample. It follows then that the young couples in our study shared a strong desire to consolidate themselves as couples and they were less concerned about differentiating themselves from heterosexual couples and practices. The strong motif apparent in Weeks et al. (and also Dunne, 1997; 1999) whereby same-sex couples not only saw their relationship as different to that of heterosexuals but as better (in terms of equality, freedom, communication etc.) is a much weaker theme in our interviews. As we noted in Chapter 3, our couples tended to take as their reference point their parents' relationships rather than heterosexual couples in general. Clearly, these were heterosexual relationships; however, our couples did not tend to generalise from these specific biographical experiences in order to construct a stereotype of heterosexual coupledom against which they set themselves. Often they borrowed readily from their parents' practices, sometimes they chose to avoid some aspects, but where they saw their parents as happily married they tended to want to achieve the same quality of relationship regardless of its heterosexual nature.

This focus on the quality of their relationship, rather than specific practices, manifested itself most clearly in the interviews when we asked the couples (together) to reflect on what would make a 'good' day in their relationship and what would make a 'bad' day. This question unexpectedly tapped into Swidler's ideas about prosaic love and about the need for ongoing relationship-building. With the possible exception of two couples (one lesbian couple whose relationship seemed quite fragile, and one gay couple who were work-obsessed), all of the couples responded to the question about what a good day would be by offering a mixture of the following ingredients:

1. A day off work (typically a Saturday or Sunday)
2. Being alone together
3. Chilling, walking, watching a DVD or reading
4. Talking/communicating/cuddling.

It was as if they were all reading from the same script, and to that extent their responses were quite surprising. These two accounts are typical:

Holly (114b):   Just getting to spend all day together and getting to share experiences together that we enjoy. So whether that's walking or if we're at home it might be talking to each other, playing board games, we don't do that very much right now, but we do enjoy it.

Ellen (114a):   We sort of go through phases. Just curling up on the sofa and reading.

Jeremy (206a):   But I mean I just like, I like weekends where we can both actually, where we're not working or doing anything and it's just me and Stewart and we can you know, buy the Sunday paper and just do normal things and do a bit of DIY together or, you know, make Sunday lunch together and just do normal, that's me as a good day and you?

Stewart (206b):   Yeah.

The couples almost universally preferred to spend the day in their own company doing (what they referred to as) simple or ordinary things. They embraced the idea of just being together in a companionable way. Walking together was very high on the list of desirable things to do. Sometimes this would be with the dog, but the main attraction seemed to be the allure of experiencing things (even very little things) together. The togetherness made the mundane activity (e.g. making lunch, playing Scrabble) become infused with meaning and purpose. But there were two other vital ingredients in addition to togetherness. The first was uninterrupted time and second was talking.

Uninterrupted time

For all the couples, the best of times was when they were not working so they could be together; but, more importantly than this simple proximity, it was when the stresses or worries associated with work did not intrude on their time together. They made the point that the time should be 'stress free', without external commitments, and without the frazzle of the working week leaking into their consciousness. That couples want to have time together is not in itself a new finding. As Warren (2003) notes:

> Sullivan (1996: 96) has shown that the most enjoyable time for couples is leisure time that is spent together. As a result, couples make efforts to 'co-ordinate time' to optimize their joint time. The couples interviewed by Hochschild (1997) also reported that they endeavoured to arrange their schedules so that they could have 'intense periods of togetherness'. Opportunities for such *synchronized* family leisure are linked firmly to the location of that leisure time over the day and the week; the *chronologic* dimension.
>
> Warren (2003: 735)

However, it was not simply time that our couples wanted; there had to be a quality of attentiveness to each other during these periods. The yearning for 'us' time (as one couple put it) was incredibly strong and it was during those periods that the couples felt that they could harmonise with each other again after the stresses of paid work, sometimes child care, and time apart.

What was also striking in these accounts were the stories about 'bad' days which seemed to be the 'flip side' of the good days. Again almost universally, bad days in these narratives came about as a result of the overflow of work and stress. Very few couples saw their interpersonal conflicts arising from factors internal to the couple. Rather, they saw conflict as arising directly from the intrusion of paid work into their home and personal space. Thus, the typical story was one where one member of the couple was worried about something at work and he or she brought that worry home with them and 'took it out' on their partner.

Brooklyn (121a):	It's when I come home stressing about work and money [...] and infect Sara with my stress.
Sara (121b):	Your stress is contagious.
Brooklyn:	Yeah I know.

In this context, days off work or holidays were vital repair time because they allowed the couple to retrieve their relationship from the distorting effects of too much work, feeling harried (Southerton, 2003) or feeling tired (Widerberg, 2006).

A great deal has been written on the subject of time in the context of work/family balance and also in terms of the harmful effects of a long-work-hours culture (Brannen, 2005; Fagan, 2001; Hochschild, 1997). Yet what appears to be a different insight arising from our interviews is the way in which 'unpolluted' time together is perceived as an opportunity to restore a relationship which is vulnerable to the excessive demands of life outside the couple. Without time together, the couples would, it seems, lose their compatibility. Indeed, it was common for them to say they became irritated with each other at times when they had not had enough time together over the previous weeks or months. This pure time together was a way of forging companionship and reminding the couples why they liked each other. It was very much a part of Swidler's practices of prosaic love.

This is why we refer in this section to *capsule couples* because, at this point in their relationships at least, they clearly felt a need to be alone. At these times the presence of others hindered the consolidation process. In remarking on this, the couples routinely pointed to how ordinary or mundane or simple their needs and pleasures were:

Pam (119b):   [Laughs] We went for a big walk; went to the supermarket [laughs].
Moreen (119a):   Pam likes to go to the supermarket [laughter]. And then I cooked a nice tea.
Pam: And we watched a film.
Moreen: Yeah. We're the boringest people in the whole world [laughter]. It's really disturbing. [Laughter]

The laughter which usually accompanied these 'confessions' of ordinariness is interesting and suggests that most couples were aware that there is a normative expectation that same-sex couples should be doing rather different, more exciting, things. But even the few who included trips to the theatre or museums were clear that the point of doing such things was to do them together. The sheer ordinariness of these weekend activities is difficult to align with the idea that same-sex couples shoulder the burden of creativeness and fluidity in their relationships. Indeed, it is possible to argue that these couples craved the mundane and the micro-personal rather than the fluid, the challenging and the macro-political canvas. They sounded similar to almost any young couple, and their desire just to be together seemed so common that, in *this* dimension at least, it appears more important to acknowledge sameness rather than difference across the hetero/homosexual 'divide'.

Talking

The second defining element of the capsule couple, namely talking, may also be more suggestive of sameness than difference. We found that the lesbian couples thrived on talking to each other, while for the male couples talking seemed to feature not as a pleasure in itself but as a requirement of relationship 'repair work'. Hence:

Annabel (124a): If we're out and we go for a walk around the lake and that, we just talk. I don't know, I think four years, nearly four years married and we can still talk.
Kenzie (124b): We can still talk.
Annabel: Constantly.
Kenzie: We never really run out of things to talk about. I know, it's strange isn't it?

Caroline (112a): We do spend a lot of time talking to each other you know?

But more rarely:

And – and we talk like – more than any other couple we've ever heard of.

Ian (218a)

The young female couples in our study emphasised the importance of talking for their relationships. Talking seemed to be pleasurable in itself and also a vital way to overcome differences and disagreements. While male couples stressed the importance of communication in relationships, talking during 'couple time' really only seemed to become important when they had misunderstandings. Ironically, they spoke more spontaneously about the *absence* of talk in their relationships while the lesbian couples spoke spontaneously about the *presence* of talk. This meant that with the male couples it was 'not talking' that carried a particular significance rather than actual talking. This meant that if one of the men in a couple was worried or annoyed about something he would actively not talk. Silence or shutting oneself away was a clear demonstration that something was wrong. Actively not talking was therefore quite different to companionable silence which seemed to be the preferred condition for most of the male couples. The female couples on the one hand engaged in both active-talking and active-not-talking in equal measure; it was as if this was a simple continuum. The men, on the other hand, seemed to operate more on a different continuum from companionable silence through to active-not-talking.

Talk takes many shapes and forms, however, and there are pitfalls inherent in reconstructing the stereotype of strong, silent men versus chatty, garrulous women. Giddens (1992), for example, has suggested that it is (heterosexual) women who seek disclosing intimacy in relationships while (heterosexual) men avoid it. Mansfield and Collard's (1988) study found the same phenomenon. So it might seem that the same-sex couples in our study are following the same gendered scripts of talking women and silent men. However, while gendered scripts may be powerful influences, what emerges from our interviews is a more complex picture of different sorts of talking and communicating. For example, 'bickering' between couples seemed to be a constant form of communicating and even bonding. Bickering is often seen as a sign of problems between couples, yet in our interviews it was reflected on quite positively as a safety valve and/or a form of humorous bonding.

Otto (212a):	I think we bicker a lot.
Phil (212b):	All right, we bicker. We've never had a major argument, never, have we?
Ian (218a):	I mean we bicker 'cause everybody bickers. You know, it's like 'Why haven't you done the dishes?' 'Well, 'cause I can't be bothered and I'm tired'. And I'm like 'Well, I cook the dinner, you do the dishes'. [To] me, that's healthy bickering because it keeps you going.
Barbara (111a):	And so sometimes, you know, one of us will say a ridiculous comment or be a bit grumpy and then that'll start, like, a bickery kind of fight which might then escalate into kind of accusing, 'Well, you didn't do the washing up and you owe me twenty quid,' all that kind of thing.
Nicole (111b):	[Laughs]

For both male and female couples, too much bickering was a sign that they were out of kilter with each other because of a lack of 'us' time. It was also a common response to see bickering as a way of complaining about different expectations or standards around housework and tidiness. In these situations, bickering itself was not necessarily positive but it allowed individuals to voice the things that got on their nerves, the other could retaliate and a kind of set piece of dialogue would ensue. The couples mostly seemed to accept that bickering did not change anything, but it allowed them to express irritation without it escalating into anything too serious. What is more, when speaking about bickering (especially about household matters) the couples inevitably laughed and were able to reflect on the process of airing gripes. Interviews themselves can induce a degree of reflexivity on the part of interviewees and this self-awareness may not always be part of everyday interactions; but in these cases it was nearly always clear that the couples had a shared understanding of the purpose of bickering. This does not mean that bickering could not be harmful or negative in a relationship. For example, some couples said that their definition of a bad day was when they bickered the whole time and could not get out of the cycle of complaint. But the majority experienced bickering as something that could be overcome (by a hug or a smile) and that was not damaging in the way that full-scale rows could be.

Bickering as a form of engagement or communication was something that both male and female couples engaged in. It was not scripted in gendered ways as talk in the form of disclosing intimacy might be. Moreover, it seemed to be just as important in the process of sustaining prosaic love as did disclosing intimacy or companionable silence. If everyday loving requires hard work, then dealing with bickering must surely be part of this labour. This raises the issue of whether the concept of a gendered 'emotional asymmetry' (Duncombe and Marsden, 1993: 224) is as useful as was once argued. The idea of a gendered division of emotional labour has clearly identified women as the ones who carry the burden of managing emotions within a relationship and in that sense carry the burden of prosaic love also. However, when we look at the interiority of same-sex relationships, we find broadly the same kinds of issues occurring for men as for women. Both the men and the women had to learn how to manage their partner's moods, both had to learn how to deal with degrees of incompatibility and both had to work to maintain the relationship. In effect, both parties had to work out a choreography of emotions in order to deal with the moods and feelings of the other. Most of our couples knew what to do when one of them came home stressed or was engaged in active-not-talking, and this usually meant allowing the stressed partner time to relax rather than insisting on talk. Certainly, there were cases of considerable inequality in this choreography of emotion work. For example, one partner might have been seriously ill or trying to cope with unemployment which could give rise to additional emotional demands. However, the inequalities were not grounded directly in gender and, returning to Weeks et al. (2001), this does suggest an important degree of freedom from the conventions of heterosexual intimacy and relating. This suggests to us that it is a mistake to look for emotion work in *only* the obvious places and in the most conventional forms (e.g. in talk about feelings). Our interviews showed that men (in same-sex couples at least) were having to do the everyday work of prosaic love and they were having to work to accommodate the other just as much as the women were.

The concept of the capsule couple that we use derived from our analysis of what our same-sex couples had to say about good times and bad times. Because they expressed so clearly their desire to be alone together and to build their relationship through doing things together, they conjured up an image of a fairly tight and inward-looking capsule. But, as we have seen in Chapters 4 and 6 where the prioritisation of the couple above other relational form was discussed, the strength of the ideal of the couple was apparent elsewhere in our data. In addition, we asked the couples to respond independently to a series of questions on who they would turn to in different moments of need. We gave four scenarios: the first was about whom they would turn to if they needed emotional support; the second was who it would be if they were unhappy in their relationship; the third was who it would be if they were physically ill; and finally who it would be if they needed to borrow money. We gave them a range of possible people including the open category of 'other' and we also said they could choose as many of the categories as they wished. On the question of who they would turn to if they needed emotional support, 96 per cent of the women and 96 per cent of the men said it would be their partner. Only four of the men said that they would also turn to parents or friends as well as to their partners, while one man said it would just be his parents, and one man and two women said it would just be friends. Overwhelmingly, therefore, these individuals saw their partners, and only their partners, as a source of emotional support. The same was true for the question on illness, with 98 per cent of the women saying it would be their partner and 96 per cent of the men saying this. This finding is perhaps less surprising because it is most likely that one would look to the person one is living with at such times. Nonetheless, it shows that there were the same expectations placed on the men as the women to provide physical care in times of illness. In the other categories, the picture was a little less stark but still showed a prioritising of the couple 'unit'. If they were unhappy in their relationship, 70 per cent of the women and 72 per cent of the men would turn to their partner with the remainder turning mainly to friends or occasionally sibling and/or parents. This finding suggests that there is a strong ethos of trying to sort out relationship problems together for these couples, which also fits closely with the practices of prosaic love discussed above. It also fits with ideas of disclosing intimacy because clearly the majority of couples felt they should deal collaboratively with the problems they might be having in their relationship rather than taking them to an 'outside' third party to discuss.

The final question about borrowing money revealed the significance of intergenerational ties and the importance of the family of origin. Although partners remained the largest category that individuals would turn to (44 per cent of women and 58 per cent of men) the next largest category were parents with 38 per cent of women and 40 per cent of men turning to parents and 4 per cent of each turning to siblings. It is striking that friends did not feature particularly significantly in any responses, with women mentioning friends only 11 times (across all four questions) and men only 16 times (see Chapter 3). Friends really only featured when relationship problems were the issue. But the overall impression gained by this exercise is that the couple was essentially striving to be self-reliant, rarely looking outwards for external support. McGlone et al. (2004) found essentially the same when they studied the results of different social attitude surveys in Britain from 1986 to 1995. The respondents to these surveys would have been predominantly heterosexuals. However, they replied to broadly similar questions on whom they would turn to in times of difficulty, and partners were found to be the main source of support when compared with other categories such as parents or friends. McGlone et al., though, found that at times of illness women were less likely to rely on their husbands and more likely to rely on family or friends than men, who relied on their wives at such times. They also found that families of origin became important at times of financial need more than at any other time of crisis. In this small domain of practices, it would seem that our young same-sex couples were rather typical or 'ordinary' and that they did operate as capsule couples, relying on themselves and seeking and finding companionship predominantly within their relationships.

Beyond the couple

We have noted that in partners' narratives there is a tendency to locate their commitment to their current relationship in terms of a life stage (see Chapter 4). Most saw their marriage as arriving at a particular stage in both a relationship and in life more broadly. The couples were conscious of their peers (whether heterosexual or not) and of their siblings, moving through identifiable stages such as 'settling down' or parenthood, and they were aligning their own relationships with what was going on around them. They were also aware of their parents' 'traditional' hopes and expectations about relationships. All of these factors meant that almost all the couples we interviewed had turned their attention to the question of becoming parents.

Eight of the 25 female couples already had a child or children but none of the male couples had children. Of the eight female couples with children already, five were planning (or hoping for) another child, and of the remaining 17 couples, nine had plans either to adopt or to conceive a child through sperm donation at some time in the future. Only four positively did not want children. The male couples were in a different position, however, because those who wanted a genetically related child could only go down the surrogacy route which for most seemed rather remote. Options to adopt or foster were mentioned by eight of the 25 male couples, but these were always rather tentative plans for action in five or ten years' time:

> [A]ctually we've even, and this is probably a bit premature but, we've even you know skipped over the subject of maybe one day fostering or something. You know we haven't had an in-depth conversation about things like that 'cause it's too early days for us to talk about that and we haven't got the room anyway, but you know, I think longer term I'd be quite interested in that and I think you might be as well, so you never know.
>
> Graham (204b)

Among these young men there were those who very much did want to have children but who felt that the process of becoming parents was rather alien and outside their possible scope of action. As Oliver (210b) puts it:

> Just the ways of procuring a child for a same-sex male couple – all of them seem to be fraught with difficulties for the child and for the parents.

However, the majority of the male couples did not include parent-hood in their plans for the future. Some thought it might be wrong for gay male couples to have children. The main reason was their concern for how such a child might be treated in school, and this was often combined with the idea that there are enough children in the world already and that it would be better to adopt than to create a new life. Some simply said they thought children would not fit in with their lifestyle, particularly with holidays and 'hedonism', but one man felt even more strongly that it was wrong to have children:

> I believe in a biological evolution sort of thing. I believe gay people are a control measure to keep the population down.
>
> Ian (218a)

So although our male couples had thought about or were thinking about the possibility of having children, it did not seem as if they were influenced by a strong cultural narrative which associated civil partnership or 'settling down' with an inevitable desire to have children or become parents. The men could still find a comfortable cultural location outside the perimeters of parenthood (Stacey, 2006). The narrative of not having or not wanting children was still available to them, and for the majority this was perfectly agreeable space to occupy, as Otto's (212a) comments indicate:

> I don't have a sort of need for my genes to be carried on in any way and the older I've got I think the more certain I've become in my belief that I just don't think it's part of who I am to actually want to have children.

It was rather different for the women for whom having children was more readily envisaged, and also more likely to be seen as desirable. Of course for the female couples it was not possible to leave getting pregnant to chance or fate; they had to be active in taking steps to achieve a pregnancy or they had to start adoption proceedings. In doing so they often became reflexively engaged in negotiating diverse possibilities. Two of the couples had actually started formally down the adoption route and were being interviewed by social services. One couple had given up on adoption because it was too taxing, and instead had decided that one of them would have to conceive a child through sperm donation. Like the men, these women often thought that it was more ethical to adopt than to bring new life into the world, but few had any experience of really trying to adopt and many who spoke of it seemed rather ill-informed about the actual process. As with some of the male couples, the women often expressed a wish to have children but not immediately because they needed to be more financially secure or they needed to have a larger home to live in. For those who were postponing having children, there was no urgency to explore avenues to conception or adoption and so it is not surprising that their plans were vague. One female couple and one male couple were also facing the issue of mixed-race parentage and so were having to think about whether they could or would be able to adopt a mixed-race child. As noted above, only four of the female couples said that they actively did not want to have children, and although she too was in a minority, Olga (126b) expressed views not utterly unlike those of Otto's above:

> I think the logistics of how lesbians come to be parents really put me off. [...] I really don't like any of the donor insemination really, of those kinds of ways of getting pregnant [...] because it's not natural [...] I feel like if somebody isn't meant to get pregnant, then that is nature sending a strong signal that that it's not to be. And to me that doesn't matter about the sexuality of a parent. I feel the same way about straight people who are infertile. I don't see why they have the right to have children, and I realise that's quite an extreme view and a lot of people would be quite upset by hearing that. But I think that if you're trying to get pregnant in that way and it's not working, there's probably a good reason why, and it might be best not to interfere with it. And also this child, some day you're going to have to explain to them how they came to be. And I can't think of a way of explaining to them how we got the sperm, how we went about [it], I just don't feel comfortable with that. It doesn't seem like a very honourable thing to do in a way.

Nordqvist (2011a; 2011b) has outlined the kinds of problems that lesbian couples have to overcome if they are going to try to achieve a pregnancy through sperm donation, whether through private arrangement or through infertility clinics. Finding a sperm donor via the internet or through friends' networks is not easy and is fraught with potential legal and interpersonal difficulties. For example, it is necessary to decide what role a known donor might have in raising a child, or it may be necessary to overcome many misgivings in acquiring sperm from a stranger in a purely financial arrangement. Equally, going to a clinic can become very expensive and the selection of donors may be quite limited. In addition, the process of trying to adopt can be quite soul-destroying not least because the couple may not meet the strict matching criteria set by a given local authority, or they may not be able to endure years of waiting for a suitable placement (Treacher and Katz, 2000). These difficulties place same-sex couples in highly stressful situations if they want to have children or additional children. Two couples (Hailee [120b] and Dawn [120a], and Kathryn [105a] and Louise [105b]) seemed to be the exception to this because both already had a child and the sperm donors they used were willing to donate again so that they could have a genetic sibling. Kathryn said:

> I think we'll have two children and that's probably going to be it, children-wise. I always only thought I wanted two children. In recent years we've actually said it would be really lovely to have more children but I think because I've had health complications before, touch wood everything's ok with this baby, we just feel we've been really lucky, somebody donated sperm to enable us to have a family and it would almost be tempting fate to have any more and we shouldn't be too greedy really; we feel very lucky to be in the situation that we're in. So I think we just need two, it's more than our share sort of thing really.

By comparison, Doris (104a) and Maria (104b), who also already had one child, tried to get pregnant again by buying sperm via the internet but it failed and so they decided to settle for just one child. In this regard, same-sex couples face an entirely different set of circumstances compared with the majority of heterosexual couples. For them it is much harder to move on to what might be regarded as the 'next stage' of a relationship, and these difficulties create both opportunities and disadvantages. Among the opportunities for our couples was the sense of being unencumbered and the possibility therefore of travelling abroad or even settling abroad, especially where one partner was not British. Plans to travel were a strong theme in how these couples envisaged their futures. Another strong theme was the idea of moving to a more ideal location. This might be 'to the country', or to a more congenial city like Brighton, or just to a bigger city like Manchester. These joint projects were ways of mapping a future together so that life as a couple was also an active project, not simply a relationship.

Couples and convention

Same-sex couples have arguably been burdened with the requirement to be in the vanguard of radical political change with regard to their personal relationships. The expectation that gay men and lesbians can or should transform conventions for relating to one another has been a strong one (Auchmuthy, 2004; Hull, 2006; Stychin, 2003; Warner, 2000). Yet, as we have shown, most of our couples just wanted 'ordinary' things for their relationships. They modelled their relationships on a concept of the ordinary rather than on the radically different. So rather than expecting to find, in an empirical fashion, dramatic changes in everyday living, we suggest that studying same-sex relationships provides an opportunity to rethink some of the conventions of sociological thinking. As Heaphy (2008) has argued, there is an important difference between a sociology of reflexivity and a reflexive sociology. In a similar vein, we are arguing here that the lives of same-sex couples provide hints and prompts for sociology to rethink personal life, rather than assuming that these couples must fit into a preformed vision of what a radical personal life should be like. For example, understanding how men relate in same-sex couple relationships offers the opportunity to rethink the rigid and somewhat stereotyped idea that only women do emotion work in relationships. While the men in these relationships may have a degree of freedom from the highly gendered expectations that (still) rest upon heterosexual men, it is also the case that not assuming that gender difference is *the* difference that matters in couples allows the sociologist to see differently the interaction that is occurring. So the interaction may be slightly different, but significantly it becomes possible to develop a different sociological vision of what is happening. This shift allows us to understand 'emotionality as contingent, rather than 'essential', contexualising it within [various] environments' (Robinson and Hockey, 2011: 160). This means that rather than being fixed on finding gender difference, a sociological perspective can begin to see emotion work as contextual. As Bondi et al. (2005) argue, emotions can be understood to be relational flows between people. These relational flows are necessarily open to change across the lifecourse and in different contexts; they may be influenced by gender but they need not be determined by gender any more than by class or ethnicity.

While it is clear that the relational ideals, meanings and practices of young men and women were often gendered, it also seems apparent that comprehending their relationships provides support for an understanding of gender as an *interactional flow* rather than just an acquired characteristic. The doing of gender in relationships is both subtle and complex as we demonstrated in Chapters 4–6. Same-sex couples can change the meanings of certain interactions and thus lift the overdetermination that can at times accompany the analysis of opposite-gender relationships. This means that what a same-sex couple 'does', does not have to be somehow intrinsically radical, but their 'doing' of it facilitates a different understanding of the meaning of the interaction. Thus, the desire to simply sit on a sofa watching DVDs may not fit into the imagined radically alternative lifestyle wishfully associated with 'queer' living, but the recognition that such practices and the forms of intimacy they are linked to are so highly regarded offers a challenge to sociological frameworks on personal relationships which see little significance in the everyday. It also offers insights into how prosaic love works on a day-to-day level and, as Weeks (2007) claims, the radical potential of claiming to be ordinary.

Conclusion

Over the course of a few generations, the everyday possibilities for same-sex relationships in Western societies have altered in dramatic, but uneven, ways. In some contexts, it has become possible for same-sex couples and partners to live more mainstream lives than ever before. There are few contexts in which the mainstreaming of same-sex relationships is more evident than those in which same-sex couples now have access to the 'rights' and privileges associated with marriage. In this book, we have taken a generational view of the mainstreaming of same-sex relationships by focusing on the experiences of younger generations of women and men who have formalised their relationships by entering into civil partnerships, who mostly see themselves as married, and who model their relationships on the ordinary. In this conclusion, we revisit some of the core issues discussed in the preceding chapters to draw out further the theme of ordinariness and its implications for the sociology of (same-sex *and* heterosexual) relationships.

One of the striking findings of our research is the ways in which civil partnerships, along with the language and practices of 'ordinary marriages', have so quickly and easily been incorporated into the lives of some young same-sex couples (see Chapter 2). Given that civil partnerships were only introduced about half a decade before we conducted our interviews, the support and encouragement that many couples received for their marriages, from their families and personal communities, is also striking. This could be linked to the ways in which – among couples themselves, and their families and communities – civil partnership or marriage was seen as symbolising an existing cohabiting relationship that was often already *implicitly* recognised as akin to an informal marriage. Put another way, partners themselves and their close networks often already understood the same-sex couple to be an 'ordinary' relationship which was not so different from those of their (heterosexual) cohabiting peers. Thus, it is not the entry into legally recognised partnerships or 'marriages' that makes same-sex relationships 'ordinary'. Rather, it is the already ordinary nature of same-sex relationships in some contexts that has enabled 'gay marriage' to be so easily incorporated into day-to-day life. At the same time, for some couples the sense of living an ordinary life was enhanced by the increased visibility and acceptability of same-sex relationships that came with the broader cultural recognition of 'gay marriage'. The emphasis that many of our young couples put on the ordinariness and acceptability of their relationships points to how the 'heterosexual panorama', the 'heterosexual assumption' or 'compulsory heterosexuality' has weakened in some contexts.

Despite the fact that same-sex relationships, and 'gay marriages', are increasingly becoming a more visible aspect of the contemporary relational landscape (see Chapters 2–4), our interviews attest to the fact that same-sex couples and partners still experience instances of invalidation. While parents, families and personal communities mostly validated our couples' formalised relationships, this was not always the case. For example, some family members did not make the effort to attend the civil partnership ceremony or the celebration, and (relatively few) others were openly hostile about the relationship and civil partnership. While partners mostly emphasised their acceptance over their marginalisation, some did recount instances of symbolic violence, where their relationships were explicitly deemed unworthy of recognition and respect. Also, while many of the partners we interviewed had had positive experiences of coming out, others recounted initially struggling with this because of the fear of rejection or hostility.

Where partners alluded to the *impossibilities* of living 'fully' ordinary relational lives, this was commonly linked to their multiple positioning in terms of sexuality combined with race and ethnicity, religion, disability and/or other axes of socio-cultural difference (see Chapter 2). In other words, it seemed that a sense of being fully ordinary was more easily achievable for same-sex couples on the basis of their being white, able-bodied and from religiously liberal or secular backgrounds. Economic resources could also facilitate a fuller sense of ordinariness. This was evident where depleted resources constrained the possibilities of achieving the ideals of a mature, financially self-sufficient and home-owning 'married' couple. Given that some couples were better placed than others to achieve a full sense of their ordinariness, ordinariness could be seen as a privilege that is *not* simply or automatically given by virtue of the legal recognition of relationships. The situated circumstances in which couples and partners live their day-to-day lives clearly influences the extent to which they can choose or achieve the ordinary ideals of relationships. This raises the reconfiguring links between ordinariness and difference. Despite the commonalities between contemporary experiences of same-sex and heterosexual relationships that we have highlighted in this book, differences still matter in shaping experiences of and claims about ordinariness. This becomes clear when we consider the links between ordinariness and difference as they emerged as significant in the book.

Among our young same-sex couples, ordinariness was a claim about difference *and* commonality. Ordinariness was valued by those who believed they had been afforded its privileges *and* by those who believed they had not. Ordinariness is not only the ideal of the privileged; it is also the ideal of the marginalised, although they may be less well positioned to fully achieve it. Thus, claims about the possibilities or impossibilities of living ordinary lives and relationships are political claims about the (in)validation of lives and relationships as they are lived. Claims about ordinariness are not neutral ones, as Savage et al. (2000) have illuminated with respect to class identities (see also Heaphy, 2011). But the ideals of ordinariness as they concern same-sex relationships cannot simply be equated with the 'normalisation' or 'assimilation' of these relationships. The issue is more complex than this. In some respects, ordinariness is about claiming recognition on the basis of respectability (Heaphy, 2011; Savage et al., 2000). In the case of new generations of same-sex partners, ordinariness could be a claim to recognition via respectability on the basis of not being at the top or the bottom of a social hierarchy: a claim about not being like those at the bottom of the sexual hierarchy who lived 'shameful' sexual lives (hence, the disparaging ways in which 'gay culture' and partners' own 'promiscuous' pasts were sometimes spoken of), and a claim about not being like perceived elites at the top of the sexual hierarchy who could simply 'consume' sexuality and relationships without taking respon- sibility (hence, partners' refusals to describe themselves as sexual and relational innovators). Put another way, ordinariness could be a claim about commonality: to be like the mass of people (heterosexual and non-heterosexual) in 'the middle' who must work at creating 'mature' and 'responsible' relationships.

Ordinariness is about relational embeddedness *and* agency. This came to the fore in Chapter 3 where we discussed in detail the idea of relational biographies which, in turn, were an explicit or implicit feature of all the subsequent chapters. In these respects, claims about ordinariness could be viewed as an 'intuitive' recognition that 'who' people (heterosexual and non-heterosexual) are and 'what people do' in relationships are linked to the relational circumstances and imaginaries they grew up with, the changing circumstances in which their relating orientations developed over time, and the specific interactional contexts in which they now relate. On the one hand, partners emphasised the continuities between their parents' relationships and their own relationships. They shared the core marriage ideals that their parents' generation subscribed to: love, stability and equality. They also subscribed to the belief that all 'good' and 'successful' relationships and marriages (be they their own or their parents', homosexual or heterosexual) required a joint commitment to *making* relationships work. This could involve the joint monitoring of relationships as well as fairly constant (explicit or implicit) communication and making time to simply be together. On the other hand, partners often believed that their relationships were different to their parents' by virtue of the 'fact' that they, like their heterosexual generational peers, were better positioned than their parents' generation to realise these ideals in practice. Underpinning this was a belief that their own generation was less constrained by social circumstances than was their parents' generation. In this respect, partners often believed that, compared to previous generations, they had more freedom to choose their partners and the kinds of relationships they wanted. For the majority, this implied a greater degree of individual agency, and they saw it as 'natural' that they (like their peers, heterosexual and otherwise) should invest such agency in creating and maintaining stable couple relationships that would be at the heart of their relational lives and connections with others.

Drawing on the previous points, claims to ordinariness are linked to *practices of ordinariness*, and this raises the issues of convention and innovation. As far as relationships are concerned, convention and innovation only make sense if we accept the idea that there are hegemonic models and scripts for relating that circulate in the culture and that we are all familiar with. For the sake of argument, we provisionally accept this proposition. The links between practices of ordinariness and conventional practices were a central theme that emerged in Chapters 4–7. Not all couples adopted conventional approaches to their relationships, but that many did was evident in the ways in which they ceremonialised their commitments, tended to 'choose' partners from broadly similar backgrounds, assumed and were committed to sexual monogamy, and were focused on couple-centred relational lives. However, as opposed to seeing this as evidence of how younger generations of same-sex relationships are more likely than previous same-sex generations to simply or blindly *follow* relating scripts, we argue that it highlights the extent to which partners and couples today (same-sex and hetero-sexual) can be actively *invested* in convention. From this perspective, married couples are not 'unreflexive' followers of conventional scripts, but are active (and sometimes highly reflexive) scriptors of convention. Put another way, they are not without agency. Rather, reflexivity and agency can be focused on the production of convention rather than its undoing. In this regard, the majority (but not all) of the same-sex couples we interviewed actively refused to be at the vanguard of the kind of relational innovation and experimentation that have been associated with previous generations' same-sex relationships. This, we suggest, is linked to the ways in which their biographies are anchored or embedded in the relational worlds in which they grew up.

The active investment in convention and embeddedness underscores the work or labour entailed in practices, 'performances' and claims of ordinariness. There were several dynamics unpinning this. As these were young couples who, for the most part, were in their first legally committed relationship, there was undoubtedly a pressure to be seen to have a successful relationship and to be doing it 'right'. As we have seen, couples also linked their current relationships and marriages to their development as mature relational actors, and the capacity to com-petently perform convention could be read as indicative of maturity. Also, these were couples who had only relatively recently formalised their relationships and the intensity with which they approached their (mostly monogamous) relationships was undoubtedly linked to the afterglow of having formalised their commitment (often in very public ways). Along with this, they were narrating their relationships to an interviewer, and via her to a public audience, and this will have shaped the form and content of their personal stories. Many of these dynamics, combined with the culturally and biographically embedded nature of relational ideals and practices, are likely to have influenced the conventional stories they told, as well as the conventional lives they lived. Yet, the intense labour involved in doing, performing and claim-ing ordinariness via the production of convention underscores the ways in which convention itself is actively made. Partners also seemed to engage in a notable degree of work in smoothing the tensions between their subscription to the conventions that support the 'naturalness' of couple and married relationships and their implicit recognition of other possible realities (for example, they could in principle, but did not in practice, *choose* non-monogamy, to be single, to prioritise rationality over the discourse of romantic love in accounting for their choice of a partner and to acknowledge the 'naïvety' of their faith in lifelong commitments in the face of the well-documented contingent nature of ordinary relationships).

This provides a perspective on the work or labour that contemporary relationships involve that is somewhat different to the ways in which these issues have tended to be framed in existing sociological studies of heterosexual and same-sex relationships. Put briefly, the emphasis in previous studies of conventional heterosexual relationships has been on the burden of physical and emotional work that falls to women in marriage and relationships with men. In studies of innovative same-sex relationships, the emphasis has been on the more equal sharing of the physical and emotional work that relationships involve. Our study does not necessarily contradict these findings but also suggests something else: that by shifting away from a reductive conception of gender we can begin to grasp the other kinds of work that relationships involve, and develop a vital conception of relational power that is perhaps more suitable for comprehending new, generationally situated, relational possibilities. In this book, we hope to have illustrated the value of this with respect to the new generational experiences of same-sex couples, but we also believe it has value in examining the reconfiguring possibilities open for heterosexual relationships.

Appendix 1: Researching Same-Sex Marriage

This book is based on a research project, 'Just like Marriage? Young Couples' Civil Partnerships', which was carried out in 2009 and 2010. It was funded by the British Economic and Social Research Council (ESRC, reference RES-062-23-1308). In studying personal accounts of formalised same-sex relationships, and by focusing on younger generations' experiences, we aimed to provide insights into historical continuities and changes in meanings and practices of commitment, and to link these to broader developments in marriage and same-sex relational cultures. Therefore, we sought to generate data which would allow us to analyse young same-sex couples' formalised commitments from the perspective of couples *and* individuals, and to situate couple accounts in terms of partners' socio-culturally shaped biographies. This, we hoped, would allow us to explore the reconfiguration of same-sex relational life that we believe to be linked to broader reconfigurations of gender, sexual and marriage relations. In this appendix, we outline our approach to the study (but see Heaphy and Einarsdottoir, 2012, for a more detailed discussion of our methodological approach).

The main body of our research was based on joint and individual interviews with 50 couples, 25 female and 25 male, who had formalised their relationships through civil partnership. The interviewees were aged up to 35 when they entered into civil partnership, and were aged between the early 20s and late 30s when we interviewed them. At the point of the interviews, the length of civil partnerships varied from one month to just over 5 years, averaging around 23 months. The length of relationships ranged from less than six months to over ten years. Fifty partners were aged between 25 and 35 when they entered civil partnership, 43 partners were aged between 30 and 35, and seven partners were aged under 25 at the time of the civil partnership.

The geographical scope of the research was mainland Britain. Couples were recruited with the help of registrar officials. We contacted local registrars across the UK to inform them about the study and to ask for their assistance in recruiting. In the main, the local offices were enthusiastic and helpful in offering their support. In practice, this entailed us sending them information sheets about the study that they would then forward to couples who had entered into civil partnership within the previous year (they did not have access to information from previous years). If couples were interested in taking part in the study they would contact a named member of the research team directly. Despite the very specific nature of the sample we sought to build, this strategy was successful in recruiting 38 couples in England (three from the North East, five from the North West, 16 from London and 14 from elsewhere in the South East). We recruited one couple from Wales, and with the help of the General Registry Office for Scotland recruited 11 couples in Scotland.

While the majority of couples lived in cities and large towns, this was not always the case, and some couples lived in rural locations. The vast majority defined their ethnicity as 'white British' (70) or 'white other' (21). The remaining nine identified as Arabic (1), black (1), mixed black (1), Pakistani (1), mixed Asian (1), Chinese (1) and other mixed (3). In terms of income, about 50 per cent of the interviewees earned below the national average, about 25 per cent earned the national average income or up to £10,000 more than this, and about 25 per cent earned significantly more than the average (see Chapter 5 for more detail and discussion). In short, the study included a wider diversity of economic backgrounds and socio-cultural experience than is often included in research on same-sex relational lives.

As noted in the Preface to this book, our study took *relationships* as the primary unit of analysis and not sexual identities. In narrating their relationships, participants often made reference to their sexual identity (and in some cases several identities), but it was sometimes the case that a specific sexual identity was not explicitly articulated as such. The study did not seek to impose or fix sexual identities. Nevertheless, we were interested in the ways in which partners discussed and defined their sexualities (or not) in narrating their relationships. Among the men, 44 partners described themselves or their relationships as 'gay', while six did not mention any sexual identity as such. Among the women, 28 partners described themselves of their relationships as 'gay', 13 used 'lesbian', two used 'bisexual', and seven did not mention a sexual identity as such. However, the ways in which these terms referred to sexual identity varied enormously. Some used 'gay' to refer to all same-sex relationships irrespective of their gender make-up. Others used 'gay' in a descriptive way to refer to women and men who were attracted to people of the same sex. Others still, but used 'gay' to refer to a fundamental sense of self. 'Lesbian' was also be used in a range of ways: to distinguish women's and men's same-sex relationships, to descriptively refer to same-sex relationships between women or to refer to women who were attracted to other women and to describe a fundamental self-identity.

From the outset, we were keen to study young couples' relationships and experiences in ways that assumed as little as possible about their structure, organisation and quality. Thus, we set out to explore how the transition from being single to civil partnership is made and experienced; how formalised same-sex partnerships are defined, experienced and practised; and how same-sex 'marriages' are influenced by interlinked socio-cultural and biographical factors. In essence, we sought to explore young couples' civil partnerships as complexly situated relationships by exploring how they were scripted (see Chapter 2).

Our rationale for interviewing partners together and apart was threefold. First, previous studies have suggested heterosexual marriages to be structured in accordance with gender differences and inequalities (for overviews see Duncombe and Marsden, 1993; 1996; Dunne, 1997; Jamieson, 1998). In contrast, studies of same-sex relationships suggest them to be highly negotiated and 'more egalitarian' because of the absence of gender differences (Dunne, 1997; Peplau et al., 1996; Weeks et al., 2001; for criticisms see Carrington, 2002; Ryan-Flood, 2009; Taylor, 2009). Unlike previous studies that have tended to rely on couple or individual interviews with one or both partners (for discussion see Carrington, 1999; Gabb, 2008), we were keen to explore how a combined approach might allow for a more nuanced view of relational power. Second, we sought to study how couples intersubjectively constructed their relationships, and couple interviews allowed us to explore couple interactions in scripting and 'doing' the relationship in a situated context. Third, we sought to explore how the scripting and doing of relationships were embedded in partners' (non-)negotiation of biographically rooted personal scripts for relating, and the individual interviews allowed us to explore these scripts. All three interviews were conducted by the same researcher during a single visit. The interview format was quite simple, starting with the joint interview which was split into two parts. The first part of the joint interview focused on the couple's relationship story. It began with the following prompt:

> We are interested in finding out the story of your relationship from the beginning to now, how you met, what attracted you to one another and how the relationship developed.
> We would like to know the ins and out of your relationship and for the first part of this interview I would like you to tell us your own story in your own words from the beginning to now.

This task was fairly open-ended and allowed partners to 'intuitively' detail their story while the researcher was positioned as an active listener (Anderson and Jack, 1991). While the task was partly designed to minimise our influence on the couples' stories, it did not, of course, neutralise this. The second part of the joint interview followed up questions that arose from the partners' relationship story. We then moved on to the individual interviews that focused especially on finances, sexual and emotional commitments and family-making/planning.

The individual interviews began by asking participants about their previous relationship experiences and were then structured around a discussion of the above mentioned areas. For each of these topics, participants were asked to describe and provide examples of their personal approach; how their approach was similar to or different from the people they had grown up with and their partner's; and how they and their partner's approach had developed over the duration of the relationship. In analysis, making links between the individual interviews, and between the individual and joint interviews, enabled us to examine the ways in which biographically embedded personal scripts influence the construction of the relationships.

The interviews were recorded and fully transcribed, and we conducted systematic interpretative analysis of the data set in line with our major questions and the themes that emerged (see Introduction). NVivo software was used for data storage, rough coding and retrieval. This enabled us to carry out cross-sectional analysis to draw out commonalities and differences across the sample. This cross-sectional analysis was enhanced by analysis through case study. The findings were then compared to existing ones about heterosexual and same-sex patterns of relating and commitment, and the changes and continuities, differences and commonalities were identified and analysed.

Several stories can be told about any one relationship, and joint-couple and individual interviews generate three differently situated narratives: a couple one and two self ones. In terms of the research context, couple and personal stories about relationships are not simply told in interviews: they are activated, shaped and 'co-produced' in interaction with the researcher. The questions researchers ask, and the ways and contexts in which they are asked, are powerful in shaping the couple and personal stories that research participants tell. But it is not only the researcher who has the power to shape the narrative. Interviewees actively construct and perform their narratives for multiple audiences. They can be agents, and can be constrained, in telling their stories and in assembling stories to give their relationships meaning. Thus, interview narratives are the product of the situated interactional contexts in which they emerge, and involve the negotiation of agency and constraint: put another way, they involve complex *flows* of power (cf. Plummer, 1995).

While relationship stories as they are scripted in interviews are shaped by the research context, they do not come from 'nowhere'. They are linked to relationships as they are lived, and can be analysed for the intersubjective *and* subjective dynamics that shape the scripting and doing of relationships in practice. As such, interview narratives about relationships can be analysed for the flow of power in relationships themselves and how this is linked to the socio-cultural contexts in which they are lived. By researching couples where both partners were aged under 35 when they entered into civil partnerships in the UK, our research explored relationships that are historically and socio-culturally distinctive. As noted earlier, our research was concerned with the 'new' relational possibilities that have opened up for formalised (or 'married') same-sex relationships. Established research-based understandings of the differences and/or similarities between marriage and same-sex relationships, and of the power dynamics that shape their scripting, are not straightforwardly applicable to these new relationships. Likewise, established methodologies for exploring power in relationships are unlikely to grasp the complex flows of power that these relationships involve and how they are linked to changing socio-cultural contexts that are reconfiguring contemporary relational possibilities.

Hitherto, by relying mostly on couple *or* individual interviews, and by focusing on the 'truths' they generate, couple studies have contributed to two strong sociological narratives about relationships: that gender power determines how heterosexual relationships are negotiated and scripted in practice, and that the absence of gender in same-sex relationships is linked to 'freer' and more equal negotiation and scripting. Our joint approach to interviewing young 'married' *and* same-sex couples, and our narrative approach to analysis, suggest something else: that in light of changing relational possibilities, there is a need to rethink how we conceptualise and study the negotiation and scripting of relationships along with the power dynamics they involve (be they formalised, married, and/or same-sex relationships). Our study, and this book, implicitly argues the value of an interactionist methodology, based on joint and individual interviews and orientated towards narrative analysis, as a strategy for exploring changing relational realities.

Appendix 2: Biographies of Interviewees

The women

101a Amina is a 30-year-old woman who identifies as Arabic. She met her current partner Josha less than two years ago and they have now been in a civil partnership for five months. Their marriage was instigated by Amina's non-EU citizenship. Amina and Josha live together in Amina's flat in North of England. She rarely sees her family of origin who live abroad.

101b Josha is Amina's partner. She is a 22-year-old of Pakistani origin. On completion of her studies, she is expected to marry a man. Her relationship with Amina is kept secret from her family of origin, and both she and Amina know that their marriage is temporary. Josha has never been in a relationship with a woman before.

102a Outside of the age range. Not included in the main analysis.

102b Outside of the age range. Not included in the main analysis.

103a Radinka is a 31-year-old white EU national. She moved to England where she met her current partner Kamilia. Three years into their relationship they decided to marry. Radinka and Kamilia live in a shared household in the South East of England. They want to leave the city. They have now been in a civil partnership for eight months.

103b Kamilia is Radinka's partner. She is 29. Like Radinka, she is a white EU national. They have been in a civil partnership for eight months after a three-year relationship. Kamilia's parents live abroad and did not make it to her wedding. Neither did Radinka's parents.

104a Doris is a 35-year-old, white, British woman. She initially met her partner Maria at church, at a point when Maria had just conceived a child. She entered into a relationship with Maria some years later. A few years into their relationship they had a religious 'blessing' and entered into civil partnership four years ago. They live in London with their eight-year-old daughter.

104b Maria is a 33-year-old black woman of Caribbean origin. While her partner is middle-class, Maria is not. Maria has a daughter who was conceived through donor insemination. The biological father has never been involved in the child's life. Maria has dealt with some serious health concerns, and this has impacted on the relationship, which has become more of a struggle recently.

105a Kathryn is a white British woman. She is 37 and has been involved with Louise for nearly eight years. They entered into civil partnership about five years ago. They wanted to have a family together and are now expecting their second child. Both children have been conceived through assisted insemination. It is her partner Louise's turn to carry their child this time. She lives in the South East of England.

105b Louise is white and British. She and Kathryn are partners. She is pregnant with their second child. Louise was 30 when they became civil partners.

Her family of origin lives in the North of England. Because of the distance from where they live, they do not have much contact. But Kathryn's parents live closer. Louise does not like the area they live in and feels isolated.

106a Angela is a 31-year-old white EU national. She entered into civil partnership with Nancy a month-and-a-half ago. Before that, they had been involved for almost five years. They live in London in a shared household with two flatmates. Angela was initially very sceptical about marriage, as her parents do not have a good married relationship.

106b Nancy is a white, 29-year-old, non-EU national who lives in a shared household in London with her partner Angela. They entered into civil partnership a month-and-a-half ago. Nancy feels she was blamed for her parents' failed relationship. Her parents have divorced and live abroad, and this has led to a sense of estrangement from them.

107a Juliet is a 36-year-old, white, British woman. She entered into civil partnership with Veronica when she was 33 after a seven-year relationship. Juliet and Veronica live in the South East of England. Their relationship is an emotionally and sexually non-monogamous one.

107b Veronica is a 34-year-old, white, British woman. She met Juliet, her current partner, 10 years ago. They have been in a civil partnership for three years. Veronica has had a previous serious relationship, which she describes as very problematic. She feels lucky that Juliet has 'no baggage'.

108a Hanna is 26. She is white and British. When she met Tammy, her partner, she was still living at home with her parents. Hanna and Tammy entered into civil partnership 10 months ago. They live together in the North East of England and have just applied to adopt a child. Hanna's family of origin live locally.

108b Tammy is a 29-year-old, white, British woman. She is Hanna's partner. Like Hanna she lived with her parents when they first met. Tammy's family of origin, like Hanna's, live locally. Tammy was 'cheated' on in her previous relationship. She initially struggled to build trust with Hanna, but over time feels they have done that.

109a Zoe is 26. She is white and British. Zoe became a mother in her teens. She had no previous experience of relationships with women before she met her partner Rebecca. They entered into civil partnership 10 months ago, after nearly five years together. Zoe, Rebecca and their three children live in the North East of England. Her family of origin live nearby.

109b Rebecca is a 34-year-old, white, British woman. She was married to a man before she entered into civil partnership with her current partner Zoe. Rebecca has two children from previous relationships with men, and together Zoe and Rebecca are raising three children. They have been together for over five years and in a civil partnership for 10 months. Rebecca's family of origin, like Zoe's, live locally.

110a Stacy is a white, non-EU national. She is 34 years old. Stacy first met her current partner Theresa nearly 10 years ago when Theresa travelled from the UK for a summer job. For the next six years, they lived in two separate countries. Stacy moved to the UK just before they entered into civil partnership about three years ago. Her family of origin, all devoted Christians, live abroad.

110b Theresa is a 31-year-old, white, British woman. She is in a civil partnership with Stacy. They spent the first six years of their relationship in two different countries, but have lived together for just over three years and been in a civil partnership for the same length of time. They live together in the South East of England, but want to move abroad. Theresa's parents live locally.

111a Barbara is a 32-year-old, white, British woman. She had been involved with Nicole for just under six years when they entered into civil partnership. This was nearly one-and-a-half years ago. They live in London, but want to move to a larger property. Her family of origin live locally.

111b Nicole is a 29-year-old, white, British woman. She and Barbara are partners. They have been in a civil partnership for 16 months. Nicole has been involved with Barbara for over seven years. Nicole lives with Barbara in London. Her family of origin live close by.

112a Caroline is a 35-year-old, white, British woman. She met her partner Edith when she was working abroad. This was just over four years ago and for the last 17 months they have been in a civil partnership. Caroline and Edith live in London. Her family of origin live in the UK, but quite a distance away. Caroline would like to return to Edith's home country.

112b Edith and Caroline are partners. Edith is a 35-year-old, non-EU national. She is from a mixed-race background. Edith and Caroline were flatmates before entering into a couple relationship. About three years later they entered into civil partnership, 17 months ago. Edith was 33 at the time. Unlike Caroline, Edith has had a 'typical middle class' upbringing. Her family of origin live abroad.

113a Fay is a 35-year-old British woman and a mother of two children. She entered into civil partnership with her partner Olivia two years ago when they had been involved with each other for nearly eight years. The children were both conceived by donor insemination and the biological father has agreed no contact. Fay, Olivia and their two children live in London with both of their families nearby.

113b Olivia is a 30-year-old, white, British woman. She carried both of her and Fay's children. Olivia and Fay entered into civil partnership two years ago and have been involved for nearly a decade. She had no previous sexual experience with women. The family live in London.

114a Ellen is a 31-year-old woman of mixed white and Asian background. She entered into civil partnership with Holly a year ago after being together for nearly three years. Ellen and Holly live in London, but neither of them likes the area they live in. Holly wants to move back to her home country, but Ellen is not convinced due to her mother's chronic health conditions.

114b Holly is 26. She is white and a non-EU national. She met her current partner Ellen in the UK nearly three years ago. They have been in a civil partnership for a year now. Holly wants to move back to her home country where her parents still live. Her relationship with Ellen is her first relationship with a woman.

115a Cori is a 31-year-old, white, British woman. She first met Gillian when she was working overseas. She was 17. They have been together ever since, but spent many years living in separate countries. Cori and Gillian have been in a civil partnership for just over three years. They live in the North West of England. Cori has no previous relationship experiences with women.

115b Gillian is Cori's partner. She is a 31-year-old, white, non-EU national. When she met Cori she was still living with her parents overseas. This was

Gillian's first relationship with a woman. Cori returned to the UK and their relationship continued. When Gillian's parents found out about it, they tried to put a stop to the relationship. Gillian eventually moved to the UK. They have been in a civil partnership for just over three years. Gillian's parents still live overseas.

116a Isabel is white and British. She is 25 and entered into a civil partnership with her partner Samantha five months ago. They have been involved for just over two years now and are raising a child – who has regular contact with his father – together. Isabel finds it difficult to fit in with the existing family structure. Her parents live a long way away.

116b Samantha and Isabel are partners. Samantha is a 27-year-old, white, British woman. She is the birth mother of a five-year-old child. Samantha, Isabel and their son live together in the North West of England, near Samantha's family of origin.

117a Linda is a 34-year-old, white, British woman. She met her partner Natalie around three years ago and within a year they had entered into civil partnership. Linda comes from a religious background and has limited experience of relationships with other women. She and Natalie live in the North West of England. Her family of origin live locally.

117b Natalie is Linda's partner. She is 35 years old, white and British. Natalie has been 'out' since her early teenage years and has had a series of difficult relationships with women. Within a year of meeting Linda, they entered into civil partnership, just over two years ago now. Her family of origin live nearby.

118a Andrea is a 29-year-old, white, British woman. She has been in a relationship with Helen for nine years. They entered into civil partnership four years ago. This is Andrea's first and only relationship. They live together with Andrea's parents. Neither of them calls it home but 'the house'.

118b Helen is a 30-year-old, white, non-EU national. She and Andrea met in the UK about nine years ago and have been in a civil partnership for nearly four years. Helen comes from a religious background. She has much more experience of relationships than Andrea. They live in Wales. Helen's family of origin live overseas.

119a Moreen is 31. She is white and British. At the age of 28, Moreen entered into civil partnership with her partner Pam. By then they had been in a relationship for nearly three years. They also had a religious blessing of their relationship. Moreen and Pam live together in Scotland, but Moreen's family of origin live down south.

119b Pam is Moreen's partner. She is 27, white and British. Before she met Moreen, Pam had had no previous experiences of relationships with women. They have now been together for six years and in a civil partnership for nearly three. Pam and Moreen met at church. Pam's family of origin live around the corner.

120a Dawn is a 36-year-old, white, British woman. She met Hailee about five years ago and they have been in a civil partnership for 16 months. Dawn and Hailee have a four-month-old baby, who was conceived by anonymous sperm donation. Dawn carried the child. They live in a 'straight' and 'settled' area, as they call it, in the South East of England. Dawn's family of origin live overseas.

120b Hailee and Dawn are partners. Hailee is a 34-year-old, white, British woman, a mother of a four-month-old baby. Hailee and Dawn met through church and have been together for around five years. They entered into civil partnership 16 months ago. Hailee's family of origin do not live in the area that she lives in.

121a Brooklyn is 35. She is white and British. She met her partner Sara when she was working abroad. Within a year they had entered into civil partnership. This was 17 months ago. Brooklyn is 10 years older than Sara. They live in a shared household in London. Brooklyn has limited contact with her family of origin who live abroad.

121b Sara is a 25-year-old, black, non-EU national. She entered into civil partnership with Brooklyn 17 months ago. At that point they had known each other for less than a year. Like Brooklyn, Sara has limited contact with her family of origin who live abroad.

122a Fiona is a 36-year-old, white, British woman. She and Iris have been together for nearly 10 years and entered into civil partnership close to five years ago. Fiona is both the older and more experienced of the two with a series of 'bad' relationships behind her. Fiona and Iris live in Scotland.

122b Iris and Fiona are partners. She is 30 years old, white and British, and has been involved with Fiona for the last 10 years. They entered into civil partnership about five years ago. Her family of origin live locally.

123a Jasmine is a 28-year-old, white, British woman who lives with her partner Pheobe in Scotland. They have been in a civil partnership for 18 months. Jasmine has had serious health concerns linked to chronic illness, which has placed both emotional and financial pressure on their relationship. Her family of origin live in England.

123b Pheobe is Jasmine's partner. She is 27 years old, white and British. Pheobe and Jasmine have been in a civil partnership for 18 months. Due to Jasmine's illness, Pheobe has been the 'breadwinner'. They struggle financially. Her family of origin live in Scotland, but a long distance away.

124a Annabel is 29. She is white and British. She has been in a civil partnership with Kenzie for around three-and-a-half years. They have a nine-month-old baby, who was conceived by donor insemination. The donor is a friend of theirs. He is gay. They have a verbal agreement between them about his non-involvement. Annabel, Kenzie and their baby live in Scotland. Annabel's family of origin live close by.

124b Kenzie and Annabel are partners. Kenzie is a 31-year-old, white, British woman. She is also the birth mother of their nine-month-old baby. Kenzie met Annabel about five years ago. They entered into civil partnership within two years. Kenzie described her previous relationship as an abusive one. Her family of origin live in England.

125a Emily is a 32-year-old, white, British woman. She and Gail met nearly seven years ago. They have been in a civil partnership for 21 months and are expecting their first child. The donor is a gay male friend of theirs. Emily gets frustrated when she is not recognised as a 'mummy' to be, like her partner. Her family of origin live locally.

125b Gail is 33. She is white and British. Gail and Emily are partners and have been in a civil partnership for 21 months. They also had a religious blessing of their relationship. Gail is pregnant and suffers from extreme tiredness. They live in Scotland but Gail's family of origin live in England.

126a Mandy is a 26-year-old, white, British woman. She has been involved with Olga for nearly five years. They entered into civil partnership four months ago and live in the South East of England. Neither of them likes the area they live in and they describe it as 'exclusive' and 'pretentious'. Her family of origin live a long way away.

126b Olga and Mandy are partners. Olga is a 32-year-old, white, non-EU national. She has lived in the UK most of her life. She met Mandy around five years ago and they have been in a civil partnership for four months. One part of Olga's family of origin live in the UK and another part abroad.

The men

201a Outside of the age range. Not included in the analysis.

201b Outside of the age range. Not included in the analysis.

202a Daniel is a 34-year-old, white, British man. He lives with his partner Robert in London. Daniel was 31 when they entered into civil partnership. They have been together for nearly 8 years, although they separated for a few months. They live in London. Daniel's family of origin do not live locally.

202b Robert is Daniel's partner. He is a 32-year-old, white, non-EU national. Robert moved to the UK to continue his relationship with Daniel. They have been in a civil partnership for nearly three years. Robert's family of origin live overseas.

203a Mark is a 25-year-old, white, British man. He has been with Callum for less than a year and they entered into civil partnership just over a month ago. He and Callum live in the South of England and have been harassed by their neighbour. Mark's family of origin live a long distance away. He fled his family home because of his sexuality.

203b Callum is a 21-year-old, white, British man. He is Mark's partner. They entered into civil partnership just over a month ago after a short relationship. Callum is very close to his family of origin who live around the corner. They are in the process of moving house.

204a Andrew and Graham are partners. Andrew is a 29-year-old, white, non-EU national. He met Graham in the UK less than a year ago. They have been in a civil partnership for three months. Andrew and Graham live in London. His family of origin live overseas.

204b Graham is 35 years old. He is white and British. He entered into civil partnership with Andrew three months ago. Graham grew up in care and was 'battered around' the system as he describes it. His foster family live outside London.

205a Kevin is a 34-year-old, white, British man. He is Jorge's partner. They entered into civil partnership just over two years ago. Kevin and Jorge live together in the South East of England where Kevin has lived all his life. His family of origin live locally.

205b Jorge is 28, white and an EU national. He and Kevin have been in a civil partnership for 25 months. This is Jorge's first same-sex relationship and only sexual partner. Jorge came out to his family of origin when he entered into civil partnership with Kevin. His family of origin live abroad.

206a Jeremy is a 29-year-old, white, British man. He has been in a relationship with Stewart for about six years. They entered into civil partnership just under three years ago. Jeremy and Stewart live in the South East of England. They have a lodger. Jeremy's family of origin live nearby.

206b Stewart and Jeremy are partners. Stewart is a 27-year-old, white non-EU national. He and Jeremy have been together for six years and in a civil partnership for around three years. Stewart has no previous relationship experience. His family of origin live overseas.

207a Outside of the age range. Not included in the analysis.

207b Outside of the age range. Not included in the analysis.

208a Jan is a 27-year-old, white, EU national. Jan and Diego met in the UK and have been in a civil partnership for 15 months. When Jan met Diego about three years ago, he was involved with someone else. Jan and Diego live in the South East of England. Jan's family of origin live overseas.

208b Diego is a 26-year-old, white, EU national. He and Jan are partners. When Diego started going out with Jan, his best friend proved very 'jealous' and tried to put a 'wedge' between them. Diego gave her an ultimatum. He never saw her again. Diego's family of origin live overseas.

209a Frederik is a 36-year-old, white, British man. He has been involved with Tim for about eight years and has been in a civil partnership for just over two years. Frederik has a chronic health condition. He and Tim live in the South East of England. His family of origin live 'just around the corner'.

209b Tim is 33 years old. He and Frederik are partners. Like Frederik, Tim is white and British. He, too, has a chronic health condition. His family of origin live in a different part of the UK.

210a Ben is a 32-year-old, white, British man. He was 29 when he entered into civil partnership with Oliver after a five-year relationship. They met abroad where they both worked. Ben was bullied at work and struggles with anxiety. They live in the South East of England where Ben's family of origin live.

210b Oliver is Ben's partner. He is aged 30 years, white and British. While Ben is receiving treatment to manage his anxiety, Oliver looks after most of Ben's personal needs. They also had a religious blessing when they entered into civil partnership nearly three-and-a-half years ago.

211a Edwin is a 27-year-old, white, non-EU national. He met Ivan in London and they have been in a civil partnership for nearly three years. Edwin and Ivan live in a shared household in London. Edwin's family live overseas.

211b Ivan is Edwin's partner. He is 30 years old, white and British. Ivan entered into a civil partnership with Ivan almost three years ago. They find it difficult to make ends meet in London where they live. Ivan's family of origin live in a different part of the UK.

212a Otto is a 32-year-old, white, British man. He met his partner Phil about eight years ago. They have now been in a civil partnership for 19 months. Otto and Phil lived separately for many years before they decided to share a home. They now live in Scotland. Otto's mother lives locally.

212b Phil was 34 years old when he entered into civil partnership with Otto 19 months ago. Like Otto, Phil is white and British. Phil's family of origin live in a different part of the UK.

213a Felix is 34 years old. He is white and British. Felix entered into civil partnership with Cameron when he was 30. Before that they had known each other for nearly four years. They live in the North of England but are moving abroad. His family of origin live a long distance away.

213b Cameron is a white, British man. He is the same age as his partner Felix: 34. They have been in a civil partnership for almost four years. Cameron is taking up the offer of employment overseas. Felix is moving abroad with him.

214a Albert was 29 when he entered into civil partnership with his partner Duncan. This was four years ago. He is white and British. Albert and Duncan live in Scotland. His family of origin live in a different part of the UK.

214b Duncan is Albert's partner. He is a 35-year-old, white, British man. Duncan and Albert have been together for over 11 years and in a civil partnership for four years.

215a Frazer has been in a civil partnership with Todd for 16 months. He is 28 years old, white and a non-European national. He and Todd live in Scotland. His family of origin live overseas.

215b Todd is a 31-year-old, white, British man. He entered into civil partnership with Frazer 16 months ago after a nearly seven-year relationship. His family of origin live in a different part of the UK.

216a Peter is a 38-year-old, white, EU national. He met his partner Victor in the UK about nine years ago. They have been in a civil partnership for just under four years. Peter had never been involved with anyone else before he met Victor. They live together in Scotland. Peter's family of origin live abroad.

216b Victor is a 36 year-old. He is white and British and entered into civil partnership with Peter when he was 32. Unlike Peter, Victor comes from a working-class background. His family of origin live locally.

217a Henry is 32-year-old, white, British man. He entered into civil partnership with Kurt four months ago. They met almost two years ago. Henry fell seriously ill a few years ago and lost much of his mobility. Henry and Kurt live in the South East of England. His family of origin live in a different part of the UK.

217b Kurt is 34. He is Henry's partner and they have been together for nearly two years. Like Henry, Kurt has a disability. Kurt's previous relationship was 'closeted'. Their neighbours persistently bully them. Kurt's family of origin live a long distance away.

218a Ian is 31 years old. At 27, he entered into a civil partnership with Neil. Ian is white and British. He has been in a civil partnership with Neil for four-and-a-half years and lives in Scotland. Ian is the proud 'parent' of numerous pets.

218b Neil is Ian's partner. He is 32 years old, white and British. Neil had been involved with Ian for nearly two years when they entered into civil partnership. Neil is unsure if it is appropriate for them to be in an open relationship, as they are, given that they are married. His family of origin live in a different part of the UK.

219a Benjamin has been involved with Leroy for around 10 years. He is 29 years old, white and British, and has been in a civil partnership for one year. Benjamin had a very traumatic coming-out experience and tried to commit suicide on several occasions. They live in the South East of England, but his family of origin live in a different part of the country.

219b Leroy is a 35-year-old, white, British man. He and Benjamin have been together for a long time and in a civil partnership for a year. Leroy suffers from a rare health condition and has been out of work for the last two years. His family of origin live a long distance away.

220a Eric and Nathan are partners. Eric is 36 years old, white and British. Eric and Nathan have been in a relationship for about 14 years and in a civil partnership for four. Eric works and partly lives in another European country. He has a chronic health condition. Eric's mother lives in the UK. He has no contact with his father.

220b Nathan is a 39-year-old, white, British man. He described his previous relationship as an abusive one. Nathan and Eric have been in a civil partnership for four years. Nathan lives alone in Scotland. His family of origin live elsewhere in the UK.

221a Lucas is 34 years old. He is white and British. Lucas has been involved with his partner Theo for 15 years. They have been in a civil partnership for just over a year. This is Lucas's first relationship with a man, but he was involved with a woman for nearly five years before he met Theo. Lucas and Theo live in the North of England. His family of origin live in a different part to the UK.

221b Theo is Lucas's partner. He is 33 and entered into a civil partnership with Lucas 13 months ago. Theo, who comes from a strong Catholic background, has had no sexual relationship other than that with Lucas. After all the years with Lucas, Theo's family of origin do not know about the nature of their relationship. They live in a different part of the country.

222a Eugene comes from a strong Catholic background. He is a 26-year- old, white, non-EU national. He has been involved with Haiden for nearly four years. They entered into civil partnership one-and-a-half months ago. Eugene and Haiden live in a shared household in London. Eugene's family of origin live overseas. He still has not told his parents about the nature of his relationship with Haiden.

222b Haiden is a 30-year-old, white, British man. He met Eugene abroad when they were both studying overseas. Haiden has had no previous sexual relationships. His family of origin live in a different part of the UK.

223a Miguel is a 28-year-old non-EU national of a mixed-race background. He has been involved with Robin for nearly four years, but they spent most of that time apart. Miguel and Robin entered into civil partnership four months ago, just after Miguel moved to the UK. Miguel's family of origin live overseas.

223b Robin is Miguel's partner. He is 35 years old, white and British. Robin's parents were initially not 'overjoyed' about his civil partnership with Miguel, but they are 'kind of' happy for Robin now. Robin and Miguel live in London, but Robin's parents live a long distance away, in an area that Robin describes as 'conservative'. He has been in a civil partnership for four months.

224a Chung is a 33-year-old Chinese man. He met Warren nearly six years ago and they have been in a civil partnership for three months. They have spent long periods apart. Unlike Warren, Chung has an extensive network of gay friends, which has caused arguments between them. Chung's family of origin live overseas. He is not out to his family of origin and they do not know about his relationship with Warren.

224b Warren is a 25-year-old, white, British man. He entered into civil partnership with Chung just three months ago after nearly six years together. Warren met Chung abroad and they have spent long periods of living apart. Warren has had no previous relationships with men. They live in London. Warren's family of origin live in a different part of the UK.

225a Herman is a 21-year-old white EU national. He entered into civil partnership with OJ a month ago after they had been together for nearly two years. When Herman and OJ met, Herman was in another relationship. They live in London, but Herman's family of origin live overseas.

225b **OJ** is Herman's partner. He is the older one of the two, 27, white and Scottish. OJ and Herman just recently entered into civil partnership, but have been involved for nearly two years. OJ describes his previous relationship as 'volatile'. His family of origin live in a different part of the UK.

226a **Trevor** is a 34-year-old, white, British man. He and Wayne are partners. They met just under a year ago and have been in a civil partnership for six months. Their relationship is heavily influenced by their intense work commitments. They live in London. Trevor's family of origin live in a different part of the country.

226b **Wayne** is Trevor's partner. He is 32, white and British. He and Trevor have been involved for less than a year. They entered into civil partnership six months ago. His family of origin live in a different part of the UK.

227a **Garry** is a 32-year-old, white, British man. He has been involved with Umberto for nearly four years. They entered into civil partnership four months ago. Garry's father has never come to terms with Garry's sexuality and has banned him from seeing his mother who is chronically ill. Garry and Umberto live in London, while Garry's family of origin live in a different part of the country.

227b **Umberto** is a 30-year-old EU national of a mixed-race background. His family of origin live overseas and have never come to terms with Umberto's sexuality. This is Umberto's first relationship. They celebrated their civil partnership with friends. He and Garry live in London.

Bibliography

Adam, B. D. (2006) 'Relationship innovation in male couples', *Sexualities* 9(1): 5–26.

Adam, B. D. (2004) 'Care, intimacy and same-sex partnership in the 21st century', *Current Sociology* 52(2): 265–279.

Adam, B. D. (1987) *The rise of the lesbian and gay movement*, Twayne Publishers.

Adam, B. D. and Sears, A. (1996) *Experiencing HIV: Personal, family, and work relationships*, New York: Columbia University Press.

Adkins, L. (2002) *Revisions: Gender and sexuality in late modernity*, Buckingham: Open University Press.

Allan, G. (2004) 'Being unfaithful: His and her affairs', in J. Duncombe, K. Harrison, G. Allan and D. Marsden (eds), *The state of affairs: Explorations in infidelity and commitment*, London: Lawrence Erlbaum.

Altman, D. (1982) *The Homosexualization of America: The Americanization of the homosexual*, New York: St. Martin's Press.

Altman, D. (1971) *Homosexual oppression and liberation*, Outerbridge & Dienstfrey.

Anderson, K. and Jack, D. C. (1991) 'Learning to listen: Interview techniques and analyses', in S. Berger Gluck and D. Patai (eds), *Women's words: The feminist practice of oral history*, New York: Routledge.

Ashby, K. J. and Burgoyne, C. (2008) 'Separate financial entities? Beyond categories of money management', *The Journal of Socio-Economics* 37: 458–480.

Atkinson, P. and Delamont, S. (eds) (2006) *Narrative methods*, London: Sage.

Atkinson, P. and Housley, W. (2003) *Interactionism*, London: Sage.

Auchmuthy, R. (2004) 'Same-sex marriage revived: Feminist critique and legal strategy', *Feminism & Psychology* 14(1): 101–126.

Badgett, M. V. L. (2009) *When gay people get married: What happens when societies legalize same-sex marriage*, New York: New York University Press.

Barker, N. (2006) 'Sex and the Civil Partnership Act: The future of (non) conjugality', *Feminist Legal Studies* 14(2): 241–259.

Bates Deakin, M. (2006) *Gay marriage, real life*, Boston, MA: Skinner House Books.

Bauman, Z. (2003) *Liquid love*, Cambridge: Polity.

Bauman, Z. (1992) *Intimations of postmodernity*, London: Routledge.

Bech, H. (1997) *When men meet: Homosexuality and modernity*, Cambridge: Polity.

Beck, U. (2000) 'Zombie categories', in J. Rutherford (ed.), *The art of life*, London: Lawrence and Wishart.

Beck, U. and Beck-Gernsheim, E. (2002) *Individualization: Institutionalised individualism and it social and political consequences*, London: Sage.

Beck, U. and Beck-Gernsheim, E. (1995) *The normal chaos of love*, Cambridge: Polity Press.

Benjamin, O. and Sullivan O. (1996) 'The importance of difference: Conceptualising increased flexibility in gender relations at home, *Sociological Review* 44(2): 225–251.

Berger, P. (1990) *The sacred canopy: Elements of a sociological theory*, New York: Anchor Books.

Berger, P. and Kellner, H. (1964) 'Marriage and the social construction of reality', *Diogenes* 12(46): 1–24.

Bersani, L. (2010) *Is the rectum a grave and other essays*, Chicago: Chicago University Press.

Blasband, D. and Peplau, L. A. (1985) 'Sexual exclusivity versus openness in gay male couples', *Archives of Sexual Behavior* 14(5): 395–412.

Blasius, M. (1994) *Gay and lesbian politics: Sexuality and the emergence of a new ethic*, Philadelphia, PA: Philadelphia University Press.

Blokland, T. (2005) 'Memory magic: How a working-class neighbourhood became an imagined community and class started to matter when it lost its base', in F. Devine et al. (eds), *Rethinking class*, Basingstoke: Palgrave Macmillan.

Blumstein, P. and Schwartz, P. (1983) *American couples: Money, work, sex*, New York: William Morrow.

Bondi, L., Davidson, J. and Smith, M. (eds) (2005) *Emotional geographies*, Aldershot: Ashgate.

Bourdieu, P. (1977) *Outline of a theory of practice*, Cambridge: Cambridge University Press.

Brannen, J. (2005) 'Time and the negotiation of work-family boundaries: Autonomy or illusion', *Time & Society* 14(1): 113–31.

Burgoyne, C. (1990) 'Money in marriage: How patterns of allocation both reflect and conceal power', *The Sociological Review* 38(4): 634–665.

Burgoyne, C. and Morison, V. (1997) 'Money in remarriage: Keeping things simple – and separate, *The Sociological Review* 45(3): 363–395.

Burgoyne, C., Clarke, V. and Burns, M. (2011) 'Money management and views of civil partnership in same-sex couples: Results from a UK survey of non-heterosexuals', *The Sociological Review* 59(4): 685–706.

Burgoyne, C., Clarke, V., Reibstein, J. and Edmunds, A. (2006) '"All my worldly good I share with you"? Managing money at the transition to heterosexual marriage', *The Sociological Review* 54(4): 619–637.

Bury, M. (1997) *Health and illness in a changing society*, London: Routledge.

Butler, J. (2002) 'Is kinship always already heterosexual?', *Differences: A Journal of Feminist Cultural Studies* 13(1): 14–44.

Buunk, B. P. and Dijkstra, P. (2004) 'Men, women and infidelity: Sex differences in extradyadic sex and jealousy', in J. Duncombe, K. Harrison, G. Allan and D. Marsden (eds), *The state of affairs: Explorations in infidelity and commitment*, London: Lawrence Erlbaum.

Calhoun, C. (2000) *Feminism, the family, and the politics of the closet*, Oxford: Oxford University Press.

Cant, B. (ed.) (1997) *Invented identities? Lesbians and gays talk about migration*, London: Cassell.

Carrington, C. (2002) *No place like home: Relationships and family life among lesbians and gay men*, London: University of Chicago Press.

Chauncey, G. (1994) *Gay New York: Gender, urban culture and the making of the gay male world, 1890–1940*, New York: Basic.

Clarke, V., Burgoyne, C. B. and Burns, M. L. (2006) 'Just a piece of paper? A qualitative exploration of same-sex couples' multiple conceptions of civil partnership and marriage', *Lesbian & Gay Psychology Review* 7(2): 141–161.

Clarke, V. and Finlay, S. J. (eds) (2004) 'For better or worse? Lesbian and gay marriage', *Feminism and Psychology* 14: 17–62.

Connell, R. (1987) *Gender and power*, Cambridge: Polity.

Coyle, A. (1991) *The construction of gay identity*, unpublished Ph.D. thesis, University of Surrey, UK.

Cruickshank, M. (1992) *The lesbian and gay liberation movement.* New York: Routledge.

Davies, P. (1992) 'The role of disclosure in coming out amongst gay men', in K. Plummer (ed.), *Modern homosexualities,* London: Routledge.

Delphy, C. and Leonard, D. (1992) *Familiar exploitation: A new analysis of marriage in contemporary western society*, Cambridge: Polity.

D'Emilio, J. (1983) *Sexual politics, sexual communities: The making of a homosexual minority in the United States, 1940–1970*, Chicago: University of Chicago Press.

Donovan, C. (2004) 'Why reach for the moon? Because the stars aren't enough', *Feminism and Psychology* 14: 24–29.

Duncombe, J., Harrison, K. Allan, G. and Marsden, D. (eds) (2004) *The state of affairs: Explorations in infidelity and commitment,* London: Lawrence Erlbaum.

Duncombe, J. and Marsden D. (1999) 'Love and intimacy: The gender division of emotion and "emotion work"', in G. Allan (ed.), *The sociology of family life*, Oxford: Blackwell.

Duncombe, J. and Marsden, D. (1996) 'Can we research the private sphere?' in L. Morris, and S. Lyon, (eds) *Gender relations in public and private: New research perspectives*, London: Macmillan.

Dunne, G. A. (1999) 'A passion for "sameness"?: Sexuality and gender accountability', in E. Silva and C. Smart (eds), *The new family?* London: Sage.

Dunne, G. A. (1997) *Lesbian lifestyles: Women's work and the politics of sexuality*, Basingstoke: Macmillan.

Dupuis, A. and Thorns, D. C. (1998) 'Home, home ownership and the search for ontological security', *The Sociological Review* 46(1): 24–47.

Edmunds, J. and Turner, B. S. (2002) *Generations, culture and society*, Buckingham: Open University Press.

Eskridge, W. L. (2002) *Equality practice: Civil unions and the future of gay rights*, New York: Routledge.

Fagan, C. (2001) 'Time, money and the gender order: Work orientations and working-time preferences', *Gender, Work and Organizations* 8(3): 239–67.

Foucault, M. (1979) *The history of sexuality, Volume 1: An introduction*, Harmondsworth: Penguin.

Fraser, M., Kember, S. and Lury, C. (2005) 'Inventive Life. Approaches to the New Vitalism', *Theory, Culture & Society* 22(1): 1–14.

Gabb, J. (2008) *Researching intimacies in families*, Basingstoke: Palgrave Macmillan.

Giddens, A. (1992) *The transformation of intimacy*, Cambridge: Polity Press.

Giddens, A. (1991) *Modernity and self-identity*, Cambridge: Polity Press.

Gillis, J. (2004) 'Gathering together', in A. Etzioni and J. Bloom (eds), *We are what we celebrate*, New York: New York University Press.

Gillis, J. (1996) *A world of their own making*, Boston, MA: Harvard University Press.

Gubrium, J. F. and Holstein, J. A. (2009) *Analyzing narrative reality*, London: Sage.

Harding, R. (2011) *Regulating sexuality: Legal consciousness in lesbian and gay lives*, New York: Routledge.

Hawkes, G. (1999) 'Liberalizing heterosexuality?' in G. Allan (ed.), *The Sociology of Family Life*, Oxford: Blackwell.

Heaphy, B. (2011) 'Gay identities and the culture of class', *Sexualities* 14(1): 42–62.

Heaphy, B. (2008) 'The sociology of lesbian and gay reflexivity or reflexive sociology?', *Sociological Research Online* 13(1) 9, http://www.socresonline.org. uk/13/1/9.html.

Heaphy, B. (2007) *Late modernity and social change: Reconstructing social and personal life*, London: Routledge.

Heaphy, B. (2001) 'The (im)possibilities of living with AIDS: Incorporating death into everyday life', in Cunningham-Burley, S. (ed.) *Exploring the body*, London: Macmillan.

Heaphy, B., Donovan, C. and Weeks, J. (2004) 'A different affair? Openness and non-monogamy in same-sex relationships', in J. Duncombe, K. Harrison, G. Allan and D. Marsden (eds), *The state of affairs: Explorations in infidelity and commitment*, London: Lawrence Erlbaum Associates, Publishers.

Heaphy, B. Donovan, C. and Weeks, J. (1999) 'Sex, money and the kitchen sink: Power in same-sex couple relationships', in J. Seymour and P. Bagguley (eds), *Relating intimacies: Power and resistance*, London: Macmillan.

Heaphy. B. and Einarsdottir, A. (forthcoming 2012) 'Scripting Civil Partnerships: Interviewing couples together and apart', *Qualitative Research*.

Hennessy, R. (2000) *Profit and pleasure: Sexual identities in late capitalism*, London: Routledge.

Hochschild, A. R. (1997) *The time bind*, New York: Henry Holt.

Hull, K. E. (2006) *Same-sex marriage: The cultural politics of love and law*, Cambridge: Cambridge University Press.

Jackson, S. (1996) 'Heterosexuality as problem for feminist theory', in L. Adkins and V. Merchant (eds), *Sexualising the social: Power and the organization of sexuality*, London: Macmillan.

Jackson, S. and Scott, S. (2010a) 'Rehabilitating interactionism for a feminist sociology of sexuality', *Sociology* 44(5): 811–826.

Jackson, S. and Scott, S. (2010b) *Theorizing sexuality*, Maidenhead: Open University Press.

Jamieson, L. (1998) *Intimacy: Personal relationships in modern societies*, Cambridge: Polity Press.

Jeffreys, S. (2004) 'The need to abolish marriage', *Feminism and Psychology* 14(2): 327–331.

Kiernan (2002) 'Cohabitation in Western Europe: Trends, issues and implications', in A. Booth and A. Crouter (eds), *Just living together: Implications of cohabitation on families, children and social policy*, Hillside, NJ: Lawrence Erlbaum Associates.

Kimmel, M. (ed.) (2007) *The sexual self: The construction of sexual scripts*, Nashville: Vanderbilt University Press.

Kitzinger, C. and Wilkinson, S. (2004) 'The re-branding of marriage: Why we got married instead of registering a civil partnership', *Feminism & Psychology* 14(1): 127–150.

Klesse, C. (2007) *The spectre of promiscuity: Gay male and bisexual non-monogamies and polyamories*, Aldersholt: Ashgate.

Klesse, C. (2006) 'Polyamory and its "others": Contesting the terms of non-monogamy', *Sexualities* 9(5): 565–583.

Knapp Whittier, D. and Melendez, R. M. (2004) 'Intersubjectivity in the intrapsychic sexual scripting of gay men', *Culture, Health and Sexuality* 6(2): 131–143.

Lewin, E. (2008) 'Location, location, location: Same-sex marriage as a moving target', *Sexualities* 11(6): 777–781.

Lewin, E. (1998) *Recognizing ourselves: Ceremonies of lesbian and gay commitment*, New York: Columbia University Press.

Lewis, J. (2001) *The end of marriage? Individualism and intimate relations*, Cheltenham: Edward Elgar.

Mansfield, P. and Collard, J. (1988) *The beginning of the rest of your life?* Basingstoke: Macmillan.

Mason, J. (2008) 'Tangible affinities and the real life fascination of kinship', *Sociology*, 42(1): 29–46.

McGlone, F., Park, A. and Roberts, C. (2004) 'Kinship and friendship: Attitudes and behaviour in Britain, 1986–1995', in S. McRae (ed.), *Changing Britain: Family and household in the 1990s*, Oxford: Oxford University Press.

McRae, S. (ed.) (1999) *Changing Britain: Families and households in the 1990s*, Oxford: Oxford University Press.

McWhirter, D. P. and Mattison, A. M. (1984) *The male couple*, Englewood Cliffs, NJ: Prentice-Hall.

Miller, D. (ed.) (2001) *Home possessions*, Oxford: Berg.

Miller, D. (ed.) (1998) *Material cultures: Why some things matter*, London: UCL Press.

Mitchell, M., Dickens, S. and O'Connor, W. (2009) *Same-sex couples and the impact of legislative changes*, London: NatCen.

Misztal, B. (2003) *Theories of social remembering*, Milton Keynes: Open University Press.

Muller, A. (1987) *Parents matter: Parents' relationships with lesbian daughters and gay sons*, Tallahassee, FA: Naiad Press.

Morgan, D. H. J. (2011) *Rethinking family practices*, Basingstoke: Palgrave Macmillan.

Nardi, P. (1999) *Gay men's friendships: Invincible communities*, Chicago: Chicago University Press.

Noys, B. (2008) 'The end of the monarchy of sex', *Theory, Culture and Society* 25(5): 104–122.

Nordqvist, P. (2011a) 'Choreographies of sperm donations: Dilemmas of intimacy in lesbian couple donor conception', *Social Science and Medicine* 73(11): 1661–1688.

Nordqvist, P. (2011b) 'Dealing with sperm: Comparing lesbians' clinical and non-clinical donor conception processes', *Sociology of Health and Illness* 33(1): 114–129.

Nyman, C. (2003) 'The social nature of money: Meanings of money in Swedish families', *Women's Studies International Forum* 26(1): 79–94.

Nyman, C. and Dema, S. (2007) 'An overview: Research on Couples and Money', in J. Stocks et al. (eds), *Modern Couples Sharing Money, Sharing Life*, Basingstoke: Palgrave Macmillan.

Oerton, S. (2008) 'Old wine in new (champagne) bottles', *Sexualities* 11(6): 782–786.

Olma, S. and Koukouzelis, K. (2007) 'Introduction: Life's (re-)emergences', *Theory, Culture & Society* 24: 1–17.

Pahl, J. (1980) 'Patterns of money management within marriage', *Journal of Social Policy* 9(3): 313–35.

Pahl, J. (1990) 'Household spending, personal spending and the control of money in marriage', *Sociology* 24(1): 119–138.

Pahl, J. (1989) *Money and marriage*, Basingstoke: Macmillan.

Pahl, R. and Spencer, L. (2004) 'Personal communities: Not simply families of "fate" or "choice"', *Current Sociology* 52(2): 199–221.

Parsons, T. (2011) 'Very Nazi reaction', *Daily Mirror*, 22 January 2011: 13.

Peplau, L. A., Venigas, R. C. and MillerCampbell, S. (1996) 'Gay and Lesbian Relationships' in R. C. Savin-Williams and K. M. Cohen (eds), *The lives of lesbian, gays and bisexuals*, New York: Harcourt Brace College.

Plummer, K. (1995) *Telling sexual stories*, London: Routledge.

Plummer, K. (1983) *Documents of life: An introduction to the problem and literature of a humanistic method*, London: Allen and Unwin.

Radstone, S. (2000) 'Working with memory: An introduction', in S. Radstone (ed.), *Memory and methodology*, Oxford: Berg.

Rauch, J. (2004) *Gay marriage: Why it is good for gays, good for straights, and good for America*, New York: Henry Holt and Company.

Rich, A. (1983) 'Compulsory heterosexuality and lesbian existence', in A. Snitow, C. Stansell and S. Thompson (eds), *Desire: Politics of sexuality*, London: Virago.

Riessman, C. (2008) *Narrative methods for the human sciences*, London: Sage.

Rosenfeld, D. (2003) *The changing of the guard: Lesbian and gay elders, identity, and social change*, Philadelphia: Temple University Press.

Robinson, V. and Hockey, J. (2011) *Masculinities in transition*, Basingstoke: Palgrave Macmillan.

Roseneil, S. (2002) 'Queer frameworks and queer tendencies: Towards an understanding of postmodern transformations of sexuality', *Sociological Research Online* 5(3), http://www.socresonline.org.uk/5/3/roseneil.html.

Rubin, G. (1992, orig. 1984) 'Thinking sex: Notes for a radical theory of the politics of sexuality', in C. Vance (ed.), *Pleasure and danger: Exploring female sexuality*, London: Pandora.

Ryan-Flood, R. (2009) *Lesbian motherhood: Gender, families and sexual citizenship*, Basingstoke: Palgrave Macmillan.

Savage, M., Bagnall, G. and Longhurst, B. (2000) 'Individualization and cultural distinction', in M. Savage (ed.), *Class analysis and social transformation*, Buckingham: Open University Press.

Shipman, B. and Smart, C. (2007) '"It's made a huge difference": Recognition, rights and the personal significance of civil partnership', *Sociological Research Online* 22(1): January.

Simmel, G. (1990, orig. 1900) *The philosophy of money*, London: Routledge.

Smart, C. (2008) '"Can I be bridesmaid?": Combining the personal and political in same-sex weddings', *Sexualities* 11(6): 761–776.

Smart, C. (2007) *Personal life: New directions in sociological thinking*, Cambridge: Polity Press.

Sonnenberg, S. J. (2008) 'Household financial organisation and discursive practice: Managing money and identity', *The Journal of Socio-Economics* 37: 533–551.

Southerton, D. (2003) '"Squeezing time": Allocating practices, coordinating networks and scheduling society', *Time & Society* 12(1): 5–25.

Simon, W. and Gagnon, J. H. (2004) 'Sexual scripts: Origins, influences and changes', *Qualitative Sociology* 26(4): 491–497.

Somers, M. R. (1994) 'The narrative constitution of identity: A relational and network approach', *Theory and Society* 23: 605–649.

Stacey, J. (2006) 'Gay parenthood and the decline of paternity as we know it', *Sexualities* 9(1): 27–55.

Stacey, J. (1997) *In the name of the family: Rethinking family values in the postmodern age*, Boston: Beacon Press.

Stocks, J., Diaz, C. and Hallerod, B. (eds) (2007) *Modern couples sharing money, sharing life*, Basingstoke: Palgrave Macmillan.

Stychin, C. (2006) 'Not (quite) a horse and carriage: The Civil Partnership Act 2004', *Feminist Legal Studies* 14: 79–86.

Stychin, C. (2003) *Governing sexuality: The changing politics of citizenship and law reform*, Oxford: Hart.

Sullivan, A. (ed.) (2004) *Same-sex marriage. Pro and con: A reader* (Rev. ed.), New York, NY: Vintage Books.

Sullivan, A. (1996) *Virtually normal*, New York: Vintage Books.

Sullivan, M. (2004) *The family of women: Lesbian mothers, their children, and the undoing of gender*, California: University of California Press.

Sullivan, O. (1996) 'Time co-ordination, the domestic division of labour and affective relations: Time use and the enjoyment of activities within couples, *Sociology* 30(1): 79–100.

Swidler, A. (2003) *Talk of love: How culture matters*, London: University of Chicago Press.

Taylor, Y. (2007) *Working class lesbian life: Classed outsiders.* Basingstoke: Palgrave Macmillan.

Taylor, Y. (2009) *Lesbian and gay parenting: securing social and educational capital*, Basingstoke: Palgrave Macmillan.

Thomson, R. (2009) *Unfolding lives: Youth, gender, change*, Bristol: Policy Press.

Thomson, R. Bell, R., Holland, J., Henderson, S., McGrellis, S. and Sharpe, S. (2002) 'Critical moments: Choice, chance and opportunity in young people's narratives of transition to adulthood', *Sociology* 6(2): 335–354.

Treacher, A. and Katz, I. (2000) *The dynamics of adoption*, London: Jessica Kingsley.

Van Every, J. (1995) *Heterosexual women changing the family: Refusing to be a wife!*, London: Taylor and Francis.

Vogler, C. (2005) 'Cohabiting couples: Rethinking money in the household at the beginning of the twenty first century', *The Sociological Review* 53(1): 1–29.

Vogler, C. (1998) 'Money in the household: Some underlying issues of power', *The Sociological Review* 46(4): 687–713.

Vogler, C., Brockmann, M. and Wiggins, R. (2006) 'Intimate relationships and changing patterns of money management at the beginning of the twenty first century', *British Journal of Sociology* 57(3): 455–482.

Vogler, C. and Pahl, J. (1994) 'Money, power and inequality within marriage', *The Sociological Review* 42(2): 263–288.

Warner, M. (2000) *The trouble with normal: Sex, politics, and the ethics of queer life*, Cambridge, MA: Harvard University Press.

Warren, T. (2003) 'Class- and gender-based working time: Time, poverty and the division of domestic labour', *Sociology* 37(4): 733–752.

Weeks, J. (2010) *Sexuality*, London: Routledge.

Weeks, J. (2008) 'Regulation, resistance, recognition', *Sexualities* 11(1–2): 27–33.

Weeks, J. (2007) *The world we have won*, London: Routledge.

Weeks, J. (2005) 'Remembering Foucault', *Journal of the History of Sexuality* 14(1/2): 186–201.

Weeks, J. (1995) *Invented moralities: Sexual values in and age of uncertainty*, Cambridge: Polity Press.

Weeks, J. (1977) *Coming out: Homosexual politics in Britain from the nineteenth century to the present*, London: Quartet.

Weeks, J., Heaphy, B. and Donovan, C. (2001) *Same sex intimacies: Families of choice and other life experiments*, London: Routledge.

Weston, K. (1991) *Families we choose: Lesbians, gays and kinship*, New York: Columbia University Press.

Weston, K. (1995) 'Get thee to a big city: Sexual imaginary and the great gay migration', *GLQ* 2(3): 253–277.

Widerberg, K. (2006) 'Embodying modern times: Investigating tiredness', *Time & Society* 15(1): 105–120.

Wilkinson, S. (2004) 'Equal marriage', *Feminism & Psychology* 14(1): 9–15.

Yip, A. (1997) 'Gay male Christian couples and sexual exclusivity'. *Sociology* 31, 289–306.

Yip, A. K. T. (2008) 'Researching lesbian, gay, and bisexual Christians and Muslims: Some thematic reflections', *Sociological Research Online* 13(1).

Zelizer, V. A. (1994) *The social meaning of money: Pin money, paychecks, poor relief, and other currencies*, Princeton: Princeton University Press.

Index